T0312589

What are people sa_

The Primacy of Loving

David wrote for the Catholic Universe Newspaper for very many years until its closure, so I was thrilled when he agreed to write for the newly launched Universe Catholic Weekly last year. Through his regular weekly columns on Spiritual Theology, I know from first-hand experience that David has helped countless readers to come to a deeper understanding of their faith and to the centrality of prayer in their lives. Reading David's work is always a spiritually enriching experience, and this book is no exception. I have great pleasure in commending it to readers.

Michael Winterbottom, Managing Editorial Director, Universe Catholic Weekly

I waited over 65 years for David Torkington's teaching on mystical theology. If only I had known at the beginning of my religious life what I have now learnt from him, it would have made me a far better person than the man I am now.

Fr Gregory Cistercian Monk of Our Lady of Bamenda Abbey, Cameroon

Working with David for twelve years when he was the Director of the Brentwood Diocesan Retreat and Conference Centre in London, was the happiest time in my life. After introducing me to the new biblical theology he encouraged me and others to return to the classical Dominican tradition. He did this firstly by encouraging us to attend a year-long renewal course organised and run by the Dominican fathers from the Angelicum in Rome, and then to immerse ourselves in the spirituality of the first Dominicans. Without this our reform

could not have taken place.
Sr Margarita Schwind OP, Foundress of the Dominican Sisters of St Joseph, Sway, England

Every book David Torkington writes is about prayer, true deep prayer, but so simply expressed, so colloquial, clear as spring water and as refreshing. We can so easily read about prayer, about love, about Christian service and in the emotional happiness of our reading come to think that we are actually doing what we are only feeling. Fortunately, no one is more aware of this danger than David Torkington. He is passionately committed to stripping from the reader those veils of illusion that allow what is said to be enjoyed in theory only. His books should be mandatory reading.
Sr Wendy Beckett, Hermit

I thank God because with David Torkington's course on prayer now hopefully in book format mysticism no longer seems so mysterious. It's not just for "weirdos!"
Janessa Ramos, 3x Emmy Award-winning journalist

David Torkington is spiritually generous and is a master at creatively teaching prayer with unforgettable words.
Marilyn Nash, Author and Artist

Thank you, David, I have come to realize that in my own protestant church the teaching of mystical theology doesn't exist and therefore the teaching of my church has been deprived of the essential connection between ourselves and Christ. We are truly poor. I always felt that I was outside my own church because I saw Christ and heard Him speaking to me. Well, that is just me. Keep doing what you are because your teaching will one day save the church we both love.
Rev Anneli Sinkko, Australia

The Primacy of Loving

The Spirituality of the Heart

The Primacy of Loving

The Spirituality of the Heart

David John Torkington

CIRCLE
BOOKS

Winchester, UK
Washington, USA

JOHN HUNT PUBLISHING

First published by Circle Books, 2022
Circle Books is an imprint of John Hunt Publishing Ltd., No. 3 East St., Alresford,
Hampshire SO24 9EE, UK
office@jhpbooks.com
www.johnhuntpublishing.com
www.circle-books.com

For distributor details and how to order please visit the 'Ordering' section on our website.

Text copyright: David John Torkington 2021

ISBN: 978 1 80341 120 0
978 1 80341 121 7 (ebook)
Library of Congress Control Number: 2021949608

A CIP catalogue record for this book is available from the British Library.

Design: Matthew Greenfield

UK: Printed and bound by CPI Group (UK) Ltd, Croydon, CR0 4YY
US: Printed and bound by Thomson Shore, 7300 West Joy Road, Dexter, MI 48130

We operate a distinctive and ethical publishing philosophy in
all areas of our business, from our global network of authors to
production and worldwide distribution.

Contents

Foreword   1
Introduction – The Way Back to the Future   7

Part 1 – Vocal Prayer and Meditation   17
  Chapter 1 The Unquenchable Fire of Love   19
  Chapter 2 Listen to St Teresa of Ávila   22
  Chapter 3 The Paramount Importance of
    Daily Prayer   27
  Chapter 4 Introducing Christian Meditation   31
  Chapter 5 Lectio Divina – Divine Reading   36
  Chapter 6 The Essence of Prayer – Gently Trying   40
  Chapter 7 Mystical Premonitions   45
  Chapter 8 Making the Impossible Possible   50
  Chapter 9 The Prayer Without Ceasing   54

Part 2 – Introducing Mystical Spirituality   59
  Chapter 10 Christian Mystical Contemplation   61
  Chapter 11 The Meaning of Mystical Theology   66
  Chapter 12 Early Christian Mystical Spirituality   71
  Chapter 13 The Mystical Prayer of the Early
    Christians   75
  Chapter 14 The Beginning of Mystical Prayer   80
  Chapter 15 Purification in the Desert   84
  Chapter 16 From the Prayer of Quiet to the
    Spiritual Betrothals   89
  Chapter 17 The Meaning of Contemplation   94
  Chapter 18 From Paradise Lost to Paradise
    Regained   99

Part 3 – A Brief History of Christian
Mystical Spirituality   105

Prelude 107

Chapter 19 A Handful of Heretics 108

Chapter 20 Monasticism to the Rescue 113

Chapter 21 St Bernard – A New Dawn 119

Chapter 22 The Franciscan Spring 124

Chapter 23 The Primacy of Love 129

Chapter 24 The Primacy of Love in
Catholic Reform 135

Chapter 25 The Curse and Consequences
of Quietism 140

Chapter 26 Devout Humanism 146

Chapter 27 The Modern Malaise 151

Chapter 28 When a Historian Becomes His-story 157

Chapter 29 St John Henry Newman's New Spring 163

Chapter 30 An Unexpected Personal Climax 168

Part 4 – Christian Mystical Contemplation **179**

Chapter 31 When Two Histories Meet 181

Chapter 32 Spiritual Weightlifting 188

Chapter 33 Love Is All You Need 196

Chapter 34 The Beginning of Contemplation 201

Chapter 35 Sweetness and Light 206

Chapter 36 From Light to Darkness 210

Chapter 37 From Darkness to Light 214

Chapter 38 The Interior Castle 219

Chapter 39 The Dark Night of the Soul 224

Chapter 40 Union with the Three in One 229

Chapter 41 Confirmatory Signs of the Mystic Way 234

Chapter 42 True Imitation of Christ 239

Chapter 43 The Language of Love 244

Chapter 44 The White Martyrdom that
Leads to Union 249

Chapter 45 How to Pray in Mystical
Contemplation I 254

Chapter 46 How to Pray in Mystical
Contemplation II   259
Chapter 47 How to Pray in Mystical
Contemplation III   264
Chapter 48 How to Pray in Mystical
Contemplation IV   269
Chapter 49 God's Holy Angel   274
Chapter 50 Death to the Demons Within   279
Chapter 51 The Fruits of Contemplation –
The Infused Virtues   284
Chapter 52 Renewal and Family Love   289
Chapter 53 To Contemplate and Share the
Fruits of Contemplation   294
Chapter 54 Traditionalism and Tradition   302
Chapter 55 Contemplation Made Simple   311
Chapter 56 Obedient Men   318
Chapter 57 Humanism Rides Again   324
Chapter 58 Not by Suffering but by Love   330
Chapter 59 Marcus Aurelius Rides Again   340
Chapter 60 The Last Minute of Extra Time   357
Chapter 61 The Father of Counterfeit Mysticism   367
Chapter 62 Followers of the Counterfeit Mystic   374
Chapter 63 Contemplation Is for Children Too   383
Chapter 64 Practising the Prayer of the Heart   391
Chapter 65 The Ascetism of the Heart   397
Chapter 66 From Stumbling Blocks to
Stepping Stones   402
Chapter 67 In the Trying Is the Dying   408
Chapter 68 Into the Redeeming Christ   413

Dedication

To my mother, and to my wife, Bobbie, and to my recusant forebears, without whom this book could not have been written.

David Torkington has sold over 400,000 books and been translated into 12 languages.

He is the author of:

Wisdom from the Western Isles – The Making of a Mystic

Wisdom from The Christian Mystics – How to Pray the Christian Way

Wisdom from Franciscan Italy – The Primacy of Love

How to Pray – A Practical Guide to the Spiritual Life

Prayer Made Simple – CTS booklet

Dear Susanna – It's Time for a Christian Renaissance

Inner Life – A Fellow Traveller's Guide to Prayer

A New Beginning – A Sideways Look at the Spiritual Life

His website is https://www.davidtorkington.com

Biblical references are from The Jerusalem Bible 1996 edition

Foreword

The name Peter the Lombard (1096–1160) probably means nothing to the general reader, but his influence on Catholic theology cannot be overemphasized. He was born in Italy over nine hundred years ago, where I was received into the third order of St Francis. His brilliant overall summary of authentic Catholic theology was held in such regard that all future scholars had, not only to read it, and review it, but make commentaries on it as the primary way they prepared themselves for future academic acceptance, and achievement. Those who first commentated on them, as part of their theological training like St Albert the Great, St Thomas Aquinas, St Bonaventure and a galaxy of other great names, came to be called the scholastics, and the large body of theological knowledge that they generated came to be called scholasticism.

I mention him because I believe that what Peter the Lombard did for, what was then called the new Scholastic theology, will be what David Torkington will do for what could be called the New Mystical Spirituality. Peter the Lombard's theology was not of course new. It was totally based on the scriptures and the theology of the early Church, just as David Torkington's spirituality is totally based on the mystical spirituality of the early Church too. In order to understand exactly what the author means by mystical, in contradistinction to the way it is misused by myriad pseudo-mystics today, let me explain what he means, for it is essential in order to understand this book. The need to understand the ancient mystical teaching of the Church is also vital today because even within the Church and from the highest authorities, contemplative life is under attack like never before.

The very essence of the "Spirituality of the Heart" that Jesus bequeathed to the early Church, was a new type of prayer that came to be called mystical prayer. The word mystical comes from the Greek and it simply means unseen, invisible, or secret. Christ taught this new type of mystical prayer to his first followers, for it was the prayer that he himself used to communicate with his Father. In the Jewish religion in which he was raised, prayer was predominantly audible for they would pray out loud. This inevitably led to some hypocrisy, so Christ advised his followers accordingly. "When you pray," he told them, "go to your private room and, when you have shut your door, pray to your Father who is in that secret place, and your Father who sees all that is done in secret will reward you" (Matthew 6:6).

Later, this secret, unseen, invisible or mystical prayer was given a totally new dimension and power. This happened after the first Pentecost, when all who received the Holy Spirit were drawn up and into the mystical body of Christ, where they would reside in future. Here they would pray in, with, and through him to the Father, who, as Jesus had promised, would reward them. He rewarded them by pouring out onto and into them all the infused virtues and gifts of the Holy Spirit. It is these secret, invisible or mystical gifts that would enable them to say with St Paul, "I live now not with my own life but with the life of Christ who lives in me" (Galatians 2:20). It was in this way that Christ continued his work by converting a pagan Roman Empire into a Christian empire through those who radically and daily opened themselves to allow him to possess them.

In this personal mystical prayer that took place alone in the "inner room" the faithful would travel along a spiritual journey called the "Mystic Way". On this hidden, secret journey, like Christ the first Mystic, they would have to experience what it felt like when God seemed to be far away and terrible temptations and distractions would all but overcome them. This is what Christ had to experience for himself, in the desert, in the Garden of Gethsemane and on the Cross. However, there would be other moments when he would be overwhelmed with joy as he prayed with his own family, his disciples and with his apostles on Mount Tabor. A later mystical writer, St John of the Cross, would describe what it was like in the dark times in his book *The Dark Night of the Soul*, and St Teresa of Ávila would describe what it was like when darkness was replaced by light and travellers would come to experience the presence of God in moments of unalloyed joy. These divine visitations were described in her master work *Interior Castle*. What she describes there can be found as experienced by St Paul, when he wrote about the visions and revelations that he received and described, when he was raised into what he called the "third heaven" that he identified with paradise regained (2 Corinthians 12:1–5). This is described by St Teresa of Ávila and called the prayer of "Full Union" or even "Ecstasy" in her famous mystical masterpiece. It is this mystical prayer that St Teresa of Ávila said was the very soul of the Church, that is now under serious and systematic attack. Who would wish to belong to a Church without a soul?

Although David admitted that he spent years reading books on spiritual theology, it was in fact through his parents that he came to understand the true meaning of the "Mystic Way" like never before. After his mother died his father told him that in the last years of their married life together he and his mother loved each other more deeply and more perfectly than at any other time in their lives. In the first days of what he described as their adolescent love, they were drawn to each other by powerful waves of emotional and passionate feelings. They acted like the boosters on a spaceship to raise it off the ground on its way to its final destination in outer space. Just as these powerful boosters fizzle out, so too do the powerful boosters of adolescent love, in every marriage.

Now, said David's father, it was what happened between the moment when these powerful emotional feelings fizzled out, and the perfect love that they experienced at the end of their life, that made this perfect love possible. And what did happen in these crucial roller-coaster years to make perfect love

3

possible? For many years, no decades, unknown to onlookers, unseen even to their closest friends and relatives, they practised selfless sacrificial or mystical loving, whether they felt like it or whether they did not, come hell or high water. It was this totally other-considering mystical loving that gradually enabled them to be bonded ever closer together, until as perfect a union as is possible in this life, was the joy of their last years together.

David remembered something that his mother said to him that he would never forget. She said if she and his father had not already been married, then their marriage could so easily have floundered and failed. She was referring to the marriage that they had entered into when they were baptised. It was their marriage to Christ that gave them access to the grace of God that continually sustained and supported their weak human love and enabled them to overcome the obstacles that could have impeded if not prevented, the union that they finally attained. If he had told his parents that they were mystics they would have laughed, but like so many other parents who had to battle against the "slings and arrows of outrageous fortune" to find the peace that they finally attained, they were indeed mystics. They were quite clearly married mystics from whom celibates called to the mystic way could well learn what they have long since forgotten.

First enthusiasm or first fervour at the beginning of both human and divine loving is clearly visible to the lovers themselves and to onlookers too, but the secret self-sacrificial loving that is the making of any marriage, whether it takes place in a human or a divine marriage cannot be seen. This is so important that I must emphasize again that this loving is called mystical, because it is secret, unseen, or invisible loving. It is practised daily through selfless living, and giving, as the spiritual life develops in the years that leads to perfect love. This loving is also called mystical for a Christian, because it takes place in and continues to grow within the Mystical Body of Jesus Christ, where it is united with Christ's own love of his Father that he practised while he was on earth and is now brought to perfection as he is in heaven. This gives to mystical loving, learnt in prayer by both married and celibate lovers alike, a power and a purpose unknown to purely human love alone.

The body of knowledge gathered together and written down by those who have travelled along the mystic way to help others is called mystical theology. God's plan is not just that we should be drawn up into Christ's life but be taken up into his action. That is why throughout the book David reminds the reader to keep the words of the great Jesuit liturgist Josef Jungmann before your mind.

> Christ does not offer alone, His people are joined to Him and offer with Him and through Him. Indeed, they are absorbed into Him and form one body with Him by the Holy Spirit who lives in all.

As this book will show, the mystical teaching that was once commonplace in the Church was seriously undermined by a heresy called Quietism over four hundred years ago, and with disastrous consequences for the family founded by Jesus Christ, called the Church. As any contemporary observer can see, once love is taken out of any family catastrophic consequences ensue, not just for the married couple but for the children and for society at large. This book has clearly been written to help bring back love, the true selfless sacrificial mystical loving that can alone restore the family of Christ, his Church, to what it originally was.

Like the theology of Peter the Lombard, the mystical theology contained in this book might have been forgotten. However, it is not new, it has just been newly presented to a Church that has sadly forgotten the real nature of love, as the secular world has forgotten it. In the early Church, entering into the mystical body of Christ and sharing in his mystical loving of his Father was the very essence of early God-given Christian mystical spirituality. Because it required a perfect union with Christ for this loving to be made perfect, imperfect human beings needed to be purified by daily taking up their cross to follow Christ. This practice came to be called "white martyrdom", for it meant dying to self in all that they said and did each day, inside and outside of the prayer that was the place where they personally encountered their Risen Lord.

It is my hope that, as in the past great saints and theologians rose up to review, commentate on, develop and propagate the works of Peter the Lombard for the greater good of the Church, the same will happen today with this work. It is also my prayer that a new body of mystical writing will therefore ensue to build up a library of teaching in modern language, to make known and popularise again the holy and ancient teachings of the Church on mystical theology. The current wave of anti-mystical edicts coming from the very highest authority in the Church who are trying to destroy the contemplative life that is the life blood of the Church, must be stopped. We must return without delay to the profound mystical tradition upon which our Church was first founded. This is the only way to do for the Church what no other teaching can do, for once love is lost only love found and reintroduced can do for any family what nothing else can possibly do. Families were made by love in the first place; they were made for love, and to propagate love above all else. That is why it is the teaching of Mystical Theology that can alone teach us and continually sustain, us in doing what Christ himself called the "one thing necessary", for our own personal sanctification, for the sanctification of the Church and for the world for which Christ founded his Church in the first place.

Sr Bernadine OSF, 4th October, 2021, Feast of St Francis of Assisi

Introduction

The Way back to the Future

The letter was direct and to the point. I was given the sack and would have to vacate the property by the first of January 1981. Although I was made the Director of what was then the only Retreat and Conference centre in London by the Bishop twelve years before, the property did not belong to the diocese. I had lost my job, my position and my home, and without any warning. At least I had the deep inner satisfaction of knowing that I had been sacked for doing what was right, but this was of little practical help in the strange limbo land in which I suddenly found myself.

But there was no time for self-pity, because seven other people had also lost everything, and I had a responsibility to support them. They were the Dominican sisters who had all, in one way or another, helped to run Walsingham House, as the centre was called. Influenced by the theological and spiritual courses run at the centre, and a year's long renewal course run by their Dominican brothers in Rome, they understandably wanted to return to the Dominican Tradition founded by St Dominic. So, when a new mother general began to force everyone to adopt the latest socio-psychological techniques in order to renew their congregation, her first action was to sack me for encouraging and supporting those who resisted her plan for renewal. The seven sisters left en bloc and with the help of a Jesuit canon lawyer, Fr Lachy Hughes, successfully appealed to Rome.

I mention this little interlude in my life, because for the first time I encountered two trends or movements which still influence the Church today. The first trend turns to tradition to change the world, the second turns to the world to change tradition. The first is theocentric, the second is anthropocentric. The divinely inspired spirituality that is the subject of this book came a poor second to the man-made "spiritualities" that were cherry-picked and implemented by amateurs from the latest psychosociological sciences. On some they were no more than a passing fad but for others they had a devastating effect. At the time I had no idea how the anti-contemplative ethos and invective that inspired these reformers would spread like fungus underground. Nor did I have any idea that it would eventually mushroom in an unprecedented manner, not just with the encouragement of, but with the active support of the highest authorities in the Church. It would seem that they are bent on doing to death what is the very soul of the Church. Although Henry VIII destroyed the monasteries, he did not, nor could he, destroy their mystical life, for so many of the monks and friars fled to the continent to continue their contemplative life there. But it seems those in authority in the Church today are trying to extinguish, at source, the heart and soul of contemplative prayer which is, as it always has been the life blood of those who are united in the mystical body of Christ.

I was blissfully happy in my position as the director of a retreat and conference centre and could not conceive where I would go next, or whether or not I would have a home, or even a job to go to. But after a few weeks, the telephone rang to offer me a new post as the Dean of Studies at the National Catholic Radio and Television Centre in London. I accepted once I was sure that the future of the Dominican Sisters was secured. In the short term they were to take over another retreat centre in partnership with the Montfort Fathers in Ashurst on the edge of the New Forest in the South of England. Thanks to the financial intervention of a layman, Mr Michael Bird, they would soon become the nucleus of a new congregation at their own Priory in Sway, in the middle of the New Forest. Their story highlights the way forward for others who are prepared to put their trust, not in the wisdom of man, but in the wisdom of God.

The trustees at the Catholic Radio and Television Centre were presided over by Cardinal Basil Hume and included the six other Archbishops of England, Scotland and Wales, but I do not know who chose to employ me. Apart from a few talks that I had given on what is still called "thought for the day" in the middle of the BBC prime time news and current affairs programme, and a few interviews for the BBC World Service, I had no experience of the media at all. I spent the next six months learning my trade and the job was fluid enough for me to continue to accept invitations to speak from all over the world. One advantage I had over others was that, as the law of compensation decrees, the dyslexia that held back my literary development gave me a verbal fluency that made up for my deficiency with the written word.

We had two studios, one each for radio and television. As Orson Welles said, the great mystery is that the camera loves some people and not others. It did not love me, but I had an affair with the microphone although it did not lead to wedding bells. My training not only helped me to help others, but to help me as a travelling speaker, and much later when I became a full-time writer. Most of the courses were to help priests, religious, bishops and even cardinals how to present themselves on the radio or the television, most particularly when asked to give short talks like "thought for the day". But the courses were open to all priests who were encouraged to seek help for their weekly sermons.

In order to fix the mind from the beginning and keep it on course, the speakers would have to write down in exactly seventeen words, what they had to say. So, let me begin by telling you, and reminding myself of precisely what I wish to say in this book in seventeen words. This book has been inspired by the work of St John Henry Newman. Like him, I will go back to the sources of our faith at the very beginning of Christianity. However, I could not possibly do what he did, and on such a vast scale. I will do something far more modest, but hopefully something that is inspiring and helpful, although I could not hope to rival the incomparable use of one of the greatest exponents of the English language. This is what I will do, in no more than seventeen words and they are: Successful renewal depends on returning to the God-given spirituality introduced into the early Church by Christ himself.

There are many other Christian spiritualities that developed later, but they are only as good as they reproduce the one and only God-given spirituality that Christ introduced into the early Church. All later spiritualities are only reproducing this spirituality for different people, in different circumstances, and in different ways of life. If they deviate substantially from what is the perfect paradigm that we find in its original purity in Apostolic times, then they should be abandoned. Whenever these later spiritualities set about renewing themselves, the sign of their authenticity will always be the way in which they return to the sources that originally inspired them in the first place. Benedictines for instance derive their original inspiration from the faithful community in Jerusalem immediately after the Resurrection. Dominicans find their inspiration from the apostolic way of life as lived by the first apostles. Franciscans are inspired by and base their way of life on the life as lived by Jesus and his disciples both before and after the Resurrection.

I will continue in the subsequent chapters to stress the divine origin of primitive Christian spirituality, which I have also detailed in the first twelve chapters of my book *Wisdom from the Christian Mystics – How to Pray the Christian Way*. So-called "new spiritualities" are raising their heads within the Catholic Church as I write. Many totally contradict the teaching of Christ, which was as essential to the early Catholic Church as they still are today. Realizing that a spirituality that was inspired and introduced by Christ himself cannot be challenged, a subtle and hardly perceptible reintroduction of Arianism is on the agenda of some modern heretics. In other words, if Christ is no more than just a man, albeit the greatest man who ever lived, and especially sent by God, then he would see that what was right for the Church two thousand years ago, would not be right for the Church today. In short, he would be introducing new modern agendas that "sophisticated" modern Catholics wish to introduce. This insidious infiltration of Catholicism has already begun in the Church from top to bottom. Whilst not openly proclaiming that Christ was only a man, they simply mention him less and less in all matters spiritual. The worst heresy that Christianity has ever known, Arianism, is again on the agenda. The continual failure to appreciate the hypostatic union in recent years has done untold harm to the fullness of the truth for which Christ died such an agonising death.

The first priest to whom I turned for spiritual help was a Doctor of Divinity who also taught Church history. His name was Fr Gabriel Reidy OFM, and he was the most erudite man I have ever met. His advice set me back on the right path for the rest of my life. Later in an oral examination he asked me whether lay spirituality was originally monastic, or mendicant spirituality that had filtered down to the laity, or was religious spirituality in fact, lay spirituality, finding a new and different embodiment in those who took vows. My answer was that lay spirituality had its origins in religious spirituality. When he later told me I was wrong, he said most religious would agree with me, and all too many lay people still believe this to be the case. Rather than being encouraged to become semi-detached members of a later, albeit invaluable spirituality for celibates, he said the laity should be encouraged to return to the God-given spirituality that was initially introduced by Christ himself, for the majority, who were predominantly members of ordinary Christian families, like their counterparts today. In essence, there is only one God-given spirituality from which all other spiritualities derive, and if any later spiritualities substantially deviate from it, or only partially or selectively observe it, then they are themselves misunderstanding it, and misguiding others who trust in them. The truth is that since the Church became over clericalized after the ascendancy of Constantine, this vital truth has been forgotten. Furthermore, when the newfound freedom in the Church that led to laxity in the fourth century began to spread, the monastic spirituality that was used to bring about renewal, though good in itself, was not necessarily the ideal way to replace the family-orientated spirituality that prevailed in the early Church.

Long before religious life came into being in the guise of Monasticism, thanks to St Antony (AD 252–356), Christian Spirituality was predominantly devised for and lived by lay Christians. Religious life as we know it today did not exist. That the Mass and the sacraments were administered by a predominantly married clergy in the early Church was to be expected as part of the natural evolution of Christianity from the Jewish religion from which it arose. However, the spiritual reasons why celibate clergy gradually became the norm are as valid today as they were in the past. A return to married clergy therefore as the norm, plays no part in the suggestions for renewal that are put forward in this book. Nor is my emphasis on lay spirituality intended to undermine or disempower the hierarchical structure of the Church, but rather to re-empower its authority that derives from tradition and thrives on holiness.

Like Judaism, from which it derived, Christianity was primarily a domestic spirituality in which the family was paramount. Why not therefore, go back to discover what can immediately be applied to our lives, rather than trying to understand and live it through the spirituality of a religious order that was not primarily founded for lay people living in the world. We can still be inspired by religious orders and look to them for help and guidance in our spiritual search for God and in our prayer life, but it is we who must apply the principles of our faith and the way we sanctify our lives, as our first Christian ancestors did. It is from studying the way they practised what they called "white martyrdom" in such a way that their whole lives became the Mass, the place where they continually offered themselves through Christ to God, in and through all that they said and did, that we can learn to do the same in our day. Although I will be spending many chapters detailing the unique teaching on prayer of the great Carmelite Doctors of the Church, St John of the Cross and St Teresa of Ávila, I have not tried to base my own daily spiritual life on the way in which they lived their semi-monastic life within their religious communities. Instead, I have tried to base my daily spiritual timetable around the way in which Jesus lived with his first disciples both before and after the Resurrection and how it continued to develop, most particularly for, and by lay people, in those first Christian centuries. What was primarily done for the Church in later centuries under the influence and inspiration of religious orders, was done in the first Christian centuries by lay people inspired and animated from within by the dynamic action of the Holy Spirit.

This lesson needs to be realized and understood today, for what was primarily done by lay people in the early Church, can be done again today. It is sadly because of the failure of some of those on whom we used to depend in the past, that the task of spiritual renewal depends more on lay people today than at any other time in the history of the Church since the death of Constantine. The history of Catholic Spirituality has its ups and downs, it highs and it lows, its peaks and troughs, like a roller coaster at a fair ground. After the Roman Emperor, Theodosius the Great (AD 379–395), proclaimed that henceforth Christianity would be the official religion of his Empire, it would no longer be predominantly the family, but senior celibate clerics and religious orders who would take pride of place. It would be them who would take the lead in spiritual renewals and rescue the Church from the many downs, lows, and troughs into which it would sink in subsequent centuries.

On the surface it would seem that the family was marginalised and had all but lost the influence it had in the first Christian centuries. However, in the history of spiritual renewal there will always be a great Pope or Bishop, a famous Abbot or founder of a religious order, or even simple souls who became great saints, mystics or prophets, who took the lead and triggered what later came to be seen as epoch-making spiritual renewals. They were able to do this because they came so close to God in profound mystical contemplation that they were given the inner security and strength to journey on, enabling them to become dispensers of the love they received to others. This would not have been possible without the love they received from the families into which they were born. St Bonaventure put it simply when he said, "Contemplation is learned at the mother's breast". Whether this is physically or metaphorically true, the love that a would-be saint receives in their family is nearly always the psychological foundation for what they finally become.

It was when the Church found herself in some of her greatest spiritual downfalls that she was rescued by the love of Christ reaching out to us through the sacraments bringing about renewal, and the hope that springs from every good and loving marriage. That is because in the Sacrament of Marriage, the loving that is generated there not only regenerates the ministers of the sacrament themselves, but their children too, onto and into whom their love overflows. It is here that these children, through the love they are given, receive the inner security to journey on in both secular and spiritual marriages when the clouds begin to threaten darkness and gloom. If it were not for the love that I received in my family, most especially from my mother, I would not have had the strength to finish my schooling thanks to the dyslexia that impeded me, never mind to move on to the higher studies and to persevere in the spiritual marriage to which I committed myself when my well ran dry. It takes great inner strength and security to persevere, not just for months, but for years in mystical purification, for as my good friend Sr Wendy Beckett said, "Waiting alone in semi-darkness for God to do whatever he pleases, sums up what it means to follow Christ."

We are facing today one of the greatest crises ever in the history of the Church, and there seems little if any evidence to show that those who came to the rescue before are poised to save us from impending disaster. It is time for the domestic Church to rise and do what it did for the Church in the first Christian centuries. That is why I have primarily written this book for lay Catholics and detailed the same spirituality that inspired and sustained those first Christian families in the early Church. The future of the Church depends, perhaps more than ever before, on the original Christ-centred spirituality that must once more be generated in our families. If we cannot see that the family is at present the last bastion against the Church's own destruction, then I can assure you that its enemies have. It is for this reason that the enemies of the Church are at present launching the most fierce and vicious attack on the family ever known in the history of the Church, or for that matter in the history of humanity. It is here, in the domestic Church that we must rally together and mutually support one another before trying to do for the modern pagan world, what the first Christian families did for the ancient pagan world. However, it can only be done by totally committed lay people if they are prepared to cast off the garb of being little more than mere nominal Catholics. If they are prepared to "put on Christ" and abandon themselves daily to the Holy Spirit in an ever-deepening and ever-developing prayer life, then the long-awaited renewal will at last have begun.

Keep the dogmatic teaching of the Church always before you and a good Catechism to explain it. For, as St John Henry Newman said, we need an educated and committed laity today more than at any other time in history. That is why he wrote:

I want a laity, not arrogant, not rash in speech, not disputatious, but a laity who know their religion, who enter into it, who know just where they stand, who know what they hold and what they do not, who know their creed so well that they can give an account of it. I want an intelligent, well-instructed laity. I wish you to enlarge your knowledge, to cultivate your reason, to get an insight into the relation of truth to truth, to learn to view things as they are, to understand how faith and reason stand to each other, what are the bases and principles of Catholicism. You ought to be able to bring out what you feel and what you mean, as well as to feel and mean it.

If, as St Jerome insists, that "to be ignorant of the scriptures is to be ignorant of Christ" then regular, if not daily turning to the scriptures is of paramount importance. It is through the prayer that is generated here that we will be led on to come to know and love the person to whom we have abandoned ourselves. When there is evidence that more and more people are hearing and following the call to follow Christ along this way, and I see more and more evidence that this is the case with each passing day, then you can be sure that Newman's "new spring" has at last arrived. It is perhaps thanks to him more than anyone else that we have learned the way back to the future.

David Torkington

The Feast of the Stigmata of St Francis, 17th September, 2021.

Immediately before receiving this gift, St Francis received the revelation of the Primacy of Love.

Part 1

Vocal Prayer and Meditation

Chapter 1 The Unquenchable Fire of Love
Chapter 2 Listen to St Teresa of Ávila
Chapter 3 The Paramount Importance of Daily Prayer
Chapter 4 Introducing Christian Meditation
Chapter 5 Lectio Divina – Divine Reading
Chapter 6 The Essence of Prayer – Gently Trying
Chapter 7 Mystical Premonitions
Chapter 8 Making the Impossible Possible
Chapter 9 The Prayer Without Ceasing

Chapter 1

The Unquenchable Fire of Love

The first Jews used the symbol of unquenchable fire to depict the all-consuming power of God's love. The first Christians, however, believed that this love was now embodied in the Risen and glorified body of Jesus, as he rose from the dead on the first Easter day, and they used the radio-active energy of the sun to symbolize its saving power. This was most particularly manifested when Jesus released this love on us all on the first Pentecost day like a supernatural tsunami of loving. That is why the name Sunday came to be used by the first Christians to describe the most important day of their week, because the sun became for them a symbol of the Risen Christ. Like most Christian symbols they are no more than a shadow of the reality that they symbolize. If you wish to compare the energy released by the Sun to the love released by Our Lord at Pentecost, you will have to add to it the energy released by all the other stars in the firmament concentrated together. Multiply that energy by infinity and transpose it into love, into pure unadulterated loving, and you are not even halfway there!

This is the loving that bonded the Father to the Son from all eternity, released on the first Pentecost to draw us back into the Father who first conceived us, in and through the Son who released it. When St John said, "God is Love" (1 John 4:8), he was not trying to give a definition of what love is in itself as a Greek Philosopher would do, he was describing in his own language that God is Loving; that is what he is, and that is what he does, continually. Unlike the sun this love radiates outward and into all who would receive it, not just during the day, but day and night, to the end of time. If you think I am indulging in pious hyperbole then think again. No man-made myth, no fairy tale has ever told any story like this. No dreamer has ever dreamed such an incredible truth as this – yet it is the greatest truth ever told by the greatest man who ever lived.

Before the Resurrection, Jesus was limited by the physical body into which he freely chose to enter. His choice meant that he could only be in one place at a time, so meeting him would have been as difficult as meeting any major celebrity in our time. But that has all changed, because the same other-worldly love that raised him out of this world on the first Easter day enables him to re-enter it on every day. So now he can enter into us, so that he can make his home in us, and we can make our home in him as he promised at the Last Supper. All this is possible, not in some distant pipe dream, but here and now in the present moment. That is why Jean Pierre de Caussade, the great Jesuit mystic said, "The present moment contains far more than we have the capacity to receive, for it is full of infinite treasures."

These infinite treasures are all contained within the love of God as it first strikes the human heart and then like a prism distributes them to every part of the human personality. These spiritual treasures are not only full of the love we need, but the virtues too, that love generates within us enabling us to return this love in kind to God, and then share what we receive with others. He calls the here and now the "sacrament of the present moment" because it is the only moment where time touches eternity. It is the only moment where the love of God can reach out to us and we can reach out to him, to begin and to continue the journey for which every human being yearns deep down within them. It is the journey to the ultimate mystical marriage for which we all yearn, where our love and the love of Christ become one, in the Three in One, and to all eternity.

This is what we call the "Good News" because it is the best possible news that anyone can ever hear. But the bad news is that the infinite love that is continually available to us is different from all other forms of energy because love cannot be forced. We know this from our own experience as human beings. No matter how we love someone or how much they might love us, if that love is not welcome, if it is not received and reciprocated then it will have no effect at all, no matter how powerful it may be. It is the same with God's love. That is why from the very beginning the first question asked by the great saints and mystics is not, "How do we love God?" but "How do we freely choose to turn and open ourselves to receive his love?"

It is only then that his love can begin entering into our love in such a way that it can suffuse and surcharge our human loving with the divine. Then it can begin the ascent, in, with and through Christ, through whom this love is given, to contemplate the Father, in whom our final destiny is brought to perfection. But, and there always seems to be a "but" when we hear good news; if we do nothing to try to receive God's love then nothing will happen except that instead of going forwards in the spiritual life we will go steadily backwards. Prayer is the word used in the Christian tradition to describe what we do each day to turn and open ourselves to receive this love.

Chapter 2

Listen to St Teresa of Ávila

Making the spiritual ascent into God is rather like trying to run up a downward escalator. The moment you stop moving steadily forwards is the moment when you start moving steadily downward. Going forwards means finding daily time to do what St Peter told his listeners to do when he was the first to announce the good news that God's love had been unleashed on the first Pentecost Day. He told them to keep turning and opening themselves to God's love every moment of their lives. Speaking to them in the language they could understand, he used the word "repent". In Hebrew there is no such word for someone who has repented, but only for someone who is repenting. It is a continuous on-going process that pertains to the very essence of the Christian life. This repenting or turning and opening oneself to receive the love of God has to be learned, and the place where it is learned has traditionally been called prayer.

That is why there is nothing more important in our lives than prayer, because without it we cannot receive the only love that can make us sufficiently perfect to enter into the life of the Three in One to which we have been called. That is why St Teresa of Ávila said there is only one way to perfection and that is to pray and if anyone points in another direction they are deceiving you. There is nothing therefore more important than prayer. When human beings love their love is both physical and spiritual, but as God has no body his love is entirely spiritual. As a mark of respect we have come to call his love the Holy Spirit. As we keep turning and opening ourselves to receive the Holy Spirit in prayer, he continually draws us up like a supernatural magnet into Christ and then, in, with and through him into the life of the Three in One to contemplate and enjoy the Father's love to all eternity.

Many years ago, I was privileged to attend a retreat given by Cardinal Hume. After agreeing with St Teresa he went on to define exactly what he meant by prayer. He first quoted and then slightly modified the definition given in the penny Catechism. "Prayer", he said, "is trying to raise the heart and mind to God." The word he introduced to the old definition was "trying", to emphasize that the essence of prayer is in the trying.

The quality of our prayer is ultimately determined by the quality of our endeavour. It was for this reason that the great mystic and mother Saint Angela of Foligno said that prayer is the School of Divine Love. In other words, it is the place where we learn how to love God by trying daily to raise our hearts and minds to him. I intend to introduce you to the different means and methods that tradition has given us to help us to keep trying to turn and open our minds and hearts to God in this book, but first let me say this. There are no perfect means to help us keep trying to raise the heart and mind to God, just different means. What helps you at the beginning, may not help you later. What helps you in the morning may not help you in the evening. What helps me, might not help you. Remember the famous words of Dom John Chapman, "Pray as you can and not as you can't." The acid test is, does this means of prayer help me to keep trying to raise my heart and mind to God?

One thing I promise will happen when you seriously set aside some daily space and time for prayer. You will find that no matter what means of prayer you choose to use, you will be deluged by distractions. After a few weeks of distractions and temptations buzzing around in the head like a hornets' nest, many people decide they cannot pray. They then tend to pack up giving a special time for prayer, and only turn to God in extremis when they are in trouble. Here is the secret of prayer that has to be learned from the outset. The very distractions that you think are preventing you from praying are the very means that enable you to pray. That is why St Teresa of Ávila said that you cannot pray without them. Each time you turn away from a distraction to turn back to God, you are in fact performing an act of selflessness; you are saying no to self, and yes to God. If in fifteen minutes you have a hundred distractions, it means that one hundred times you have made one hundred acts of selflessness. Gradually, if you continue to do this day after day, then acts of selflessness lead to a habit of selflessness that helps you to pray better and better.

This is why St Angela of Foligno said that prayer is the School of Love where loving is learned by practising selfless loving. If you have many distractions and you keep turning away from them, then you will accomplish straight As when the examination comes around. If, however, you only have two; one is dreaming about where you are going for your next summer holiday and the next is worrying about how to earn the money to travel there, then that is a different matter. Let us suppose that when you settle down to pray you fall asleep. Is that prayer? No. On the other hand, let us suppose that the moment you are preparing to pray you are swept up into an ecstasy. Is that prayer? No. In the first case you were doing nothing, and in the second case God was doing everything. Strictly speaking you were not praying at all in either case. Prayer is what happens between the sleep and the ecstasy where you are continually trying to raise your heart and mind to God, and in so doing learning how to love in the School of Divine Love.

St Francis of Assisi said that it is in giving that we receive. In other words, as we try to give ourselves to God in prayer he gives himself to us. In our very endeavour to turn away from distractions in order to raise our hearts and minds to God, our endeavour becomes the channel through which our love rises to God and God's love descends into us. It is only then, as our weak human love is suffused and surcharged by the divine that we can begin to love God like never before. Then we can begin to observe the new commandment that Jesus taught us, which is to love God with our whole heart and mind, with our whole body and soul. At first glance it might be thought that this is not a new commandment, but the old commandment that the Jews in the Old Testament were taught. Yes, it was given to the Jews in the Old Testament, but they could never observe it as God wanted them to until Jesus came to show them how.

When St Peter told the crowd that the love of God promised in the Old Testament was on that very day being unleashed upon all, he told them to repent or to turn and open their hearts and minds to receive it. However, he told them to do something else too. He told them to be baptised, to undergo the new initiation ceremony. This initiation would not so much mark their entrance into a new organisation, institution or religion, but their entrance into a person, the person of Jesus himself now Risen and glorified. So now when they were told to continue repenting, trying to raise their hearts and minds to God, they would do it in Christ. But that is not all, for the same Holy Spirit whom he sent would so enter into their prayer that now they would be able to pray with him, and through him to the Father who had sent him in the first place. The daily battle against distractions now takes on a new meaning, for now it enables us to participate in Christ's death and Resurrection by daily dying ourselves each time we say "no" to self and "yes" to God. Once prayer is seen in this context then what was originally seen as a pointless activity can be seen as the most important activity that we can ever perform. After all, how can we expect to find that learning the most important thing that any human being can learn is easy, namely loving God, the first of the new commandments that Christ gave us. Learning to love in the School of Divine Love is the most important thing that we can learn, not just for our happiness on earth, but for our ultimate happiness hereafter.

The selflessness learned in prayer helps us outside of prayer too, as the habit of selflessness enables us to love others, our families, our husbands and wives, our children and others, too, who have need of our love. Now we see that the second of the new commandments becomes possible, that we should love others as he loves us. This can only become possible when, as we try to love him in prayer, our endeavour becomes the channel that enables his love to enter into us and into our loving, enabling him to love others through us, as his love gradually begins to suffuse our love with his own.

Eventually, as Christ is born again in us, the love received from him overflows outside the special times set aside for prayer to irrigate everything that we say and do in the rest of our lives. In this way we gradually begin to practise the prayer without ceasing, as every moment of our day becomes the time and place where we try to love God in all we do, and through him those we try to love. The sacrifices involved in doing this become the offerings that we take with us to Mass. This is the moment when, with the rest of the Christian community we offer up to God, in, with and through Christ, all the sacrifices that we have made as we tried to pray without ceasing throughout the previous week. These sacrifices added to the great sacrifice of Christ himself, enable God to fill us with his love in return, for it is indeed in giving that we receive. It is important to emphasize that the capacity to receive his love in return will not just be determined by the quality of the love that we try to generate once we have entered the church, but by the quality of the love that we have generated in the prayers, the good works, and the sacrifices that we have made during the previous week. These are the sacrifices that, when offered at Mass, determine the measure of the love that we will receive in return. It is this love that will enable us to go out and make the rest of our lives into the Mass.

Chapter 3

The Paramount Importance of Daily Prayer

If we are beginning a journey upon which our whole future depends, it is of paramount importance to understand exactly where we are going. When we begin to pray seriously, St Teresa of Ávila makes it clear that our destination is what she called the Mystical or Spiritual Marriage. The Greek Fathers called this same destination *divinization* or *theosis*.

In order to understand the way ahead, imagine a great classical archway that rises on two sides and meets at the centre keystone at the apex of the arch. The left side represents vocal prayer, the right side contemplative prayer that begins with meditation. In a balanced spiritual life, both grow and rise to perfection simultaneously meeting in the keystone which is Christ. Both are essential in an authentic life of prayer, as can be seen in the life of Christ.

We know for a fact that Christ used vocal prayers from his earliest years and continued to use vocal prayer to the end of his life, whilst at the same time being totally engaged in mystical contemplation. We know that he prayed using vocal prayer at least five times a day if not more, with his disciples, at home, at mealtimes, whilst travelling, as well as in the Synagogue and the Temple. However, from the moment he was born into this world, he was in his divine nature totally engaged in contemplating the infinite loving Father who sent him and to whom he would return with as many as would follow him. At times he would have to retreat to lonely places totally alone on the mountain side, into the inner room, into the garden "where it was his custom to pray". Here he would have longer periods of time to relish what he was receiving from his loving Father and to allow the love that he was receiving in his divine nature to percolate through ever more fully into his human nature. In this way he was enabling the two forms of prayer to become one, in what came to be called the "prayer without ceasing" which reaches its consummation in the mystical marriage.

We do not have a divine life like Jesus, but we do have an inner life that can develop into a contemplative life. This contemplative life takes us up and into Christ's own contemplation of his Father that began on earth, and which continues now in heaven. Here, our contemplation is fitted into his contemplation where his ecstatic joy becomes our ecstatic joy too. But let us begin at the beginning with the left-hand side of the archway in my analogy. Then I will return to the right-hand side, showing how meditation comes to its summit in what some have called Acquired Contemplation, or the Prayer of Simple Regard. This develops into the God-given contemplation that rises through purification under the guidance of the Holy Spirit into the Mystical or Spiritual Marriage that St Teresa of Ávila describes in her masterwork *The Interior Castle*.

Most of us, like Jesus, are taught set prayers by our mothers that we use for the rest of our lives. We add to them and are taught further prayers and devotions like the Rosary, the Stations of the Cross and innumerable other pious practices. Then, as we progress in the spiritual life, what were at first set prayers that we used to recite, are put into our own words as our intimacy with Christ deepens. Jesus made it clear that he wants us to become his brothers and sisters. He even went further when he said at the Last Supper that he wants us to become his friends. As this realization begins to register, vocal prayer understandably becomes correspondingly deeper and deeper and more and more intimate. Then finally the most profound realization of all begins to dawn. Christ wants this friendship to be as close as that of married couples, only even more penetrating, because as Jesus said at the Last Supper, "If anyone loves me he will keep my word, and my Father will love him, and we shall come to him and make our home with him" (John 14:23). This profound realization leads to deeply personal encounters with Christ in the language of love.

In the early Church it would take two years of preparation before a person was initiated into the Christian community. During this time, they were taught predominantly vocal prayers that were said at least five times a day. These prayers were derived from the Jewish prayers that Jesus was taught and which he used when he prayed with his disciples. Later, the disciples would teach the first Christians to use them too. However, after the sending of the Holy Spirit these prayers were said in a new context as the Holy Spirit drew all who were open to receive him into the mystical body of Christ. That is why these traditional prayers and new ones that were added were all prayed, in him, with him, and through him to the Father. It is these prayers that would be used daily by the first Christians for two years before they were baptised on Easter night and taken up into the Mystery of Christ with others who had undergone the same training in practical daily prayer.

The more you become acquainted with the lives of the saints the more you will become aware of the mystical dialogues that took place between them and their "Tremendous Lover". Some of these, like the dialogues of St Catherine of Siena were written down. Sometimes Christ would appear to them in person with revelations that were not just for them personally, but for the rest of us, like the revelation to St Francis of Assisi about the primacy of love, and the revelation to St Margaret Mary about that same primacy of love, as embodied in the Sacred Heart. The point I want to make is that when vocal prayer is taken seriously and deepens daily, it becomes what the Divine Office is meant to be for priests and religious.

It is of paramount importance to be taught and to practise the daily prayer and the prayers that should underpin every authentic Christian's spiritual life, as practised by Jesus and his disciples before the Resurrection and by all his devoted followers after the Resurrection down to the present day. They are vital, as I tried to show with the analogy of the Archway. I want to stress this point to encourage readers to put into practice more formal prayers, so that when the time comes for purification in the dark night you will have in place a regular and practised pattern of daily prayer. It is this daily prayer that will sustain you when mystical prayer seems to have plunged you into darkness from which there seems to be no escape.

If our daily vocal prayers are genuinely inspired by the Holy Spirit, they will automatically mirror characteristic themes such as sorrow for sin, expressions of faith, sacrifice, offerings, acts of praise, thanksgiving and adoration that are the very essence of the Mass. Just as the act of worship opens the community to receive the fullness of God's love in the Mass, so it also opens everyone to that same love in the daily personal prayers that enable our whole lives to become the Mass. In other words, the place where we offer minute by minute, hour by hour, day by day all we say and do, all our successes our failures, all our joys and all our sorrows and sufferings to God through Jesus. Therefore, for the man or woman of faith, every moment is the moment when we both offer our selfless loving to God to receive his loving in return, in, with and through Christ in whom we live and move and have our very being. This is how every moment becomes a sacrament, the "sacrament of the present moment" where time reaches out through love to touch eternity.

Vocal prayer can become the very foundation of all prayer in which we can always find solace and support when the contemplative way seems to lead nowhere but into dark nights when the well runs dry. But I will return to this later.

Chapter 4

Introducing Christian Meditation

The whole point of authentic Christian meditation is not just to come to know and love the most divine and loveable of human beings who once walked on this earth. The truth is far more profound, for the very same Christ whom we are coming to know and love in our meditation on his life in the past, is alive and present to us here and now. He is not only near us now but, as St Augustine put it, he is "as close to us as we are to ourselves". This is the meaning of the Resurrection. Love of its very nature wants union; it wants to be united with the one who it loves. It is not possible to be united with someone who once lived, but only with someone who is alive now. That is why, as meditation enables a person to come to know and love Jesus, as he once was, it gradually leads us into contemplation where we can be united with him as he is now, Risen and glorified. Then, in, with and through him, we can be united with the Father who is our final destiny.

Nevertheless, at the beginning when we first begin to meditate on the Christ of history, it may seem that we who have not known him face to face are at a disadvantage. Although that cannot be denied, we are nonetheless greatly advantaged in another way. The continual and intimate personal relationship, day by day, hour by hour, minute by minute that was not possible even to his closest disciples two thousand years ago, is open to us here and now. Getting to know Jesus whilst he was on earth, inevitably involved coming and going, meeting and departing. Not even his nearest and dearest could be with him all the time. However, after the Resurrection all that changed. Now, raised outside the limitations of space and time, he can be with everyone at one and the same time, and furthermore he can be with us all the time, because he can be with us from the inside through love.

The Resurrection did not mean that Jesus became transformed into some sort of disembodied spirit other than the man who walked the highways and byways of Palestine, as he was at pains to make clear. That is why he showed the marks of his suffering to his disciples, made those who doubted touch him and shared food with them. Whatever else happened to him at his glorification, his human nature was still fully intact, as was his divine nature. If he was not the same person as before, it was not because he was less of, but more of a man, because his glorification meant that all his human qualities were brought to perfection through the love that totally penetrated him through his divine nature. These qualities were refined, distilled and transformed by the love of God who raised him from the dead. Now he can continue his work on earth through those who are prepared to receive him. William of Saint-Thierry, a Benedictine monk and a good friend of St Bernard who was his mentor, once said, "You will never love someone unless you know them, but you will never really know them unless you love them." If you wish to go deeper into the spiritual life therefore, you have to learn first of all how to come to know and love Jesus Christ. The more you come to know him, then the more you will come to love him. The question is, how do we come to know this adorable human being now so that we can come to love him over two thousand years after he lived on earth? How do we communicate with him every day of our lives?

There is nothing mysterious about human communication. How does anyone come to know anyone else except by using words? The spaces between people are bridged by words. They enable us to find out more about them, to draw closer to them and, if they are loveable, to love them. Therefore Christians have always regarded the Gospels with such reverence because they enable us to come to know and love the man who was the perfect human embodiment of God's infinite loving. When we learn to listen to his words, we learn to listen to God. When we learn to love him, we learn to love God. When we meditate on the Gospels we enable the Christ of history not just to come alive in our imaginations and in our memories, but in every moment of our daily lives now in the twenty-first century. This is the very essence of our faith. The Christ of ancient times has now become the Christ of all times. His new transformed and transfigured body means that he can, not only be close to us every day of our lives but enter into us just as it enabled him to enter into the Upper Room after his Resurrection despite solid walls and bolted doors. No physical barrier can prevent him doing what he came to do, what he wishes to do more than anything else. And what is that? It is for him to enter into us now, and for us to enter into him, as he promised at the Last Supper. Please read slowly and prayerfully the whole of chapter 14 of St John's Gospel to read about not just what Christ wished to do in the past, but what he wishes to do now in the present.

Long before we were married to another human being we were married to Christ when his life flooded into our lives at Baptism. When Christ said that the Kingdom of God, which for us begins at baptism, is like a wedding feast, that is precisely what he meant. He does not mean that we are like the guests who will all be having a good time, but like the bride who will experience the joy of being united with him, the bridegroom. It is for this reason that the Fathers of the Church use the analogy of one of the most beautiful love poems ever to have been written, "The Song of Songs" or "The Song of Solomon". However, just as married life becomes a sham if the married couples stop loving one another after the marriage ceremony, the same is true of our marriage to Christ. Any happily married couple greet each other with love the moment they wake in the morning, and the love that binds them together supports and sustains them both throughout their daily life until that love is sealed with a loving kiss at the end of that day. One way or another they are continually in each other's hearts and minds even when they are not in each other's arms. The same must be true of our marriage with Christ and that is why after greeting him at the beginning of our day, the Morning Offering can enable us to be with him and he with us at every moment of the forthcoming day, in all we say and do.

What cannot be true of our relationship with our husband and wife can be true of our relationship with Christ because he is not only with us, but in us, and we are in him at every moment of our lives as St Paul discovered on the Road to Damascus. If we claim to be Christians, but day after day passes by without us speaking to Christ, our spiritual marriage will soon become a sham and then a scandal. Our neighbours will soon begin to think, if not to say, "If this is what Christianity does for its believers then I'll manage very well without it." For practising Christians, the love generated in their spiritual marriage with Christ overflows into their physical marriage with their husband or wife and it overflows onto their children too. The reason why Catholic marriages have traditionally been seen as the ideal, is not so much because the couples believe in the same teachings of the Church, but that they have been brought up to practise selfless giving. This will have been learnt as they freely give their time to express their love of God in Church and in private prayer and in trying to love their neighbours, especially those in need.

This selfless giving will have firstly been learnt at home through trying to love their parents and their brothers and sisters. In short, the selflessness practised for twenty years or more before their marriage to another human being is the best guarantee of a successful marriage that depends on a habit of selflessness more than on anything else. It is this that will enable the couple to generate a supernatural quality of love, not just for themselves, but for their future family too and those who will be inspired by that family.

It was this quality of love that astounded the ancient pagan world into which Christianity was born and was responsible more than anything else for the conversion of a pagan world into a Christian world in such a short time. This same quality of love can do the same for the near pagan world that we live in today. All we must do is to enable Christ to reach out to that world through us. If we only radically open ourselves to receive him then he will do the rest.

Chapter 5

Lectio Divina – Divine Reading

In vocal prayer, despite the time given to brief moments of silence, we have been doing most of the talking. However, for prayer to lead on to generate the quality of love that will alone permanently change us for the better, we must learn to listen. If our spiritual life is to deepen we need to learn to stop talking and listen, to be silent and to allow ourselves to be loved. This is why all authentic Christian prayer begins not by flinging ourselves into obscure states of transcendental awareness, but by trying to listen to God's words as embodied in the words of Jesus Christ. This is how the early Christians used to pray in a method of prayer that later came to be called *Lectio Divina* or the divine or sacred readings. It was so called, not just because they believed the words they read were inspired, but because they also believed that they too would be inspired by the Holy Spirit as they read them. They believed that through these sacred readings they would be led on and into a profound dialogue with Jesus that would lead them on and into "the love of Christ, which is beyond all knowledge, where we are filled with the utter fullness of God" (Ephesians 3:18–19).

Whatever other methods of prayer we may at times find helpful, we must never forget and always turn back to the Scriptures as the Christian prayer book *par excellence.* In the Middle Ages, a Carthusian monk called Guido coined four Latin words that have been used ever since to describe the four steps of *Lectio Divina* or Christian Meditation. They show how they can lead serious-minded Christians onward to experience the love that surpasses all understanding. These Latin words are only used to sum up the way ordinary Christians prayed from the earliest of times, enabling people who had not known Jesus personally to love him. The words are *Lectio* – Reading, *Meditatio* – Reflecting on what is read, *Oratio* – Reacting in prayer to the sacred texts and *Contemplatio* – Relishing, while reacting in fewer and fewer words, and then in silence, to the love that is experienced. Many of the early Christians knew whole passages, if not all the Gospels by heart. They had no other prayer books to hand, nor did they have need of them. When the first Christians used the scriptures, most particularly the New Testament, they were not interested in how much they read, but in how deeply they penetrated the sacred texts in their search for wisdom.

The wisdom for which they searched was not a body of facts, but a body – a mystical body full of loving, who continues to love now as he did when he was on earth. They would read a few verses at a time going over them for a second and a third time, poring over them, entering more profoundly into their dynamic inner meaning. Then they would pause in moments of deep interior stillness to allow the same Spirit who inspired the scriptures in the first place, to inspire them too, with knowledge and love for the man who had come to redeem them. When they had savoured one text, they would reverently move on to another, and then repeat the process, leaving pauses for silence for the impact of the words to seep into the very marrow of their being. As this prayer grew more and more intense, the moments of silence would become more and more prolonged, and as love blossomed, words would naturally give way to periods of profound inner contemplative loving.

Now before going any further, I want to make an important point that we should never forget. When we say that God created us in his image and likeness, we mean that it is God's love that is deepest in us, despite what nature and nurture has done to distort it. When least distorted, it not only mirrors God's love, but in some mysterious way it embodies it deep down within us. And it is from this love that *a primeval prayer* rises and takes the form of a desire to touch and experience the ultimate source of all love which is God. It is this God-given desire to return to the One who made us that I want to highlight because it is the continual and ongoing impulse that must be supported and sustained by the various methods of prayer that I will propose. The methods will change, but the God-given desire that they support will never essentially change except in its strength. All that will happen is that the desire that is so subtle to begin with becomes stronger and stronger, as it is fuelled and finally purified, to attain the union for which it craves. It is because this inner spiritual growth cannot be seen that it has been called from the beginning a hidden, secret, or mystical growth or journey. The word mystical is derived from the Greek word that simply means secret. A person who gives over their life to taking part in this secret hidden journey came to be called a mystic. The study that specializes in studying this journey and in guiding people through it is called Mystical Theology.

Let me now return to describing how this journey begins before describing how it continues and finally reaches its completion. It begins with God who is responsible for making his love the very ground and foundation of our being – his own image and likeness within us. It is from this foundation that the primeval desire, or prayer, as I have called it, arises quite naturally to reach out for that for which it was created, the ongoing, ever increasing and never ceasing infinite loving. Although this desire may always be there, the influence of nature and nurture may make it more pronounced at some times, rather than at others. Even though it is always there, it will inevitably wax and wane like the moon unless something is done by us to sustain its continual presence.

In order to do this, we need to construct a spiritual way of life for that purpose in which we endeavour to do all in our power to nurture this God-given desire. If this is not done then the desire that can literally become our salvation will continue to wax and wane throughout our lives without changing us one jot or one iota. But the only love that can nurture, sustain, and perfect this

God-given love is God's love itself. That is what Jesus gave to his first disciples both before and after the Resurrection. However, this was not possible in quite the same way for the second wave of followers who never saw him in person. It was for this reason that an entirely new way of prayer was designed for the very first time. It was designed to introduce those who had never known Jesus in person to meet him in what came to be called "meditation".

Those who knew Jesus in person told new followers all about him as they were being prepared for membership of the first Christian community. Sometimes at weekly Mass there would be more than one apostle or disciple who would captivate their listeners, telling stories of all that Jesus had said and done. Then evangelists like Matthew, Mark, Luke and John and others would write their recollections down so that later followers like us could take part in this new form of prayer that teaches a person how to come to know and be united with Jesus through love. Then finally by entering into his secret or mystical body, they in their day, like us in our day could unite with God himself through mystical contemplation.

For the Fathers of the Church, the prayerful reading of the scriptures was a sacred mystery or a sacrament. It was a unique sacrament, because anyone could turn to it at any time of the day or night. In the first centuries when Greek, not Latin, was the language of the Church, meditating on the scriptures was seen as one of the other great mysteries or sacraments after baptism, because it could lead the faithful on through meditation into Jesus Christ, the flesh and blood embodiment of God's love. It can and will do the same for us today. The scriptures are there ready and waiting, all we must do is to turn to them to read them slowly and prayerfully to enable us to love Christ ever more deeply, and the Holy Spirit will do the rest.

Chapter 6

The Essence of Prayer – Gently Trying

Prayer is a process of continual inner conversion that involves gently trying to turn, open and surrender the heart to God. As the process is practised, the heart is made accessible to the heart of God, and his love shafts down to purify and empty it so that Christ can come to birth again in us. I do not want to start hair-splitting, but I think it is very important to distinguish between what is the essence of prayer and what are the means to prayer. People are always asking me to advise them what method of prayer to adopt, or more usually to bless the prayer pattern that they have already adopted. Some people fritter away their lives searching for the spiritual equivalent of the Philosopher's Stone, the magic formula for prayer which will infallibly lead to mystical contemplation, or to whatever other spiritual "goodies" they have set their hearts on. The truth of the matter is, there is no perfect means of prayer. There are just different means to help us to keep gently trying to turn and open our hearts to the only One who can make us new. Methods and techniques of prayer are like props. Their purpose is to help a person to keep on loving, to keep turning back to God. If the Rosary helps to do this, if the stations of the Cross or some other devotional practice is useful then that is fine. Others may find the slow meditative reading of the Scriptures helpful, responding to them in their own heartfelt prayer, or by using ancient prayers like the Jesus prayer. Saying prayers from the liturgy, like the Gloria from the Mass or even the great Eucharistic prayers themselves, said very slowly and prayerfully can be used.

The important point to remember is, there is no magic formula, no infallible method or technique. There are just hundreds of different ways of prayer to do one and the same thing. A means of prayer is good for you if it helps you, here and now, to keep gently turning your heart back to God. What might help you at the beginning of your spiritual journey may be of no use later. What helps in the morning may not help in the evening. What helps you one minute might not help you the next. So please move from one method to another with complete freedom. Remember that these methods are only means. Beware of the "here today and gone tomorrow" gurus who have a fixation about a particular means of prayer which they enjoin upon everybody without question as a panacea. They know nothing about the spiritual life. If they did, they would know that methods of prayer change as people change and as prayer develops with the years. Remember the words of Dom John Chapman, "Pray as you can, not as you can't."

Let me now put the microscope upon the greatest mystic who has ever walked upon the face of this earth to catch him in the act of praying. Here we see yet again, this time even more clearly, the essential ingredients of authentic Christian prayer. At the end of his life, Jesus knew that his hour had come. He knew that in a short time he would be betrayed by one of his own. He would be dragged in front of the Jewish authorities to be accused of being a blaspheming liar. He was to be dressed like a fool and paraded in front of that debauched dilettante, Herod. He was to be stripped by the Romans, flogged literally within an inch of his life, dragged through the streets like a common criminal, and then hung up naked and bleeding, to die on a Roman gibbet. His humanity rebelled at the very thought of it; he was in desperate need and so now, in his hour of greatest need, he turned for help to his Father in prayer.

He goes into the garden "where it was his custom to pray", and there throws himself down upon the ground to beg for the help and strength to remain steadfast to the end. Then he tries to turn and open himself to receive help and strength from his Father, but he is overwhelmed by a thousand and one distractions, taunted by temptations that threaten to come between him and the love of his Father. Where do the temptations come from? What is the source from which these temptations arise? They come from the memory, from the imagination, from the feelings that all batter upon the mind, bludgeoning it with blows that all but bring it into submission.

Firstly, his memory looks back over almost thirty years. How many times in those years did he come to Jerusalem? How many times did he approach other major cities in Palestine and see there on the rubbish tip outside the city gates slaves, criminals of every sort hung up on post and crossbeam, half flayed alive, slowly choking to death. Then his imagination comes into play as he begins to imagine that this will be happening to him the next day. He begins to realize more poignantly than ever the atrocious agony that he will have to endure at the hands of his own people, and before the loving gaze of those who love him most. He is bathed in blood, sweat and tears, and his deepest feelings are aroused and they rise up to batter his mind, to beleaguer it with a thousand and one questions. Why, for what purpose? Or at least, why this way, and not another? The temptation to take a shortcut that tested him in the desert, tests him now to the limits of his endurance so that he begins to pray. "Father, if you are willing, take this cup away from me" (Luke 22:42). Then the Holy Spirit enables him to pray time and again, "Let your will be done, not mine," until he becomes the prayer he makes, the will of God made flesh.

This is real prayer. He relentlessly turned and opened himself to the Father and was repeatedly emptied of every thought, word and desire that stood in the way of the total surrender he made and re-made in that hallowed place. The angel of consolation who came to comfort and support him brought moments of light to his darkness, giving him the help and strength to go on surrendering himself in prayer. In the process of his final prayer, he was given the power and the strength to go out of that garden, to bring what he preached to others to perfection in the final moments of his life on earth. What was learned with the heart in Gethsemane was put into practice with his whole being on Calvary. Now we can see the real meaning and inner nature of Christian prayer; see how it is the school in which the heart is trained and disciplined in the selflessness that leads us into the selfless sacrificial prayer of Jesus. It is the place where we learn to participate in his death and Resurrection. It is the place where true imitation leads to an identification that enables the Risen One to be present to the world through us.

To follow Christ means to take up our daily Cross even if compared with his it is no more than a matchwood cross. To do this, we need to do what he did by turning to God our Father for help and strength as he did in Gethsemane. It is here in our prayer that we, like him, have to experience temptations and distractions as he did, but this must never put us off. Remember always that as we endlessly try to turn away from these obstacles, they no longer become obstacles but the means by which we show our love for God by turning our hearts and minds back to him, no matter how powerful these distractions or temptations become. This is how our stumbling blocks become stepping stones to receive the quality of love that only God can give us. This then is how the repentance that St Peter called upon us all to practise on the first Pentecost day is practised repeatedly. It enables us to be more and more open to receive the same Holy Spirit whom he and his fellow apostles received, eventually making all things possible. With love, all things are possible that were once quite impossible without it. Prayer is the place where in praying as Christ did in Gethsemane, we practise today what St Peter called upon his listeners to practise almost 2,000 years ago.

The love that we continually express for God by turning away from temptations and distractions, by continually saying no to self and yes to God, will enable his love to enter into us to do in us what is quite impossible without it. That is why St Teresa of

Ávila said that you cannot pray without them! If God gives us profound experiences of his love in prayer to change us, then that is his gift and his gift alone. Our part is to keep turning to him in prayer so that he can give us this gift of his love, his Holy Spirit, who can alone transform us into the image and likeness of his Son Jesus Christ.

Chapter 7

Mystical Premonitions

After the Protestant Reformation, a new terminology began to replace the older monastic terminology used for the beginning of mental prayer devised by Guido the Carthusian (1114–c.1193). The reading of the scriptures was no longer mentioned as the first rung on the ladder of prayer that leads to contemplation – *Lectio* was of course not forbidden, but after the Reformation it was frowned upon by the Church, at least for the laity for fear they would misinterpret the scriptures as the reformers did. It was also feared that they may make use of some of the many new translations of the Bible in which orthodoxy had intentionally been "lost in translation". In the new terminology then, Meditation not *Lectio* was the first step in mental prayer. What was called *Oratio* before now came to be called Affective Prayer when the emotions were moved by the loving and adorable person of Christ as the person praying began to realize that Christ's loving was directed towards them personally. As in human loving words are gradually used less and less as union comes ever closer. In his book *Women in Love* D.H. Lawrence writes, "Words travel between the separate parts, but in the perfect One there is a perfect silence of bliss." Prayer then becomes simpler and simpler and is therefore understandably called Prayer of Simplicity or Acquired Contemplation or the Prayer of Simple Regard when all a person wants to do is to be lost in the loving gaze of the one whom they know and experience as loving them now.

The first step therefore in mental prayer was called Meditation and it included the prayerful reading and reflection on the scriptures for those immune to the dangers of falling into the errors of the reformers. Others were encouraged to read the lives of Christ written by some of the great spiritual writers or to make use of the many meditation manuals or the exercises of St Ignatius or devotions like the Way of the Cross or the Rosary. We are living today in a completely different spiritual climate when we should all be encouraged to begin as the first Christians began with the scriptures themselves, for there are now so many good and reliable translations to choose from. However, it must be said that like St Augustine, many of us first experienced the love of God in his creation long before we were introduced to any systematic form of mental prayer. In fact it was these experiences that so moved us, as they moved St Augustine, that made us seek God in himself. This is the point at which a genuine searcher is led on, like St Augustine, to a more formal form of mental prayer where God's love made flesh is to be discovered in the Gospels in the most perfect human being who ever lived.

Like many of us, St Augustine first encountered the love of God mirrored in the enchanting landscapes created on earth and the beautiful fauna and flora that filled them. So too in the great artistic works of the men and women who tried to reflect their beauty and grandeur in their paintings and their music and in their artistic masterpieces. But like so many others who would follow him, St Augustine's fascination with the reflections of God's glory would lead him onward to his greatest masterwork, God's love-made-man in Jesus Christ. The beginning of his search then was prompted by what I can only call mystical premonitions that many of us may well have experienced too. They come more directly from God and involve brief albeit fleeting experiences of what, or rather of whom, we want to experience all the time, but for our human weakness. Here is the classic example of the point I am trying to make, taken from St Augustine's Confessions:

> When first I knew you, you lifted me up so that I might see that there was something to see, but that I was not yet the man to see it. And you beat back the weakness of my gaze,

blazing upon me too strongly, and I was shaken with love and with dread. You called and cried to me and broke open my deafness and you sent forth your beams and shone upon me and chased away my blindness. You breathed fragrance upon me, and I drew in my breath, and do now pant for you. I tasted you, and now hunger and thirst for you. You touched me, and I have burned for your peace. So I set about finding a way to gain the strength that was necessary for enjoying you. And I could not find it until I embraced the mediator between God and man, the man Christ Jesus, who is over all things, who was calling unto me saying, I am the way, the truth and the life.

The experiences that St Augustine first enjoyed were common to many before and after him, although few can explain the experiences as he can. Many people have enjoyed what are sometimes called "natural" mystical experiences to which I have just referred, but they find it difficult to express them. Whilst the poets spend all their time trying to transpose them into words and capture them in sublime poetry, Augustine rushes on to seek the source from whom they came. St Augustine spent years coming to know Jesus by poring over his every word in the Scriptures and by responding in his own words until a sort of spiritual conversation developed in his prayer life. To begin with the knowledge was predominantly intellectual but it gradually became more and more emotional as he experienced the love of Christ reaching out to envelop his mind and heart and his whole being. Now he began to respond in the language of love (Affective Prayer), as his deepest feelings awoke to the love he experienced reaching out to envelop him. Finally, when everything had been said that needed to be said, he found that all he wanted to do was to be still, to savour in silence what he had received in a deep but heartfelt contemplative stillness (Acquired Contemplation). What happened to St Augustine will happen to all who follow his example. This contemplative stillness is similar to the experience of those who come to the heights of human love as John Donne describes so beautifully in his poem "The Ecstasy".

> We like sepulchral statues lay;
> All day, the same our postures were,
> And we said nothing, all the day.

It is into a similar silence that we must go if we wish to journey on, in, with and through Christ to contemplate the glory of the Creator himself. That is why when we begin to meditate in earnest as St Augustine did, we must begin not just with the scriptures in general, but with those parts of the sacred books that enable us to meet the person of Christ – the most loveable and adorable human being ever to have walked on this earth. The Gospels make it clear that his personal and ever-ready love is not just for those he met in person while he was on earth, but for each of us in person for whom he came, for whom he died and for whom he rose from the dead. And the purpose of this love is to take us up in, with and through him to the place where the primeval desire for the fullness of love that we first experienced long ago will find its fulfillment.

In short, begin your meditation by primarily using the Gospels to centre your whole attention on the person of Jesus so that knowledge can gradually turn to love. Affective Prayer begins when the sparks of love that are generated there begin to lead upwards and into the Risen Christ. Here the sparks of love that were produced in us are united to the infinite flame of love that burns in him now. For although our meditation begins by turning to the Christ who once lived to ignite our love for him, that love then rises to be united to him as he is now in his risen glory. It is possible to love someone who once lived in the past, but it is not possible for that love to unite us with that person now. We can only be united in love with a person who is alive and loving us now. That person is Our Risen Lord whom St Augustine not only knew was alive and living amongst us now, but who was, in his words, "closer to us than we are to ourselves".

But for this closeness to become a deep personal and loving union we must learn to love him repeatedly and ever more deeply. Never be deceived into thinking that the Risen Christ is some sort of purely spiritual realization of the person that he used to be on earth. It must always be remembered that he still has a real physical body that is even more perfect than the body known to and loved by his friends who were close to him whilst he was on earth. The truth is that it was even more perfect, because all the loveable human character traits and all the captivating human feelings, emotions and passions seen in the selfless giving of himself for others, are in fact all brought to perfection in him in his glorified body. They are all brought to perfection in him by the power of the same love of God who raised him from the dead and can be both experienced and received by those who are open to receive his love now.

All these realizations will eventually lead to the desire, not only to love Christ, but to enter into him now, for union with the fullness of love is the ultimate destiny and desire of every human being. In prayer this desire is set alight with the sparks that eventually light the flame of love that sets us afire with the love of Christ, enabling us to contemplate the Father, in, with and through him. It is called Acquired Contemplation to distinguish it from pure mystical contemplation.

Chapter 8

Making the Impossible Possible

In the prayer that leads from meditation to contemplation, the deep human desire for love that has always been there is gradually transformed. It is set alight by reflecting and ruminating on love – God's love. This love is made visible to us as we see it embodied in Jesus Christ, and as it is expressed in all that he said and did in his life, death and Resurrection. Gradually, as meditation deepens, the same Holy Spirit who gave birth to Jesus and inspired and animated all that he was and all that he did begins to suffuse and surcharge our weak human love. At first, sparks of love are generated that gradually become a single flame that reaches out to the love that burns in Christ, until the flashpoint comes when his love and our love become as one. This, the high point of meditation, is called Acquired Contemplation, the Prayer of Simple Regard, or Prayer of Simplicity. It is experienced in the mind, the heart, and the body, as our whole person is deeply enthralled by love.

For this whole process to take place in what St Angela of Foligno called the School of Divine Love, time must be found for meditation or nothing will happen. But if time is given regularly, then in time we will receive the love that I have been describing. It will so suffuse and surcharge our love that we will be able to behave more and more like Christ, not only enabling us to love God in and through him, but to love others too as Jesus loved others; now he is able to love them through us. That is what St Paul meant when he said, "I live now, not with my own life, but with the life of Christ who lives in me" (Galatians 2:20).

I have often been asked how long it takes to arrive at Acquired Contemplation. It simply depends on the time we can give for the sort of meditation that I have been describing.

With daily regularity one or two years at the most, but few of us can do this when family life is at its most demanding. In perfect conditions, and with help, it can take much less. Before the heresy of Quietism (1687) undermined mystical theology as I describe later, the noviciate was seen as the place where young religious would be taught the meditation that would lead them to Acquired Contemplation. This was seen as the ideal, because Acquired Contemplation does not last for long before the prayer is suddenly led into Mystical Contemplation, and for this sudden new departure, help, explanations and the support of a competent novice master or novice mistress is needed.

The spiritual life seems to have become so complicated that you feel you need a couple of degrees in theology just to understand it before you can attempt to live it. Yet it is essentially simple; so simple that you need the simplicity of a little child to see it. There is only one thing that is necessary, and that is love. Not our love of God, but his love of us. In other words, Christianity is firstly a mysticism, not a moralism. It is not primarily concerned with detailing the perfect moral behaviour that we see embodied in Christ's life and then trying to copy it, virtue by virtue in our lives. That is stoicism, not Christianity and it is doomed to failure. Christianity is primarily concerned with teaching us how to turn and open ourselves to receive the same Holy Spirit who filled Jesus. The more we are filled with his love then the easier it is to return it in kind, as the divine suffuses and then surcharges human love so that it can reach up to God and out to others. Then, and only then are we able to love God with our whole heart and mind and with our whole being and to love our neighbour as Christ loves us.

The trouble is we make the same mistake with Christ as we do with the saints. We read their lives backward. We read about their rigorous way of life, their superhuman sacrifices, and their heroic virtues, and believe that the only way we can be like them is to do likewise. If we only read their lives forward instead of backward then we would see that they were only capable of doing the seemingly impossible because they first received the power to do it in prayer. If we try to be and do what they did without first receiving what they received in prayer, then our brave attempts will inevitably end in disaster. True imitation of Christ or any of his saints means firstly copying the way they did all in their power to receive in prayer the Holy Spirit who inspired and strengthened them with his love; to do what is impossible without it. That is essentially all we must do. That is why the spiritual life is so simple if only we have the simplicity of a little child to see it.

Although it is true that you cannot have a mystical life without an ascetical life, asceticism for a beginner is quite simple. Do not give up anything you like or enjoy except when it prevents you from giving quality space and time to God in prayer each day. If you think it is too easy then try it and stick to it and you will soon find it is not quite as easy as you thought. Do not let first enthusiasm fool you into heroics that you will never sustain. When you have persevered for long enough you will gradually begin to receive and then experience the love that will enable you to do what is quite impossible without it.

When we fall in love and begin to experience being loved, then there is nothing we would not do, nor any sacrifice we would not make for the person we love. We positively look for things to do, the harder and the more exacting the better, to enable us to show the real quality of our love. What was impossible to a self-centred egotist only a short time before becomes not only easier but also our greatest pleasure. It is the same in the spiritual life. The exemplary behaviour, the extraordinary self-discipline and the heroic sacrifices made by those who begin to experience the love of God are not the results of arrogant stoics trying to make themselves perfect. They are the actions of those desperate to express their love in behaviour that could not be maintained for long without the love that sustains them from within. All the little pleasures and pastimes that were thought indispensable before, suddenly become dispensable, and with the greatest of ease.

When the love of God strikes a human heart it strikes it as a simple ray of light strikes a prism. Just as that light is then diffused and transformed into all the colours of the rainbow, so the love of God is diffused and transformed into all the virtues and supernatural gifts that are needed. All this happens simultaneously, as the love of God suffuses our own imperfect love, making it possible for us to love God in return and the neighbour in need, in all that we say and do. In short, first seek God and his Kingdom which is love, and everything else you want or desire will be given to you.

Chapter 9

The Prayer Without Ceasing

The first Christians were urged to pray constantly, and this prayer became known later as the "prayer without ceasing", "Pray constantly; and for all things give thanks to God, because this is what God expects you to do in Christ Jesus" (1 Thessalonians 17–18). The Morning Offering and its implementation is the place where the whole of the forthcoming day can be dedicated to loving God through a continual process of prayer, self-sacrifice and the service of others. For the early Christians, this daily endeavour was offered together with the daily endeavours of all their brothers and sisters at their weekly Mass. What they received together as they offered all the sacrifices made during the previous week, enabled them to receive all the graces that would sustain them spiritually in the forthcoming week. If we only follow their example then our lives will be irrevocably changed, as we exercise our priesthood every day of our lives so that the whole of our lives becomes the Mass, the place where we continually offer ourselves through Christ to the Father. When this profound and mystical spirituality is practised within the mystical body of Christ by all, from the Pope at the top to the humblest lay person at the bottom, then everyone will be always open to the love of the Holy Spirit. In the early Church when a higher percentage of Christians than at any other time in history were committed to living out this mystical spirituality, their very presence had an enormous influence on the Greco-Roman world in which they lived. The unprecedented example of unbridled selfless charity and all the gifts that charity brings with it converted the ancient pagan world into a Christian world in a comparatively short space of time. The same can be done today. But only the Holy Spirit can do it. It is our privilege to allow him to do it through us, through the quality of our daily prayer life.

If you read the liturgists and the historians of early Christianity who had such an influence on the Second Vatican Council, great emphasis is placed on public liturgical worship. However, this emphasis has often been to the detriment of the personal and daily prayer that enabled the first Christians to participate in the liturgy with such effect. This aspect of early Christian spirituality is regrettably all too often dealt with only as a footnote, or as a brief appendage under the heading of "daily devotions of the early Christians", or some other such title. It is quite evident that before, during and after the Council otherwise well-meaning scholars, theologians, liturgists and historians have failed to grasp the crucial importance of the personal daily spiritual endeavour of ordinary Christian men and women, most of all in their daily prayer life.

When I was a small boy during the Second World War, I remember the sirens going off shortly after the Mass had begun. The priest simply carried on, nor did the people rush to the shelters despite the sound of bombs dropping all around us. It was the most intense and prayerful Mass I had ever attended. Everybody prayed in those days before, during and after the Mass. The following Sunday our parish priest said that the imminent threat of death enabled us all to experience the Mass as our forebears had experienced it in penal times when at any moment priest and people could be carried off to their death by secret agents of the King or Queen. The same was true for the first Christians when the Mass that we can take so easily for granted could mean imprisonment, torture and death for those who took part in it. But nothing could keep them away from offering themselves with their brothers and sisters in, with and through the One who had given his life for them. However, only Christ can make that offering effective because it is made in, and together with his offering.

In repeating St Peter's words, "You are a chosen race, a royal priesthood, a consecrated nation, a people set apart," our parish priest explained why the early Christians were so aware of their priesthood. They did not just exercise their priesthood at Mass each Sunday, but with the love they received at Mass, they tried to exercise it at every moment of every day of their lives. Then, when they returned the following week, they would offer up all the sacrifices they had made, to receive from God in return, far more than the little they had given. In this way, they would be caught up in an endless cycle of giving and receiving, death and resurrection, that would fit them ever more fully into the mystery of Christ, to receive his love in ever greater measure. St Justin who was born in 100 AD, described what happened at Sunday Mass in his day. After the priest prayed at the end of the great Eucharist prayer, "Through Him, with Him and in Him, in the unity of the Holy Spirit, all glory and honour is yours, almighty Father, for ever and ever," the Amen of the faithful would all but take the roof off.

St Jerome who was born almost two hundred years later said that in his day this Amen resounded all around the Basilica like a thunderclap. Why? because from earliest times the first Christians exercised their priesthood of self-sacrificial loving which was offered to God, in, with and through Christ himself, in whom they lived and moved and had their very being. It was this priesthood that they celebrated each Sunday when they went to Mass, and the great Amen enabled them to affirm the very essence of the profound spirituality that bonded them together with Christ, and in, with and through him with the Father. Although I was only young at the time I have never forgotten his words. Nor did I forget what he said to me later when I asked him what Amen meant. The word comes from the Hebrew, and means "I agree", "let it be so". The way this Amen all but raised the roof of churches in the early days of Christianity, sums up perhaps more than any other word or action, save martyrdom, the faith of our earliest ancestors and how they joyfully practised it.

The early Christian liturgy was deeply inspiring, vibrant and spiritually re-energising, not because it was correct in every detail, or verbally faultless, but because it depended on the daily personal prayer of the faithful, and the profound mystical spirituality that it generated. It was this that transformed all and everything they said and did into the "prayer without ceasing". The daily personal spirituality of the first Christians was intense and all-consuming. It contained one vital ingredient on which the whole success of Christianity depended, and still depends. Whether the believers were at prayer, at least intermittently throughout the day, practising regular fasts or serving the poor, they were essentially turning away from self and towards God. In doing this they were practising at all times the repentance that St Peter had called upon everyone to practise on the first Pentecost Day, so they could at all times be open to receive the Holy Spirit. This is what they meant and understood by the "prayer without ceasing" that is to be practised every day of the week and offered at the end of that week, in, with and through Christ to our Father in heaven.

The highest and most profound knowledge of God comes not through knowledge alone, but through love – our love. This happens when through prayer our love is suffused and surcharged by the divine. That is why, when at the end of his life St Thomas Aquinas experienced the love of God with such all-consuming power, he said something astounding. He said that all he wrote before, namely his great *Summa Theologica* was no more than straw compared with the new knowledge that comes through the love that is wisdom. The consequences of what he said are even more astounding for us personally. Very few of us have intellects like St Thomas Aquinas. Even less have even a fraction of the knowledge contained in his great magnum opus, but if we only learn to open ourselves to receive God's infinite love that comes to us in prayer, then something dramatic happens. The Holy Spirit will give even the simplest and humblest of us the profound knowledge that is even beyond the grasp of some of the most learned professors of theology.

It is, for this reason, the great mystical theologian and hermit Evagrius Ponticus (AD 345–399), whose writings summed up the teaching of the Desert Fathers with whom he lived, said, "A person of prayer is a theologian, and a theologian is a person of prayer." It is in prayer alone that true spiritual wisdom is learnt. In the nineteenth century, crowds flocked not to the great theologians of the day in search of wisdom, but to a simple country priest, the Curé d'Ars. In the same way in the twentieth century, it was to a simple Franciscan Friar, Padre Pio to whom they flocked for the spiritual help they needed, or to Lourdes or Fatima or other places where Our Lady called people to prayer, time and time again. Her message is always the same – "Turn back to prayer", for it is here that selfless giving is learned that enables our love to be suffused and surcharged by the divine. It is this love alone that can change us permanently into the persons God created us to become from the very beginning. This will enable us "to love and serve him in this life and to be happy with him in the next", as the catechism used to put it so succinctly.

Part 2

Introducing Mystical Spirituality

Chapter 10 Introducing Christian Mystical Contemplation
Chapter 11 The Meaning of Mystical Theology
Chapter 12 Early Christian Mystical Spirituality
Chapter 13 The Mystical Prayer of the Early Christians
Chapter 14 The Beginning of Mystical Prayer
Chapter 15 Purification in the Desert
Chapter 16 From the Prayer of Quiet to the Spiritual Betrothals
Chapter 17 The Meaning of Contemplation
Chapter 18 From Paradise Lost to Paradise Regained

Chapter 10

Introducing Christian Mystical Contemplation

When most readers hear the expression "mystical spirituality" they usually think of St Teresa of Ávila and St John of the Cross, and understandably so. They have both been declared doctors of the Church for their unique and unprecedented knowledge of mystical theology. That is why it is to them more than any others that we will turn to help us travel on through the purgatory of the mystic way to the Transforming Union with God that begins even in this life for those who persevere. However, they are not the greatest of mystics. The greatest is Jesus Christ, for throughout his life on earth his whole being was taken up with the mystical contemplation of his Father. This contemplation was brought to perfection after his death and Resurrection in such a way that others could join him. This would enable them to reach their completion in the ever-deepening and ever-increasing joy of experiencing the endless loving that passes to and fro between the Father and the Son in the mystery of the Holy Trinity. It is only here that what I have called the primeval desire to love and be loved finally reaches its consummation. Let me explain these profound mysteries by returning to the world of the first Christians to see how they first came to see, understand and then enter into them.

If I told you about a place with no taxation, no income tax, no capital gains tax, no value added tax, no tax at all, it would be good news and you would want to know more. But before you start packing your bags, I have some bad news. Sadly that place no longer exists. I am talking about ancient Athens whose citizens were free of the financial furies that pursue us throughout our lives. I know it all sounds too good to be true because even Utopians need roads and bridges, civic buildings, public amenities, an army and a navy. So how did they do it? They invented a unique method of public service that expected every citizen to be responsible for financing one major public work once in their lifetime. It may be erecting a statue, building a temple or equipping a battleship to defend their shores. They would then be free of any other responsibility for life. This act of public service performed by one person for the benefit of the whole community was called their "liturgy".

So, when Greek converts were told what Christ had done throughout his life on earth and what he was continually doing now, not just for a single state or country but for the whole of humanity, they said that was the greatest liturgy that anyone had ever performed. It was the greatest act of public service ever performed by one person for the good of all humanity. When they came together on the first day of every week, the day of the sun, or Sunday, it was to experience Christ's Liturgy made present, coming amongst them as with his first disciples at the Last Supper. In him, all the love that enabled him to give every moment of his life and death for others was recapitulated and made present in his person.

That is why the first Mass was called the "heavenly liturgy". However, the first Christians did not just want to be bystanders, merely admiring what he did, they wanted to become participators by choosing to share in his unique act of self-sacrifice. That is why, throughout the previous week they tried to do in their lives what Christ did in his life. By following his example they tried to love God with their whole heart and mind, body and soul, and to love others as he did in all they said and did every moment of every day. It was this selfless giving that enabled them to receive the same love that Christ received, to enable them to continue living their own personal liturgies in the following week with ever greater love as their own love was suffused with the divine.

In the first part of their Sunday Liturgy, they were taught how to love the most loveable man to have lived on this earth, not just by listening to stories about him in the scriptures, but stories told by those who knew him personally. These stories not only fired their imaginations at the time but during the following week as they learned how to reflect and ruminate on them in a new form of prayer called "meditation". This new form of prayer filled them with a love for Jesus that grew with every passing day as they meditated on him. All love wants is not just to come close to those you love, but to enter into union with them. Although this union could not be consummated with the Jesus who once lived, it could be consummated with the Jesus who lives now, in his transformed and transfigured glory. It is at this point that this desire for union with him is swept up into Jesus as he is now, contemplating his heavenly Father, not just to share in his being, but in his action and in his sublime contemplation.

This was the first time in Christian history that meditation enabled the human desire for union with God to be transposed from the meditation on Christ as he once was, into union with him as he is now in heaven. Perhaps the best way that I can explain why and how this transition takes place is by turning to a modern metaphor. If a spaceship is to make the first part of its journey to the planet Mars it must be harnessed with sufficient power and energy to lift it off the ground and thrust it through and out of the earth's atmosphere. To this end, canisters of fuel are fixed to the body of the spaceship, but when they have done their job they must be cast off for they can now only hinder the spaceship on its journey. It is then able to continue its journey unencumbered with ever greater speed as it comes under the gravitational pull of its destination. The first Christians knew nothing about spaceships, but they soon found out by experience that once meditation had fired their hearts and minds with the love of Christ as he once was, then that love would raise them above themselves and into the Christ as he is now.

As soon as meditation leads us into contemplation, all methods of meditative prayer that helped fire our love before must be cast off because they have served their purpose. We would find it impossible to return to them. Meditation has led us on to contemplation of the Father. Although this contemplation takes place in, with and through the Risen Christ, our desire and attention are primarily directed to God the Father. That the Christ who was once the sole attention of a person in meditative prayer seems to have disappeared in contemplative prayer, often perplexes the traveller and makes some theologians question the orthodoxy of a form of prayer that seems to have bypassed Christ. Let me return to the metaphor of the spaceship again to make myself clear.

When they awoke in the morning of the launch, the astronauts looked out of the window with joy to see the spaceship that was going to make all their dreams come true. Then, on their journey one of the astronauts panicked when he awoke one morning and looked out of the window. The spaceship had gone! "Calm down," his comrade insisted, "the spaceship has not gone; you are in it, and we are on our way to meet our destiny." Far from being taken away from Christ, our prayers have been answered. We do not see him as we once did, but the union that we desired has begun to take place and we are travelling towards our ultimate destiny in God, in, with and through Christ, there to contemplate his glory for all eternity.

Meditation is a means to an end; contemplation is that end. It is our eternal destiny which we will enjoy with all we have known and loved in this life, and those whom we have never known, but who have loved Christ from the beginning. They will be our new family in the mystical body of Christ when all things are completed in him, and when all love is finally fulfilled in the love of the Three in One who originally conceived us. In mystical contemplation we are prepared for an ever deeper union with Christ by a continual purification. In this purification, there is both light and darkness. While St John of the Cross both describes and explains the darkness better than anyone else, St Teresa of Ávila both describes and explains the moments of light better than anyone else, most particularly in her masterwork, *The Interior Castle*.

Chapter 11

The Meaning of Mystical Theology

It is only in mystical contemplation that our weak human love is so purified that it enables this love to mix, mingle and merge with the love of the Holy Spirit. Then, suffused and surcharged with this love we will not only be able to enter into the mystical body of Christ but into Christ's mystical contemplation of our common Father. This contemplation is hardly perceptible to begin with. Eventually it will lead to and beyond ecstatic bliss in our minds and hearts even in this life, before overflowing into our whole being, transforming it as Christ's own body was seen transfigured and transformed on Mount Tabor.

It is in the purification that must precede the experience of God's love in mystical contemplation that the great saints, prophets and reformers are gradually transformed into the image and likeness of Christ. They were there in abundance in early Christianity and before, during and after great reforming councils like the Fourth Lateran Council and the Council of Trent. However, for the reasons that I will explain later, they were noticeable by their absence before, during and after the Second Vatican Council. I will explain why, and how, because it is due to this terrible tragedy that the Church is fighting for its life at the beginning of the twenty-first century. I will begin by outlining the very essence of this God-given mystical spirituality that animated and inspired the early Christian Church. Then I will follow this with a brief history of Christian mystical spirituality.

"Mysticism" is a word never used by the early Christians, nor by any of the Greek Fathers. In general, it is used today by many disparate groups from modern-day Neo-Platonists to myriad different forms of New Age enthusiasts. Most of them are bounty hunters seeking exotic or esoteric transcendental experiences of one sort or another for their own personal pleasure, well-being or satisfaction tending to be anthropocentric rather than theocentric. In human loving the transforming experience of being loved is the consequence or byproduct of selflessly giving oneself to another. The same is true of divine loving when our weak human loving is united to the divine loving of Christ, enabling us to contemplate God and to experience what St Paul calls the "love that surpasses all understanding". If you seek this love purely for your own pleasure and satisfaction it will continually elude you. But if you persevere in seeking it, or rather, God, for his own sake with endless self-effacing perseverance, "come hell or high water" then you will inevitably receive him and his love until it overflows into every part of you, and from you onto others.

The ancient Greeks had various religious cults to which privileged citizens belonged. The rites of initiation were so secret that severe penalties were imposed on anyone who divulged them. A great and well-loved Athenian General called Alcibiades was exiled from Athens for mimicking these rites when he and his friends imbibed too much alcohol. Because these initiation rites were so confidential, they were called the "mysteries" from the Greek word meaning secret or hidden. It was for this reason that St Paul coined the word *Mysterion* to describe "God's Secret Plan". This plan was to create us so that we could come to know and experience the ecstatic joy of sharing in the life and love of the Three in One, and to experience it with ever growing intensity to all eternity. He called it "God's Secret Plan" because it was never fully divulged in the Old Testament, although it was hinted that God had something special prepared for his people in the future.

"With this special grace I have been entrusted, not only of proclaiming to the pagans the infinite treasure of Christ but also of explaining how the mystery is to be dispensed. Through all the ages this has been kept hidden in God, the creator of everything.

So that the Sovereignties and Powers should learn only now, through the Church, how comprehensive God's wisdom really is, exactly according to the plan which he had from all eternity in Christ Jesus our Lord" (Ephesians 3:8–11).

Even when Jesus came to prepare people for the final unfolding of God's Plan, he did not reveal it fully. It was only after he sent the Holy Spirit that this plan was seen with ever greater clarity, as Jesus promised at the Last Supper. "I have said these things to you while still with you. But the Advocate, the Holy Spirit, whom the Father will send in my name, will teach you everything and remind you of all I have said to you" (John 14:25–27). The Good News that St Paul proclaimed then, was that thanks to the Holy Spirit sent on the first Pentecost Day, "God's Secret Plan" was a secret no longer for those with ears to hear and hearts to love with. If they were baptised they would be taken up into God's Secret Plan that was now no longer simply an idea, but a person, the risen and glorified Jesus Christ, the Lord. It would be in, with and through him that we would journey on to the place that God his Father has prepared for us, bringing his plan to completion.

Those who were baptised and had totally dedicated their whole lives to entering into God's plan in the Risen Christ were called mystics. However, it was only if those who chose to enter into Christ's mystical body further chose to enter into his sacred action, into his contemplation of the Father, that they became mystics in the sense that we use the word today. They would then be on the mystic way, in, with and through Christ, the Way, the Truth and the Life. It is from the word *Mysterion* then that the words "mystic" and "mystical" have their origin, as also the word the "mysteries", because they lead us into, and sustain us, as we participate in "God's Secret Plan" that he designed to bring us to perfection in the Risen Christ. When Latin took over from Greek as the official language of the Church, the "mysteries" came to be called the "sacraments". In earlier years, however, the sacred reading of the scriptures was also seen as one of the mysteries for the first Christians, enabling them to come to know and love Christ in such a way that they were led on to generate the love that leads to union with Christ in his contemplation of the Father. It was for this same reason that many centuries later, another popular way of generating the love that leads to union came to be called the "Mysteries of the Rosary".

Early Christian spirituality was designed by God himself from the beginning, who then sent his Son, Jesus Christ, to bring about on earth what was originally conceived in heaven. Having spent his time before the Resurrection explaining God's plan and how it was about to be put into operation, he instituted a profound mystical spirituality that would enable his followers to participate in God's plan to eternity. This spirituality would help and support believers in their endeavour to enter into his now glorified mystical body, to be united with him in his contemplation of the Father. The more we are purified from the self-love that prevents us from entering ever more fully into this mystical contemplation, then the more we will come to know and experience his infinite loving. But union with Christ can only be realized to the measure that inner purification has prepared us to receive it. Then, the love that we receive can be shared with the world around us, beginning with our own family and our spiritual brothers and sisters in the Christian community.

Mystical theology, therefore, teaches how the love of a sincere Christian searcher is gradually prepared for an ever-deeper union with Christ. It teaches how this union is brought about through a profound inner transformation that purifies, refines and brings our love to perfection, enabling us to become one with Christ, not just in being but in action, in his mystical contemplation of the Father. At last, what we thought we knew by faith alone becomes palpable, as in, with and through Christ we are able to experience tangibly the love that created us in the beginning and the love that will be our ultimate destination. It is this ever-deepening and ever-expanding experience of being loved that makes all the difference in the world. Knowledge alone is not enough. Knowledge alone will never change anyone permanently for the better. But the experience of being loved will. All this happens in the mystic way where saints are made out of sinners and where the great spiritual leaders are formed to lead us back to the contemplation that dispels darkness and bathes us in the light of God's love that makes all things new, beginning with us.

Chapter 12

Early Christian Mystical Spirituality

In the early Church, once a person heard the good news and expressed belief in Christ, baptism followed almost immediately, as you can read in the Acts of the Apostles. However, in time it was soon realized that this was not necessarily the best thing to do for the Church, or for the individual whose first emotional response could so easily wither and die without proper instruction about the meaning of their commitment. It was therefore decided that a period of two years should precede the Easter night when they would be baptised into the mysteries of Christ. In this period of preparation, the "novices" would live the same intensely prayerful lives as the baptised, fasting and practising charitable works. They would then offer these to the Lord at Mass on Sundays but would have to leave before what we now call the offertory.

When the time came for them to be baptised at the Easter Vigil, they would first all turn to the West where it was believed that Satan reigned in Hell, to denounce him three times. After this they would turn to the East from where they believed Christ would come again; opening their arms they solemnly committed themselves to him. Then, casting off their old clothes that signified leaving behind their old lives they were ready to enter into the pool that came to be called the womb of the Church. It was here they were plunged into the baptismal waters three times whilst the words of consecration to the Three in One were said by the priest. This was the meaning of the threefold immersion; they were beginning a journey in Christ which would be completed when they were sufficiently purified to participate with him in the life and love of the Holy Trinity. When they emerged from the pool they were clothed in shining white garments, similar to that worn by Christ as he rose from the dead, to make it clear that the journey they were about to undertake could only be made because now they were in the Risen Lord. It would in future only be in him, with him and through him that their journey be made possible, carrying their daily Cross as Christ did before them. That is why St Paul insisted that their baptism fitted them ever more closely into Christ's death and Resurrection. This daily dying was symbolized by being plunged beneath the waters in these rites of initiation.

During the two years of preparation, the novices were taught how to carry their daily cross by endlessly acting selflessly in the way they put God first. This would be demonstrated by praying each day at the prescribed times for prayer. Here they would express their love for Christ and continually reconsecrate their lives to him, endeavouring to love him in the neighbour in need. "Insofar as you neglected to do this to one of the least of these, you neglected to do it to me" (Matthew 25:45). This is how they were taught to observe the two new commandments that Christ gave them. However, what Jesus came to call the "new worship in spirit and truth" extended to encompass simply everything they said and did, everything they suffered or enjoyed, even the simplest of things. St Paul said, "Whatever you eat, whatever you drink, whatever you do at all, do it for the glory of God" (I Corinthians 10:31), and in doing this they would be practising the "prayer without ceasing".

It is important to understand the spiritual dynamics that underpin the "prayer without ceasing". Whatever form of prayer is made, deep down beneath what is said or done is the vital action upon which everything depends. This action is the act of selflessness. When we pray, we are continually practising selflessness, the act of selfless giving. The more we pray and the longer we pray, the more this selflessness becomes a habit of selflessness and self-sacrifice. The very distractions and even the temptations with which we battle enable us to keep saying "Yes" to God and "No" to self, opening us to the love of God that Christ unleashed on the first Pentecost Day. They were taught that once baptised and fitted into the life and action of the Risen One, all their offerings would become priestly offerings, because they were offered in the New Temple. Christ, and in, with and through him, the new High Priest, to the Father. That is why, when dressed in a white garment, they were led into the whole Christian community who were waiting to welcome them. This time they would not have to leave at the offertory, because now for the first time they would be able to offer themselves in, with and through Christ, to receive the love of the Father as never before.

In the early Church, little emphasis was given to the psychological experiences felt as the love of God began to fill their hearts and minds. The whole emphasis was on God, and not on the feelings experienced. They were there but rarely referred to except perhaps occasionally with expressions like spiritual intoxication, sober inebriety, or spiritual transportation. Even later mystics were reluctant to describe the intimate moments when they experienced the love of God. What is true of married love is also true of divine love. A mystic like St Francis would rush away into solitude when he felt the love of God overwhelming him. If he was travelling with others he would tell them to walk on and leave him alone or pull his hood over his head so that nobody could see the joy that possessed him when God's love took hold of him. The same could be said for most of the mystics and understandably so. St Teresa of Ávila did detail from her own life the psychological experiences that characterize a person's journey to mystical union, but, as I will explain later, she did this for very good reasons. To dismiss the idea of a mystical spirituality in the early Church because they do not talk about mystical states, esoteric experiences or strange mystical phenomena is utterly wrongheaded.

The Gospel said that you judge someone by their fruits. That is the real test. The story is told of two novices who approached

St Francis. The first asked him how he could tell if his prayer was authentic, to which Francis replied, "By your love of your neighbour." The second asked how he could tell when he had achieved perfect prayer, to which Francis answered, "By the love that you have for your enemies." That puts us all in our place! But apply this test to the first Christians and you will be forced to conclude that a higher percentage of them than at any other time in the history of the Church, had attained the heights of mystical prayer as that term is understood by any student of St Teresa of Ávila.

The detailing of the subjective experiences that result when God's love begins to make itself present within a person who is travelling on the Mystic Way comes much later in the history of Christian Spirituality. Mystical theology did not begin with St John of the Cross and St Teresa of Ávila, they merely detailed better than anyone else, the journey that anyone experiences who totally abandons themselves to God in the mystic way. Their analysis is as true for someone who sets out on the mystic way in the first or the twenty-first century. Although what they describe cannot be found in any systematic way in the first Christian centuries, it is nevertheless by using this later psychological analysis, and by applying it to the journey of the first Christians that we can discover deep insights into their spirituality. It can, as we are about to see, explain a mystery that has long since baffled secular historians. Namely, how could a small "heretical Jewish sect" of little consequence, convert the vast pagan empire of Rome, created and sustained by the greatest military power the world has ever known, and in such a short time?

Chapter 13

The Mystical Prayer of the Early Christians

St Paul insists that once we are baptised into Christ, we are baptised into his death and Resurrection. But unlike pagan rites of initiation, Christian baptism was not seen as a magical rite that was instantly expected to change a person. Christ's death and Resurrection that raised, transformed and transfigured him was the result of dying many times before his death on the cross as he sought to do his Father's will despite the forces of evil that were levelled against him. So too did the new Christians once they symbolically "put on" Christ at their baptism. It is only through dying many times over as we endeavour to carry our cross daily, that we are gradually taken up into Christ's life and his Resurrection where we begin to take part with him, in him and through him, in his mystical contemplation of God.

The first name for Christianity was "The Way" because it was essentially a spiritual and a mystical journey which involved dying many times over. Practising the selflessness that enables a person to be filled with sufficient grace to be united with Christ, is a long and painful process. Just because we waited for over fifteen-hundred years for this exacting purification to be detailed and described as the "Dark Night of the Soul" by St John of the Cross, does not mean that it was not a reality for the first spiritual travellers. We know without a shadow of a doubt that it was part of their journey, for without such a purification they could not have been united with Christ. Only then could they receive and experience the gift of God's love, enabling them to generate all the virtues and all the unique God-given qualities that simply amazed and dazzled the ancient pagan world.

They were not only overwhelmed to witness the sublime virtues and profound mystical teaching of the Gospels lived out in the daily lives of the Christians, but other virtues too, so prized but rarely practised in the Greco-Roman world in which they lived. I am referring to the virtues that were extolled by the Stoics who set themselves up as the spiritual gurus of the ancient world into which Christianity was born. In such a world it is only to be expected that the virtues of the warrior, courage, bravery, steadfastness, endurance, perseverance and the ability to remain dignified and uncomplaining even while suffering pain, torture and death, would be praised above all others. But despite the desire and the determination to embrace these virtues, their failure was so routine that Seneca, the greatest Stoic of them all said, "Show me the stoic".

In contrast, when Christians were persecuted all these virtues were seen as they were never seen before. Even when flogged within an inch of their lives, tortured in the most despicable ways imaginable and put to death by fire, sword or being thrown to the wild beasts, their composure was breathtaking. Time and time again jailors, torturers and executioners were so moved that they were converted to the faith that gave such staggering strength and superhuman courage and bravery, not just to strong men but to women and children as you can read in *The Acts of the Martyrs*. But so many more were converted from the vast crowds of sadistic voyeurs who came for a day's entertainment watching Christians being burnt alive, torn apart and crucified, for they could not help but marvel at seeing a superhuman form of endurance quite beyond the power of mere mortals. Not all Christians were called to "red martyrdom", but all were called to what came to be called "white martyrdom", the dying to self that involved carrying their daily cross for Christ, day after day. White martyrdom may not seem as dramatic as red martyrdom but over a lifetime it could be far more exacting, involving the purifications as described by St John of the Cross in his Dark Night of the Soul and leading to the same moments of light as described by St Teresa of Ávila.

The first Christians were called the "saints" because they tried, and so many of them succeeded in living such saintly lives. The Greco-Roman world in which they lived was rampant with outrageous immoral behaviour. Such contemporary vices as sexual depravity that was commonplace between men, was not only condemned but utterly prohibited for Christians. If such a sin or other major sin such as adultery, murder and acts of apostasy was committed, they had to be confessed publicly and forgiven. Although there was always mercy and forgiveness on the first occasion, the offenders were permanently excommunicated from the Christian community if these major sins were committed again. This did not mean they were damned, for that was ultimately a matter for God, but it did mean they could not continue to be seen as members of a community whose very presence was meant to bear witness to the presence of the Risen Christ. All this is a measure of the uncompromising commitment of those first early Christians to live the unblemished lives that Christ demanded of them.

That very many lived such lives and converted vast numbers of pagans in such a short time is as historically undeniable as it is inexplicable to secular historians. The explanation can only be found in the powerful spiritual energy or love that transformed those who persevered in their daily dying in Christ, through long and testing Dark Nights. In the words of St Teresa of Ávila, as the length and intensity, of the prayer of Quiet and then Full Union in mystical prayer becomes ever more regular and constant, then the traveller who has been changed slowly over the years, suddenly begins to change with ever greater rapidity. When their prayer becomes even stronger still and begins to overflow from the mind into the body, further experiences are made palpable causing the flesh to quiver with delight, and the whole body to tingle and even the eyes to dissolve into tears. This is the beginning of what St Teresa of Ávila calls the Spiritual Betrothals when a person experiences for a brief time what they will ultimately experience all the time, in the Mystical Marriage with Christ, if not in this world then in the next.

The receiver whose prayer has so far been predominantly characterized by silence, or at least by few words that rise out of darkness, suddenly wants to cry out with joy and give thanks, as the light of God's love begins to envelop them. Then all they want to do is to praise and glorify the God who has chosen to love them like never before, in such a way that they can actually feel and experience his love reaching out and into every part of their human being. As St Teresa of Ávila puts it – the chrysalis opens to allow the butterfly to emerge. Very soon the receiver realizes that words alone are not enough to thank God, and they feel the urge to express their gratitude in a new and total abandonment of themselves to him. This new and radical commitment must express itself in the world they now wish to convert so that others might come to know and experience the height and the depth, the length and breadth of God's love that they have come to know and experience for themselves.

Now for the first time, believers not only experience the love that will alone enable God's Secret Plan, the *Mysterion*, to be brought to fruition, but that love also enables them to see the truth. It enables them to see the truth about the terrible state of the world and to see what God wants them to do to transform it radically. And, lest they despair at their inadequacy, they are given all the virtues necessary and all the gifts that the Holy Spirit can give to this end through his love. Just as a single shaft of light contains all the colours of the spectrum, so also a single shaft of God's love contains within it all the power and the strength, all the insights and the vision, all the gifts, and the virtues to participate now in bringing about God's *Mysterion*.

In the light of reading this, re-read *The Acts of the Apostles*, *The Epistles* and the writings of *The Fathers of the Church*, and you will see this hidden mystical life at work purifying and refining the lives of the first saints, mystics and prophets. The profound wisdom found on almost every page could not possibly be the work of spiritual novices. It is the work of mystics, so far advanced on the mystic way that they were sufficiently purified to enable the Holy Spirit to use them to communicate his wisdom, not just to their contemporaries, but to their fellow Christians down to the present day.

Sadly, this golden age of Christian Spirituality fell into serious periods of decline, albeit with many glorious revivals. I will detail later what we can do to help bring back that God-given spirituality given to the early Church by Jesus Christ himself.

Chapter 14

The Beginning of Mystical Prayer

Before the 1960s, mental prayer took place behind the closed doors of a personal prayer life. However, as the charismatic movement began to spread amongst Catholics, communal charismatic style prayer became more and more popular, not least because of unusual phenomena, from speaking in tongues to slaying in the spirit. When criticised as a deviation from the normal Catholic prayer tradition, they claimed that far from being new, their way of worship was widely practised in the early Church, as verified by anyone who reads St Paul's first letter to the Corinthians, chapter twelve. They were of course quite right. The sort of communal prayer they practised was commonplace in the early Church and necessary for the establishment of Christianity.

Almost every town, city and village of the early Church would have its communities of charismatic Christians, not dissimilar to today. These charismatic communities were the spiritual powerhouses, the faith factories in which their old faith was refashioned, reworked and refitted into the new, for the vast majority of them were Jews. They used the prayers, the psalms, the chants, the hymns and the canticles they already knew, adapting them where necessary and eventually creating new prayers, hymns and music to express what now superseded their old liturgies. This new liturgy was but the external expression of the new worship that Christ gave them. This was the worship in spirit and in truth, the same worship that Christ himself offered, the offering of himself to the Father. Deep down this worship depended not just on pure and contrite hearts as the prophets had insisted, but hearts so fully cleansed that they could be united with the heart of the Risen One in whom they all lived and moved and had their being.

This worship would only rise to its fulfillment if their hearts could be so purified that the second baptism of fire could prepare them, not just to be united with the heart of Christ, but to beat in unison with his. It would be in this new form of worship that human loving would be suffused with the divine to enable new creatures to be formed in the image and likeness of Christ. It was the charismatic fervour in these communities that animated and inspired the first Christian novices and supercharged them with the determination to journey onwards. This journey would lead them through a profound purification that would prepare them for union with Christ in his mystical body and then into his mystical contemplation of the Father. The first Christians came to see that this above all was the purpose of the charismatic prayer that was so commonplace at the beginning, because almost everyone, apart from the first Apostles and their earliest disciples, were beginners. It gave the enthusiasm, the inspiration and the strength for the journey ahead where they would be reformed and refashioned into the image and likeness of the One who would possess them and work through them that his Kingdom would come on earth.

If we "fast forward", we see that this same form of Charismatic prayer that mushroomed in the Catholic Church in the 1960s is still strong in many places today. It is an important movement that has borne much fruit. However, in order to lead its members to the depths of prayer, it must also encourage daily mental prayer. In this way, propelled by the love generated in the first fervour of the beginning of the mystic way, those within the movement are better equipped to advance further on the spiritual journey.

In some places, it may be observed that Charismatic groups cling to the emotional experiences characteristic of the movement. Alone, this is insufficient to generate the depths of love with leads into the mystic way with its power to purify and refine, and thence onward to mystical contemplation. If they do not learn this deeper way, they will sadly remain undernourished like spiritual adolescents. Therefore the leaders themselves would do well to understand the mystical way of prayer in order to guide those who find themselves drawn more and more to profound contemplative stillness, as will happen naturally when they give themselves to the practice of daily mental prayer. A competent spiritual director will lead charismatics into mystical contemplation where the charismatic foundation of their spiritual life will develop beyond all expectations. Without this guidance there is a danger of substituting false forms of contemplative prayer such as centring prayer, mantras and other pseudo-mystical prayer. These will not lead to mystical contemplation as detailed by St Teresa of Ávila and other Christian mystics but will actually prevent the action of the Holy Spirit. Consequently, the purification that can alone enable a person to be united with Christ and with his contemplation of the Father can be prevented permanently. We must all learn from the mystical spirituality of the first Christians on how to progress in our prayer life after our first enthusiasm has run its course. Otherwise we will condemn ourselves to a bogus form of mystical contemplation that leads nowhere, but round and round in circles and deprives the Church of the mystics, the prophets and the saints that are so desperately needed in the Church today.

There are places where the charismatic movement has laid a more solid foundation for authentic spiritual renewal. The early fervour may have waned, but in its place, there is a genuine desire for deeper prayer and good spiritual direction. Many of the most influential Catholic institutions and some religious congregations spring out of the original fire of the charismatic renewal. It is my deepest wish and prayer that those who have experienced the blessing of the renewal, and those desiring deeper intimacy with God experience the richness of the Carmelite tradition. We should take as our guide in this journey two great spiritual writers made doctors of the Church for their unrivalled understanding and teaching on mystical theology. I am referring of course to St John of the Cross and St Teresa of Ávila. Just half an hour reading the first nine chapters of *The Dark Night of the Soul* would make it clear why the time always comes for a beginner to move forward into mystical prayer. It could be a life-changing half hour for anyone ready for real spiritual development.

Chapter 15

Purification in the Desert

Immediately after Jesus was baptised in the Jordan by St John the Baptist, "The Spirit drove him out into the desert and he remained there for forty days and was tempted by Satan" (Mark 1:13). St Matthew describes these temptations and the other evangelists show how his tussles with the devil continued in one way or another throughout his public ministry. St John uses the symbolism of light and darkness to describe this struggle that reaches its conclusion on the Cross. He writes, "After Judas had taken the bread, Satan entered into him. He went out. Night had fallen" (John 13:30).

Christ's victory over Satan and the powers of evil took place on the Cross when the powers of evil were pitted against him, but he never faltered and the moment he died was the moment when he was glorified. What he received at that moment enabled him to be united with his Father where he was able to contemplate his infinite glory. He returned to the place he had occupied from all eternity, but on his return, he took with him his human nature that had been victorious over the powers of evil. This, his human nature was now not only able to contemplate the Father, but also to transmit the love he received and experienced in return to other human beings.

This theme that begins in the scriptures with Christ being led into the desert continues through the first centuries and is to be found in its clearest manifestation in the teachings and the sayings of the Desert Fathers. In his remarkable life of St Antony, St Athanasius makes it clear that Antony and his followers went there precisely to confront and defeat Satan, as Christ did at the outset of his public ministry. As the great spiritual theologian Père Louis Bouyer puts it in his *History of Christian Spirituality*:

In primitive monasticism, the retreat to the desert is in no way a simple desire for tranquillity, for leisure or for extended contemplation in the sense this is understood in Greek Philosophy. If a monk buried himself in the desert it was with the desire of fighting the devil in what was considered his usual dwelling place.

The monk was a person possessed by a holy impatience to seek perfection. That is why he goes with all speed to the place where he can expect to find face to face and vanquish the spirit of evil, so that the spirit of love can possess him and rule where evil ruled before. It would be naive to believe that this battle was primarily a physical battle fought in the wilderness. It was the wilderness that created the utter solitude that forced the monk to face the demons within. However, before going any further I would like to say something about the devil by way of clarification. That the devil exists is the teaching of the Church. That he is seen to have attacked Christ is clear from scripture, but from the outside. It must be quite clear that the Evil One could not get inside Christ either when he was on earth or in heaven, which is good news for us. For although the Devil is the ultimate personification of Evil he cannot enter into the glorified body of Christ, so those who enter into his mystical body are safe from direct confrontation with him. Therefore, although we may be assailed by powerful temptations in the Dark Night, we are safe from direct confrontation with the Evil One. When I speak of the "demons within" I am using the phrase metaphorically. I am therefore referring to the unruly passions and urges, the consequences of original sin that keep threatening to destroy us. I am not referring to demonic creatures, agents of the devil, that dwell within us like pernicious gremlins gleefully plotting to destroy us. This is an important distinction that must be made as, beginning with the Desert Fathers this distinction can become blurred so that you cannot always tell when a person is speaking literally or metaphorically. In what follows below I will be using the expression the "demons within" metaphorically, as used in common parlance today by religious and non-religious people alike.

Nonetheless, the spiritual combat is for all who are baptised into Christ who have responsibilities that prevent them following people like Antony into solitude. They too are called to union with Christ, and they too are called to take up arms against the "demons within" so that love may rule where evil once ruled before. Once a spiritual novice passes through the first fervour that all serious searchers experience in any age, they find themselves in a spiritual desert that is located deep down within them. Here, like the monk, they have to face the demons that dwell there. No one is free of the seven deadly sins that keep their victims earthbound. The very idea that a person ruled by their demons from within can be united with the Risen Lord is totally unthinkable. It is for this reason that, once first enthusiasm has evaporated we have to undergo the purification that entails first seeing the demons that separate us from Christ, and then with God's help, vanquish them. The ensuing purification is mentioned everywhere in the writings of the early Fathers of the Church, but it is to be found in far greater detail later in the writings of St John of the Cross. He explicitly states that after first fervour, that in his day took place most commonly in a person's personal prayer life, a "novice" would have to face the sinfulness and the selfishness within. In the first chapters of *The Dark Night of the Soul*, he enumerates all the faults and failings that so far remained unseen, for the beginner is too occupied with the intoxicating vapours of sweetness and light to notice the demons within that have to be rooted out before being rooted into the life of Christ.

This can be testing at times almost beyond endurance. When at the end of a particularly painful period in his purification St Antony had a vision of Christ, he complained to him with the words, "Where were you?" Christ answered, "Antony, I was present at your side. But I waited, observing your fight. And since you have resisted so bravely, I will now always be at your side." The mystic way is a spiritual combat in which the forces of evil within have to be defeated. This purification is not always painful for there are times of joy too, when after periods of purification there are moments of spiritual delight when the one who has been actively purifying us makes his presence felt. It is then that his love can suddenly transport us to high states of spiritual experience, as St Teresa of Ávila describes in her masterwork, *Interior Castle*. In addition to St Athanasius' famous book on St Antony, we come to know more of the spirituality that St Antony and other spiritual masters taught their monks through the writings of Evagrius Ponticus (AD 345–399), a learned monk who synthesized their spirituality for posterity.

Speaking of the purification which Antony and his fellow monks had to undergo on their way to union with Christ, Evagrius called the aridity in which they found themselves after first fervour *Accidie*, and the experience of presence that follows it *Apatheia*. St John of the Cross details the characteristics of *Accidie* in *The Dark Night of the Soul* whilst St Teresa of Ávila does likewise for *Apatheia* in her masterwork, *Interior Castle*. Through a sort of spiritual hide-and-seek, believers are purified by the alternating experiences of absence and presence, light and darkness, convincing them that it is God and not they who are in control of their spiritual destiny. At times they are cast into the depth of all but despair, at other times they are raised to the heights of ecstatic joy and to almost every state between the two before purification is complete. Then, what the early Fathers called *Theosis* or Divinisation, and their spiritual descendants called the Transforming Union or the Spiritual or Mystical Marriage takes place enveloping the whole person, body, and spirit as they are possessed ever more fully by the same Spirit who possessed Christ and raised him from the dead. This is preceded by the "Spiritual Betrothals", when you can experience for some of the time what is experienced for most of the time in the Mystical Marriage itself. I hope this makes it clear that the mystic way, as experienced by the first Christians was no different from the mystic way as explained by St John of the Cross and St Teresa of Ávila, nor for that matter is it any different for those travelling along the mystic way today.

It is in this purification that the primeval desire for the fullness of love which can only be found in God is gradually purified to enable this desire to be fulfilled. However, no matter how perfectly it is honed for this purpose, human love alone can never rise to enter into God. When the purification has been sufficiently completed the Holy Spirit who has been actively involved in the whole process draws the person into Christ more deeply than ever before to be fitted into his contemplation of the Father. For it is only in, with and through him that it is possible to be united with God the Father. That is why Jesus once said, speaking of John the Baptist, that no man born of a woman was greater than he, but even the least in the Kingdom of God is greater than him. Why? Because it was only after the outpouring of the Holy Spirit that took place after the death of John the Baptist that the new people of God could be drawn up and into Christ's mystical body so that union with God could take place through him. It was only in and with him that everyone could draw close to and enter into God their common Father and their final destiny.

Sadly at the end of the Age of the Martyrs two pernicious heresies would attack the divinity of Christ and consequently, his love, the Holy Spirit. This would have disastrous consequences on the God-given spirituality that Jesus introduced to our first Christian forebears for many centuries to come.

Chapter 16

From the Prayer of Quiet to the Spiritual Betrothals

The great Franciscan theologian Blessed John Duns Scotus said that when God conceived his plan to share his life of ecstatic bliss with us, he simultaneously conceived the means by which that plan could be put into operation. He said that "If God wills an end, he must will the means." That is why he became flesh and blood in the person of his son Jesus Christ and why he had to have an immaculate Mother so that no imperfection from her nature or nurture could prevent him becoming Christ the perfect King. That was the first stage of his plan. The second stage was brought about by Jesus who in the fullness of his manhood, explained in far more detail the meaning and purpose of God's plan and how in future it would not be just for the Jews, but for all mankind. The final stage of implementing that plan could only begin after Jesus returned to God. It was only after this that his human nature could, not only be transformed and transfigured by the fullness of God's glory, what the Greek Fathers called, the *Pleroma* but become the means of transmitting the love they had seen radiating out of him, onto, and into them, and then the other Apostles on the first Pentecost day.

The Holy Spirit, symbolized by flames of fire above each of them in the Upper Room, not only entered into them but then drew them into the transformed and transfigured Christ who would receive them and all who would follow them into his new mystical body. His body now glorified was no longer limited by the laws of space and time as his physical body had been. So, like God himself in whom he now existed, he could be approached by anyone, at any time and in any century to the end of time. Once purified, our loving and Christ's loving can mix and merge

89

as one; then we can contemplate the Father, in, with and through him, beginning now in this world but continuing as our final destiny to all eternity. If this is not good news, what is? It was not just good news for them but for everyone. That is why they lost no time in rushing out to tell this to the crowds outside; the best news that mankind could ever receive. They and all who would come after them were being called to union with the All Holy and utterly Other, the God who chose to share his life with us, beginning here on earth and to all eternity in heaven.

When they rushed outside, they were so full of the love they received that people thought they were drunk. In a sense they were, but it was not the drunkenness that comes from filling themselves with wine, but from being filled with the love of God. Filled with enthusiasm to receive the same sort of wine that filled the Apostles, the crowds asked what they should do. They were encouraged to receive baptism, then spend their whole lives turning to receive the love of God that Jesus was continually pouring out upon them. This love enabled them to be drawn up continually, not just into their Risen Lord's mystical body, but into his endless contemplation of his Father. His contemplation did not just mean gazing upon the glory of God but being simultaneously drawn into that glory to be united with the God he called Father, and to experience the Holy Spirit who was the love that bound them together. He then becomes the means of transmitting the love of God to every human being who is prepared to receive it. In this sense, contemplation is not so much a means to an end, but the completion of the profound primeval desire to love and to be loved that enthrals all of us from the very beginning of our existence.

St Bonaventure once said that contemplation is first learned at the mother's breast. It is here that we receive the love of our mother that gives us the security to go out of ourselves to first gaze upon beauty, truth and goodness which is how we first meet the love of God in his creation. When a poet is transported with delight at the sight of "a host of golden daffodils" his joy is that of one who first meets God in the beauty of his creation. This form of natural mystical experience is one with which we can all identify, for who has not met God's beauty shining through his creation as we stand and stare at the beauty of a ravishing land or seascape or at the transcendent grandeur of the mountains towering above them? In order to experience the love of God more directly, albeit from an almost infinite distance, mystical writers like St John of the Cross insist that a purification must take place first or the "demons" within us will so occupy our attention that it will be impossible to gaze upon the love of God. But when we have been sufficiently purified, to begin with the experience that we have is not dissimilar from those natural mystical experiences that we may have had in the past.

In the past those experiences were sudden and unexpected and usually of very brief duration, and quite unpredictable. However, the experience that we have of God in mystical contemplation after a certain initial purification, can be predictable when we go to prayer, for a time at least, and it lasts longer and can rise to ever-increasing degrees of intensity, dwarfing what we experienced of God through the beauty of his creation. Initially, however, this is not so much by the quality of the experience, but by a new and all-engrossing intensity.

St Teresa of Ávila calls the first stage of mystical prayer the Prayer of Quiet. It is indeed a quiet and peaceful gaze upon the love of God as it first begins to make itself felt in the mind or in the *apex mentis* as some mystical writers express it. However, there are different degrees of intensity; the inner peacefulness is not always of the same strength. Sometimes there is a lifting sensation in the head when Prayer of Quiet rises to reach its peak. It is most particularly at this point that the analogy of "sober inebriation" is used. This is probably how the Apostles felt as they rushed out to tell the world what was happening on the first Pentecost. No doubt that is why they were accused of being drunk at only nine o'clock in the morning. When the first Christians used the expression "sober inebriation", or to quote St Augustine, "sober drunkenness", they were trying to say that it is similar to the feeling that you have when you have had one or two too many, but without the side effects, the foolish behaviour, the giddiness, the lack of balance and the hangover the following day. In truth, you have never felt better in your life and that is hardly surprising because you are beginning to experience what you were created for in the first place, and that which you have been craving for years without realizing it.

What St Teresa calls Full Union is essentially the same experience as that felt in the Prayer of Quiet, except that the lifting feeling that sometimes accompanies it suddenly spirals up and up inside the head. This feeling is combined with a suddenness and intensity that makes a person feel they will be rendered unconscious if it does not stop, which it mercifully does before what is feared takes place. It is usually of far shorter duration than the Prayer of Quiet, but it is so intense that for the first time there are no distractions whatsoever and it is virtually impossible to move from the spot.

The experience of Full Union can sometimes strike a person like a mystical dart outside of prayer but lasting for no more than a few seconds. You may be in the garden, a queue at the supermarket or waiting for a train or a plane when you are struck, and the brief feeling of giddiness in the head makes you wonder whether you should go to see your doctor or your spiritual director. It is as if Someone is saying, "You might have forgotten me but I have not forgotten you." These darts do not come from Cupid but from God. What is initially feared when Full Union is lifting a person to ever higher degrees of intensity can now take place, rendering a person unconscious for a greater or lesser period of time. St Teresa calls this Ecstasy. This experience is not for all and is in fact usually a sign of a certain psycho-physical weakness that causes the mind to capitulate and the receiver to faint from shock.

Rapture is the word used by St Teresa to describe the experience of Full Union or Ecstasy when it happens with such rapidity that she can only liken it to the speed of a bullet travelling up the muzzle of a musket. The majority of people who travel along the mystic way to its completion on earth do not experience Ecstasy, for it is not an essential, let alone an indispensable part of the journey. The experiences that I have been describing so far have been felt in the head. However, gradually as the purification continues they begin to spill over into the body, at first briefly and intermittently in what St Teresa calls the Spiritual Betrothals, that, as one might expect, precedes the Mystical or Spiritual Marriage.

For St John of the Cross a person is in the Dark Night or purification up to and including the Spiritual Betrothals. For the vast majority of people the night of purification continues for their lifetime on earth. Very few come to the Mystical Marriage, including very few of those who have been canonized. But the truth is that our final destination is union with God, in, with and through Christ, when what happened to him on Mount Tabor will begin to happen to us. Then the Holy Spirit will possess us, mind and body, heart and soul; how else can we be fully united with the glorified Christ to achieve our ultimate destiny? I will speak more of the Mystical Marriage later because from it we can learn much more about the spiritual life.

Chapter 17

The Meaning of Contemplation

When I was a small boy, I used to yearn for my favourite radio programme that would take me into many different and exciting new worlds. I loved to identify with the children transported into one of these worlds when their mysterious mentor would sit them down before the picture he chose for their latest adventure. He would tell them to be still, to be calm and then to begin staring at the picture without moving, without even blinking, concentrating on the scene before them. Then as they did so the picture began to come alive, becoming three-dimensional as it expanded and drew ever nearer. He would then say, "Listen to the sound of the wind blowing through the trees, the water in the streams, the birds singing, the dogs barking and the people speaking. Quick, hide behind that bush and listen to what they are saying." It was then that the adventure would begin.

This programme enabled me to understand much later the meaning of Christian contemplation. The word contemplation itself means to gaze, to stare, to concentrate on something or someone. What is central to the word is the Latin noun *templum* meaning a sacred place. For Christians then, contemplation means being in a sacred place, more precisely in a temple, or rather in the new temple which is Christ. The prefix "con" means that we are contemplating, not just in him, but with him and through him. Then the closer we come to the One on whom we are contemplating, and as purification sharpens our spiritual vision, we begin to glimpse albeit in a very distant way, something of the glory of God that God promised us as our final destiny. We are not just onlookers or bystanders, but because we have been united with Christ we become participators with him in the glory that he experienced from eternity, from where his

Father decided to create us to join him.

Because he was not afflicted from within by the "demons" that harass us from within, Christ was able to contemplate his Father's glory at all times throughout his life on earth. That is why at the Last Supper he described himself as a man of joy, and why he wanted his followers to become men and women of joy too. This did not mean that his life would be continually full of sweetness and light, for the "demons" that were never in him were in others all around him. The glory of God is the outward expression of the infinite love that St John insists pertains to the very essence of who God is. To gaze on his glory means to participate in that glory by receiving his love. But in God, love and truth are one, so that the one who receives his love will always receive his truth simultaneously, that must be both lived and proclaimed no matter what the consequences. This is not only true of Christ the first mystic, but of all who would follow him.

The love they come to experience as they contemplate the glory of God in, and with Christ, always fills the recipients with the truth too, endowing them with insights they never had before. This enables them to see the truth that they must needs express. In their innocence, they think their listeners will be only too anxious to welcome the truth, but telling the truth is a very serious and dangerous business. Would-be prophets, beware! The simple truth is not a dainty dish to set before the most dangerous animal on earth, particularly if he or she has political or religious pretensions. By choice they prefer ambrosia to eat and nectar to drink; they have little stomach for humble pie. Be warned, for if you serve it regularly enough and in large enough portions it can make them cross, very cross, and when they are very cross, they can crucify. This was not only true for Christ but, it would also be true for those who would follow him. Jesus prepared the Apostles at the Last Supper, for what was about to happen to him would also happen to them and to those who would follow him in what came to be called the "Age of the Martyrs". It would not always mean they would have to suffer red martyrdom but it would always mean embracing "white martyrdom". Jesus made it quite clear that unless his followers were prepared to take up their daily cross they could not be his disciples.

When purification is complete mystics enter immediately into the Mystical Marriage with Christ, often called the Transforming Union. It is then that for the first time they are able to experience the continual contemplation of God that Jesus experienced at every moment of his life on earth. They are able to do this because the "demons" that once ruled them from within rule them no longer and so like Christ they become continually aware of the presence of God. This does not mean their lives now become free from the suffering that warfare with the powers of evil always entails, any more than it did for Christ with whom they are united like never before. Evil might not oppose them from within in the same way as it did in the past, but they will most certainly continue to encounter it in those around them for whom the light of truth terrifies them in their darkness. They can be as terrifying to a modern Christian as they were for Christ who they crucified. It is not only total outsiders to the faith who will condemn those who proclaim the truth, but insiders too who have lost their way.

Yet despite this, Christian mystics become men and women of joy as Jesus promised, for they begin to experience a profound truth that is hidden from those who merely travel in the foothills of the mystic way. It is their joy to suffer, as it is a joy for any lover to suffer for the one they love. This joy is as infectious today as it was in the past when it inspired the ancient Roman world with the otherworldly power of love they could not resist. It brought them in their thousands to knock on the door of the Church that readily admitted them to begin their journey along the mystic way.

The most dramatic manifestation of this Christ-like joy could be seen as, like Christ, they gave their lives for the truth in red martyrdom. It might be in the smile on the face of an old and saintly man like Polycarp as he was being slowly burnt at the stake, the joy of the deacon Carpus, as he was being nailed to his Cross, the ecstasy of Blandinia as she was scorched in an oven, or the silent serenity of Felicity and Perpetua; after being flogged half to death, they were thrown to the wild beasts in the arena. But perhaps the most revealing martyrdom of all was that of the first martyr, Stephen, as he was being stoned to death, not least because the account of his death was inspired by the Holy Spirit in the Acts of the Apostles. Like all the others he was supported, sustained and strengthened from within by the Christ who lived in him. At the moment of his death he saw the destiny which all the others would attain. "Stephen filled with the Holy Spirit gazed into heaven and saw the glory of God" (Acts 7:55).

When St Dominic founded his order of friars he wanted to base their lives on the lives of the first apostles. In order to explain the very essence of what this meant, his illustrious spiritual son, St Thomas Aquinas said that the work of the Dominican Order was, "To contemplate and to share the fruits of Contemplation with others." What he said sums up the vocation of the Dominican order, but it also sums up the vocation of the whole Church. The fruits of contemplation was most certainly the lifeblood of the early Church, as they should be the life blood of the modern Church too. The first fruits like the infused virtues and the gifts of the Holy Spirt can be seen fully embodied in the life of Christ.

A more modern Dominican, perhaps the greatest spiritual theologian ever, Reginald Garrigou-Lagrange OP insisted that this vocation is for all, not just for monks in their monasteries or nuns in their nunneries who did not, in fact, exist when Christians first received their vocation from God. In fact, it was almost over three hundred years later when St Antony, the father founder of monasticism inspired the monasteries that would become spiritual oases everywhere in the deserts around him. Contemplative loving was from the beginning for all, as it still is today, for "ordinary" mothers and fathers and their whole families, for all are called to contemplation and to share the fruits of their contemplation with others. In Christ's mystical body no one is ordinary for all are called to the most extraordinary destiny imaginable. This calling to contemplation is not a sort of optional extra. It pertains to the very essence of the mystical spirituality given to us by Christ, and it is our great and grave responsibility to follow it. May God give us his grace his power, and his Holy Spirit to enable us to do it.

Chapter 18

From Paradise Lost to Paradise Regained

The very reason why Christ sent out his love on the first Pentecost day was so that it could enter into all who would receive it. This love that would draw us up into his mystical body and then into his mystical contemplation of his Father was God's plan from the beginning, so that through contemplating his glory we would ultimately be drawn into that glory. When in human love a person gazes on God's glory depicted in this man or that woman's beauty, love wants to go further. It does not just want to gaze upon them but to enter into them and as fully as possible and for as long as possible.

This profound truth is perfectly portrayed in Emily Bronte's Classic Romance *Wuthering Heights*. However, the word Romance is far too soft, too sweet, too sentimental to describe the potent primordial passions that drew the lovers, Heathcliff and Catherine together to become as one. Catherine can only describe her love, not just by saying that she loves Heathcliff, but that she is Heathcliff and he could say the same through his love for her. Their ultimate desire for love which is the ultimate desire of all lovers is depicted in the first film ever made that tried to portray this love on screen. When in death they were finally laid side by side; the individual wraiths of each rose from their tombs merged into each other to become in death what they desired in life. Then as one, they went out into their beloved paradise, the bleak Yorkshire Moors where their love was first ignited.

Like all human love at its most profound, and at its most perfect, it desires an ongoing and ever-deepening oneness that is only bounded by eternity. When, on the night before he died, Jesus said, "I am in the Father and the Father is in me" (John 14:11), he was describing that love as it is in heaven, where all love that is briefly glimpsed in human love, finds its ultimate consummation. The love that binds them together is the stuff that heaven is made of. Only moments after describing this loving at-one-ment, Jesus offers to share it with those who would follow him. He promises that if we truly love him then both he and his Father and the love who binds them together, will not only come to us but make their home in us, even in this life and to eternity. "On that day you will understand that I am in my Father, and you in me and I in you" (John 14:20).

This is the ultimate destiny of all humankind; it is for all, and this has been the continual teaching of those who have followed in the footsteps of the disciples. The next day Jesus returned to the Paradise that he offers to all, with the thief who died with him, to make it clear that no one is beyond redemption. No one is beyond being born again to enjoy the life of infinite loving that can be briefly glimpsed through human love, as a promise of the divine love which is to come when we are invited to enter into the wedding to end all weddings because it never ends. The ultimate consummation of loving then is union, not just with another human being, but with all other human beings in the love that called us into being from all eternity for that purpose. All that I have said about human love is true of divine love but in infinitely greater measure.

The person who learns to contemplate the glory of God does not just want to gaze upon that glory forever, but to enter into it for all eternity. The desire to do this has been implanted in us by God himself. Christ came not just to tell us that this is possible but to give us his love here and now so this promise can be brought about. Beginning here on earth, it can be consummated in heaven, not just briefly, not just to the end of time but to eternity. Further to this, the ecstatic bliss that we experience does not render us senseless but heightens all the senses like never before and grips our whole being, mind and heart, body and soul in the mystical and glorified body of Christ. Nor are we at any time static, but at all times dynamic, as the ecstatic bliss that we enjoy simply goes on and on deepening and expanding, as does our heart's capacity to receive it. This ongoing rapturous bliss described by St Gregory of Nyssa as Epecstasy, goes on and on in such a way that we can finally come to experience, in some measure, the love without measure, that has bonded the Father to the Son from all eternity.

This is the profound mystery that the famous Russian iconographer Andrei Rublev tried to depict in his famous icon of the three angels seated around the table on which the Holy Grail stood, beneath the Oak of Mamre. They represented the Holy Trinity who came to tell Abraham that he was to be the Father of God's own people who would one day come to share in his own life. But the icon also represents the invitation to the viewer. The chalice represents that invitation. For whoever receives the body and blood of Christ is taken up into him to come to share in the life of the Three in One. Contemplating that mystery in, with and through Christ as the prelude to entering into it, is not an optional extra for a few pious souls, but the way God has designed for everyone from the very beginning to attain their ultimate destination. The mindless vigilantes who set about stamping out contemplative prayer, good or bad, after the condemnation of Quietism, beginning at the end of the seventeenth century, were in effect undermining the only way to union with God for all, for which he initially created us. There may be many different forms of prayer that can lead a person into this contemplation, but there is, ultimately, no other way forward to union with God.

Although he was primarily writing for the enclosed members of the Discalced Carmelite reform, John of the Cross makes it clear that contemplation is for all, as do all authentic mystical writers. Despite this teaching from ancient times, the legacy of the vigilantes who have now been long forgotten, lives on to this day in the impoverished spirituality for which they have been responsible. It has seeped into those who profess the old Scholastic Theology and the new Biblical Theology despite the fact that at the heart of both of these theologies mystical contemplation as the way to union with God is fundamental. Although this was emphasized and underlined by the great spiritual theologian Reginald Garrigou Lagrange OP, it has still not filtered down to students in the seminaries, never mind students in the schools or the laity in the pews, who still have to languish on what the spiritual theologian Louis Cognet called "Devout Humanism". But I am getting ahead of myself. I will return to this later and explain it in much more detail.

Well-meaning, but nevertheless pseudo-prophets are arising as I write, to call the faithful back to the moral truths and certainties of the past and to bring back calm waters to save the Barque of Peter from the turbulent seas of feral liberalism that is threatening to destroy it. I use the word pseudo-prophets for two reasons. Firstly, because like all nostalgia, it is based on the myth that such a moral paradise existed only a short time ago, usually in the generation just before they were born. Secondly, because such a moral paradise can only be reborn as the external expression of a deep and profound mystical spirituality like the spirituality that Jesus first gave to the early Church through the first Apostles. I call it mystical because it matures in the mystical body of Christ himself where we can be taken up to share in his contemplation of the Father. The moral paradise that we desire is the result or the byproduct of the contemplation that St Thomas Aquinas calls the "fruits of Contemplation". The true prophets who we need to hear from then will not endlessly call us back to a moral paradise that we cannot conjure by human endeavour alone, but to that which comes from the grace of God. It is this grace that inspires true prophets, who like Our Lady continually calls people back to prayer, the prayer that she knows leads into true contemplation in, with and through her son, Jesus.

It is only his love given in this contemplation that can suffuse and surcharge our impoverished love with the only love that can lead us back from Paradise lost to Paradise regained. It is only here that moral perfection will be seen as the fruits of contemplation and in no other way. The only way that leads from Paradise lost to Paradise regained is through the mystic way. It is in this way that we learn to carry our daily cross and embrace the white martyrdom of daily selfless giving inside and outside of prayer. This is the only way to rise with Christ from being the children of the Old Adam which we are, to the children of the New Adam to which we have been called, in the new Paradise of God's Kingdom of Love.

Part 3
A Brief History of Christian Mystical Spirituality

Prelude

Chapter 19 A Handful of Heretics

Chapter 20 Monasticism to the Rescue

Chapter 21 St Bernard – A New Dawn

Chapter 22 The Franciscan Spring

Chapter 23 The Primacy of Love

Chapter 24 The Primacy of Love in Catholic Reform

Chapter 25 The Curse and Consequences of Quietism

Chapter 26 Devout Humanism

Chapter 27 The Modern Malaise

Chapter 28 When a Historian Becomes His-Story

Chapter 29 St John Henry Newman's New Spring

Chapter 30 An Unexpected Personal Climax

Prelude

Before explaining how meditation is transformed into contemplation and then describing how to pray in this new form of prayer, what follows is twelve chapters detailing how Catholic mystical spirituality declined due to several heresies which began in the fourth century. The restoration under St Bernard and St Francis of Assisi is detailed before explaining how decline set in again in the eighteenth century due to Quietism and Semi-Pelagianism, exacerbated by the "Enlightenment". All three are mainly responsible for the moral morass in the contemporary Church that without contemplative loving, is starved of the love that has and always will be its vital spiritual energy.

Lay readers of the last chapters may have thought, "How interesting, but of course, that is not for us but for monks, and religious." On the contrary, the mystic way or the way of the cross, or the way of white martyrdom was the only way known and practised by the first Christians long before monasticism and religious life were ever dreamed of. I wish to lead my readers back to this spirituality. It is the spirituality that Jesus introduced into early Christianity that draws all, not just into his mystical body, but into his mystical contemplation of our common Father.

Chapter 19

A Handful of Heretics

In the fourth century the God-given plan that Jesus introduced to lead people back to share in the glory of God to all eternity came tumbling down. This was because God's Plan completely depended on Christ, not just to introduce it but to become the go-between with a human and a divine nature, bonded inseparably together in what came to be called the "hypostatic union". His human love was absolutely crucial as it was that love, transformed and transfigured in the body that rose on the first Easter Day, that would draw all who would receive it onwards and upwards back into his Risen and glorified body. Take away the human nature of Jesus and the whole of God's plan would crumble, making what God had conceived from eternity impossible. The way in which God's plan was implemented in those first centuries was the wonder of the world. It should still be the wonder of the world today, if it had not been destroyed in the fourth century by a heretic called Arius who denied that Christ was God, and other heresies that I will describe later.

Arius (AD 250–336), was a Berber priest from North Africa who said that Christ was not God, but just a man. If what he said was taken seriously then the whole of God's plan could not possibly have been implemented. Mary would not have been the Immaculate Mother of God and Christ would have been no more than a pseudo-prophet making outrageous promises that could never be fulfilled. The mystery is that in the fourth century vast numbers of Christians believed Arius. At the time people no longer believed as their ancestors did that their Emperor was divine, nor did they believe that their predecessors had been divine either. This is one of the reasons why the heresy that proclaimed that Christ was not divine either was able to take root. Once it did, the profound God-given spirituality that thrived after Jesus sent his own love to inspire and animate the early Church declined, when people were led to believe that neither he nor his love was divine after all. Soon man and his well-being began to come first and God began to come second, at least in practice. Inevitably, the material world began to take precedence over the spiritual and the faith that was once so vibrant and alive soon became little more than nominal for the majority, as it is today. This was the sad state of affairs that began to set in after Constantine became Emperor.

When Constantine became the Roman Emperor after the Battle of Milvian Bridge (AD 312), his religious tolerance enabled Christians to come out in the open after many years of suffering. However, by the time Christianity became the official religion of the Roman Empire in AD 381 the "Church Suffering" became transformed into the "Church Triumphant". Sadly, the newly established Church gradually began to take on all the trappings of an imperial power that would have horrified its founder. Many now wanted to become Christians, not to die bravely through red or white martyrdom as their brothers and sisters before them, but to live the good life, and that meant a richer and more prosperous life with the best and most important jobs in town. Nine times out of ten these jobs seemed to be given no longer to the pagans, but to the "old faithful" and the new converts. The clergy themselves were tempted and even corrupted with positions of honour and high office that were closed to them before. Bishops who had once been hunted down were now raised to senatorial rank and were to be seen draped around the court of Constantine, one of the richest men on earth. The Pope was offered and often took on a rank equivalent to that of a consul with all the attendant flummery. In the hope of supernatural rewards hereafter, wealthy Christians were encouraged to donate land and property to the Church both during their lifetimes and after their deaths by way of legacies.

The new properties donated to the Church by wealthy Christians was the origin of what later came to be known as the Papal States, making the Church a temporal power in her own right within the Empire, presided over by the Pope who now became a temporal as well as a spiritual leader. In subsequent centuries this would attract men with mixed motives to the papacy.

In no time the blood of the martyrs that had been the seed of the Church that flowered, went back to seed again but this time the seed was barren or bore ambivalent fruit. Like any other institutions with power and property, it attracted the ambitious to further their own preferment, and armies of bureaucrats to maintain it and at times real armies to defend it. Inevitably, as John Wesley once put it: "Wherever riches have increased, the essence of religion has decreased in the same proportion."

These new Christians became more and more consumed with the lust for money, power, and ambition and began to worship the God who would not deter them or put too many demands on them. In this climate, it would be far more acceptable to acknowledge that the founder of their religion was no more than a man, albeit a very great man, but not God. A new breed of Christians had steadily been growing up who were not brought up in the Judaeo-Christian ethos that prevailed initially. Many came from the culture that prevailed in the Hellenistic world and many more came from a far more basic paganism that prevailed amongst the countless hordes of Barbarians who now poured into the Empire in droves. They did not find concepts like the hypostatic union easy to grasp. It was far easier to simply abandon their old gods who were at the best of times quarrelsome, interfering despots, who demanded expensive gifts and sacrifices to placate them. How much better to have just one God, the Christian God who it seemed was far more reasonable, far more understanding and far more merciful too, who did not demand expensive gifts and sacrifices. In the new Christian world order in which they now wanted to rise it became imperative to accept the Christian religion without all the religious complications that were beyond them.

For these people, the teaching of Arius was good news. It maintained that Jesus was not divine, but purely human and a later creation of God. To use the technical language of the day, Arius argued that Jesus was not consubstantial or coeternal with God the Father and that there was a time when he did not exist in any form. The heresy was so successful that at one time over eighty per cent of Christendom became Arians with disastrous effect. In the days before mass media, the only thing the Church could do to stop the heresy was to coin a slogan and then beat it incessantly like a drum, to impress the truth into people's minds. The slogan was quite simply "Christ is God", "Christ is God", "Christ is God". Orthodoxy finally won the day, but at a price. The divinity was emphasized so much that Christ and God were hardly distinguishable in people's minds. Jesus Christ, the mediator, who had been at the heart and soul of the Christian community suddenly vanished from view. It was as if Jesus had ascended into heaven again, but this time it was a psychological ascension that raised him up and out of people's minds and hearts. Jesus who was once the vital and dynamic source of Christian spirituality was all but lost to view. In the future, even the foremost Christian writers used the word Christ for God and the word God for Christ without feeling it necessary to distinguish one from the other.

Then another heresy called Macedonianism began to spread alongside Arianism in the mid-fourth century. Like Arianism, it was called after its founder Macedonius I, the Greek Bishop of Constantinople from AD 342–346, and from AD 351–360. Macedonianism was the logical consequence of Arianism. It did for the Holy Spirit what Arianism did for Jesus. If Jesus was not divine, then neither was his love, the Holy Spirit. How could a person participate in God's Plan without Christ and the Holy Spirit? The Holy Spirit was sent to draw us up into

Christ's Risen and glorified body where we would share in his loving contemplation of the Father and receive the fruits of contemplation to share with others. When Macedonianism had taken away the Holy Spirit and Arianism had taken away Christ, God might still be in his heaven, but we had no means of reaching him. The only possible way we could reach him without God's power, the Holy Spirit, was by man's power, human endeavour alone.

This led to another heresy in the fifth century called Pelagianism. It was a sort of Catholic stoicism championed by a British Monk called Morgan, named Pelagius by St Augustine who vehemently opposed him. It promoted a DIY spirituality that was always destined to fail, because as Christ insisted, "Without me, you can do nothing." And if all this was not enough, anyone who did try to rise Godward was further hampered by the teachings of two more heresies that infiltrated the Church. Whereas Manichaeism taught that the body was evil, Neoplatonism, originally taught by Plotinus in the third century, believed that the body was the prison of the soul. Before even beginning the ascent to God, Christian stoics would have to engage in some of the most extreme forms of asceticism to put to death all their bodily desires and free themselves from the evil material world that held them earthbound. As the Holy Spirit seemed to have disappeared, they had to do this alone. At least, Epictetus the founder of Stoicism, had the honesty to say, "Show me a stoic if you know one. Let my old age gaze upon what so far I have never seen." And Seneca, one of the most renowned stoics of all said, "Show me the stoic". No one can ever rise to reach God without the Holy Spirit and a spirituality that taught that God created all things and said they were good. This was pre-eminently true of the masterwork of his creation, his Son made flesh and blood to become for us the Way, the Truth and the Life.

Chapter 20

Monasticism to the Rescue

The God-given spirituality of love that was the mainspring of early Christianity was still enshrined in the monastic life after Constantine became emperor and Christianity was proclaimed the official religion of the Roman Empire by Theodosius the Great in AD 381. It was this consecrated form of life that was now used to renew the secular world that was rapidly going downhill.

The plan for renewal involved taking the spiritual life that was flourishing with ever greater fervour in the desert and using it as leaven to enable the secular world to rise from the decadence that threatened to destroy it. Far from being tainted with the laxity that was becoming endemic in the newly established Church, the nuns and monks in the desert were thriving as whole armies of the young and the disillusioned were heading there to swell their ranks. They had not only heard about the exploits of these intrepid spiritual explorers by word of mouth, but they had read the *Life of St Antony* by St Athanasius, the patriarch of Alexandria who knew Antony personally. Many had read the writings of John Cassian who lived for twelve years amongst the monks in the Egyptian desert recording their ascetical heroism, and other writings that have remained with us to this day. Now they wanted to join them, so they flooded in droves to the monasteries founded by Antony, Pachomius, Macarius and others in Egypt, as well as to those founded by Hilarion, Jerome and Melanie in the Holy Land. So too the great monastic foundations in Cappadocia in present-day Turkey, that thrived under St Basil, St Gregory Nazianzen and Gregory of Nyssa drew their followers mainly from the Christian Eastern Church.

The "plan" to renew the Church was to encourage the monks

to set up monasteries in the West on the edges of civilization or sometimes even in towns, to act like beacons of light to enlighten a secular world that was forgetting its origins. Important monastic foundations were set up in the south of France by monks including John Cassian and St Honorius and even in Rome itself, and other major cities of the Empire that were in desperate need of the spirituality of the Desert. Then the next step was to choose the holiest and most learned of the monks and make them bishops to inspire their clergy with the spirituality they in their turn would hand on to the faithful who were becoming all but spiritually destitute. When this new monastic breed of bishops found themselves alone in the world they were asked to re-evangelize, they felt isolated and insecure after the brotherly support they had received in their monastic seclusion. So, many bishops brought brother monks with them to their new surroundings to practise the way of life they had known.

This inspired other bishops like St Ambrose, St Augustine and St Martin of Tours to gather their clergy around them and introduce them to a sort of semi-monastic community for mutual support in turning to God and in ministering to the people. These priests who were not monks were nonetheless introduced to this semi-monastic way of life and came to be known as Canons or Canons Regular because they were committed to a regular rule or canon that determined their way of life.

When these bishops built their Cathedrals, as well as building monasteries next to them, they set aside a place in their Cathedrals for the sort of monastic prayer they had enjoyed in the desert where some of them were formed. Choir stalls were built so that each member of the monastic or semi-monastic community could sit, kneel or stand opposite each other to recite the Divine Office. The structure of this Office was based on the Jewish tradition that Jesus and his disciples would have followed, praying five times a day. This practice was the origin of the Divine Office, as practised in Benedictine Monasticism.

This form of monasticism gradually became the most popular interpretation of monasticism in Europe in the sixth century, mainly due to its spirit of moderation. What was, however, the very essence of monastic spirituality was the profound prayer to contemplation that inspired and animated every other facet of the monastic life and the teaching that the monks used to inspire the secular world around them. This profound mystical spirituality can be seen in the writings of St Augustine, as monastic spirituality begins to inspire those for whom the monks went into solitude in the first place. This same teaching can be seen alive and well and still inspiring monasticism two hundred years later in the writings of Pope St Gregory the Great. Their profound mystical teaching can be read in detail in Dom Cuthbert Butler's monumental book *Western Mysticism*. Quoting St Gregory, he shows that above all else it is love that is central to the mystic way, for:

> The gift of Contemplation can only be given to those who love, for the power of love is the engine of the soul, which while it draws it out of this world, lifts it on high.

That it was still alive and intact at the end of what was a long and particularly depressing period in the Church's history, can be seen in the mystical theology of St Bernard almost six hundred years later. Although monasticism as such was never specifically designed as an instrument to promote the Gospel message in the world, it was nevertheless remarkably effective. In addition to providing holy Bishops who imbibed the spirituality of the Desert Fathers, their monasteries became beacons of light in the Dark Ages to clergy and laity alike, disseminating both spiritual and secular learning, while transcribing the Christian and Pagan classics for posterity.

I think it important to remember that in his scholarly work *Western Mysticism*, Abbot Butler has shown that before St

Bernard of Clairvaux (1090–1153), the inner or hidden awareness of God's love that is experienced as a by-product of loving him, is generally called contemplation or mystical contemplation. This older and more traditional way of referring to the tangible experience of God's love is generally retained by the mainstream of Catholic mystical writers. I use the word Catholic because genuine mystical writers who perpetuate the most ancient Christian mystical tradition are predominantly Catholic. The reason for this is that the first radical Protestant reformers, and those who are still influenced by their doctrines, believe that man is intrinsically evil thus making the divine indwelling and the consequent mystical life unthinkable. Anglicanism would, in general, be a good example of an exception to this rule. In her famous book *Mysticism*, Evelyn Underhill, an Anglican, admits as much when she says, "The greatest of mystics have been Catholic saints" (p 126).

There is another great development of the monastic life that I must refer to because it had such a profound influence on the reconversion of Europe in the wake of the barbarian invasions, as well of course on the country where it grew and developed.

I became bored with overindulging myself in the south of France many years ago. I therefore, took the ferry to the island of Saint-Honorat a couple of miles off the coast of Cannes. It was here that more than fifteen hundred years ago, a community of monks arrived from the Egyptian desert. They were not just any monks, but monks who were schooled in the monastic spirituality of their father Abbot Antony, described in detail by St Athanasius in his *Life of St Antony*.

At the door to the now Cistercian monastery, there is a large plaque stating that it was here on this Island and from the monks recently arrived from Egypt, that St Patrick was schooled in the "science of the spiritual life". When he returned to Ireland it was to set up myriad monastic settlements after the style of the Antonian monks. This is a central church around which the monks, or more precisely the anchorites would build their primitive cells. The remains of such monasteries can still be seen in Ireland today and thanks to St David in Wales and St Juliot in Cornwall, at Tintagel, for instance, high up on the headland above Merlin's Cave. In his classic work *Irish Monasticism* the great Jesuit scholar Fr Ryan describes their prayer life:

A very large proportion of the Irish monks progressed so far in prayer that they were capable of unbroken contemplation. Just as contemplation was looked upon as the normal result of a spiritual life, of self-conquest and prayer, so it was expected that some among the contemplatives would reach mystical heights in their Union with God.

He then cites individual monks who like St Antony before them would withdraw into greater solitude for ever deeper union with God. But this was not necessarily the end of their spiritual journey, for as St Athanasius shows in his *Life of Antony*, the consummation of the spiritual life is in what he calls "spiritual paternity". This spiritual paternity does not just prepare the monk to become a spiritual father to his own monks but to return to the world they left many years before to share the fruits of contemplation with others. That is why St Athanasius tells us that before he died, St Antony returned to the busy streets of Alexandria to preach to those in most need of the wisdom that he imbibed in his solitude. That is why it was the natural completion of their particular brand of monasticism, for the Irish monks like Brendon, Columba and Columbanus and so many others, to set out and preach to the unconverted about what or rather Who had converted them in their many years of solitary prayer.

Without such monks like Columbanus and his disciples, the new lands occupied by the "barbarians" might never have been evangelized. If only present-day evangelists were prepared for the apostolate by contemplation, instead of by psychological gimmicks and crowd-pleasing novelties, then what was done for the Church in their day will be done again for the Church in our day.

Chapter 21

St Bernard – A New Dawn

The history of Christian spirituality is rather like a roller coaster with continual ups and downs, as renewal is followed by decline as the human spirit inevitably falters and falls despite best efforts. When monks who had attained spiritual paternity led renewal all was well, but sadly when their fervour faded, or when monks who were spiritually unprepared for the task went out into the world, it was the world that converted them to its ways and its own standards of living the "good life". So by the eighth century, Europe was awash with wandering monks, many of whom were busily undoing by their behaviour, all that was done by their illustrious forebears.

The situation was such a scandal that when Charlemagne was enthroned in AD 800, he ordered all monks back to their monasteries and decreed that henceforth all monasteries in his empire must accept and observe the rule of St Benedict. The vow of stability taken by every monk meant that the monasteries would never be able to provide Christendom with itinerant preachers as in the past. Cluniac, Cistercian and Carthusian monks would help reinterpret and reform the monastic life in subsequent centuries, but they would do little for the laity who were increasingly starved of evangelical spirituality. The Canons Regular who initially developed out of monastic life had little effect, as the diluted form of monastic spirituality on which they depended was hardly sufficient to keep them from spiritual starvation themselves, let alone enable them to feed those starving in the world. It was certainly not sufficient to generate with any consistency the profound contemplative prayer that animates the effective apostle.

If genuine and far-reaching renewal was necessary for the

Church to lead its people back to its God-given spirituality, two things would be necessary. Firstly, Christ should be repositioned back into the centre of Christian spirituality. This must be done in such a way that people could once more come to know and love him in his human nature and so be taken up into his divine nature, to contemplate the Father. Secondly, this new presentation of the old spirituality would then have to be taken into the secular world, to the ordinary people, by a new brand of religious who first practised what they were to preach to others. All this was about to start at the beginning of the twelfth century.

Sometimes in human history you feel that drums should roll, cymbals clash, trumpets sound and spotlights highlight a particularly important event or person, or both. Just such a time came in the year 1112. The place where this event was about to happen was at a newly-found monastery at Citeaux in France. The English Abbot Stephen Harding was on the verge of giving up the new venture to go back to the early Benedictine tradition in all its rigour and simplicity with the emphasis on daily manual labour in the fields when there was a knock on the monastery door. When the door was opened it was to reveal St Bernard, a young nobleman of 23 years of age with thirty-two of his friends. Like the first apostles, they were drunk with spiritual fervour. But they were not yet ready to go out to the world to fill it with what filled them. They needed to enter into solitude for their charismatic enthusiasm to be tempered through purification in the mystic way.

They had been set alight by the latest religious fashion that was consuming medieval Europe. In 1095 Pope Urban II inaugurated the first Crusade. Less than ten years later pilgrims who had been to the Holy Land on pilgrimage came flooding back, inspired and animated with what they had seen. They saw where Jesus was born, where he grew up, where he preached, where he worked miracles and where he suffered and died before rising from the dead and ascending into heaven to send the Holy Spirit. Once

Jesus in his loving and loveable human nature was back centre stage at the heart of Christianity, the faithful could come to love him, and enter into him and his mystical body. At the beginning of this new age, St Bernard was the first to follow his heart into the mystic way that would enable him to develop a new Christ-centred theology and mystical spirituality that would be the cornerstone of Christian spirituality for centuries to come. Only three years after he joined this new Cistercian reform he was sent to found another monastery at Clairvaux in 1115 where he was Abbot until his death in 1153. In his monumental study of *Christian spirituality*, Père Pourrat devotes nearly one hundred pages to St Bernard, showing his "emphasis above all on devotion to the mysteries of Our Lord's Life – the infancy, the episodes of the Passion and the Crucifixion and also his devotion to the Blessed Virgin". In the view of Pourrat, it is above all St Bernard who shaped the theology of the later Middle Ages and also of modern times.

His mystical theology was particularly innovative. In the very early Church, it was known and accepted that virgins were seen as brides of Christ. Many of the early Fathers commentated on the *Song of Solomon* to develop the idea that the Church is the bride of Christ. Even individuals in their personal spiritual search were sometimes referred to as brides of Christ, but St Bernard went further. In his famous commentaries on this deeply moving and romantic poem he goes a step further, and then embellishes his theme in some of the most lyrical language used so far to depict a mystic's relationship with Christ. The theme is that it is in the act of mystical contemplation itself that the mystic becomes in a very real and experiential way a bride of Christ. Furthermore, it is in the blossoming of this intimate bridal relationship that a person comes to the consummation of the spiritual life, the Spiritual Marriage. This same theme would be taken up by the great Scottish mystic Richard of St Victor (1110–1173) who became the influential prior of the Canons Regular of St Augustine of St Victor in Paris. Thereafter, the idea that the

Mystical or the Spiritual Marriage represented the summit of the mystic way became generally accepted. It featured in the bridal mysticism of the Rhineland mystics, then John Ruysbroeck and of course St John of the Cross and St Teresa of Ávila. Through these latter two it has come to be the accepted way of referring to the summit of the mystic way.

Although the theological and mystical writings of St Bernard had an immediate effect on his monastic contemporaries, theologians and open-minded Bishops and their clergy, it was someone else who was destined to take this new Christ-centred spirituality to ordinary people. For St Bernard and the new members of the Cistercian order, their spirituality was more than adequate to lead them to the heights of the mystic way, but their vow of stability still prevented them from taking their new-found Christ-centred spirituality to the world that was in such need. In the years after Bernard's death more and more little bands of fervent men, some of whom had been on pilgrimage to the Holy Land, dedicated themselves to living more evangelical lives and then preaching to others to do likewise.

That the renewal they were trying to bring about was necessary was beyond doubt, for the long and depressive spiritual emptiness of the Dark Ages had taken its toll on the moral fibre of a Church lacking the inner mystical life that was about to reanimate it. The text of the Fourth Lateran Council (1215) that was now on the horizon painted a gloomy picture of the woes of clerical irregularities that it was called to remedy. However, it was already decided that the many groups of evangelical men who had set themselves up to renew the Church were not fit for purpose. With the best will in the world, they had become "evangelical ranters" full of bile and vitriol for the clergy who may well have deserved their invective but it would never convert them, for only the humble can speak to the dissolute and the depraved with any hope of being heard.

The man who would do what they failed to do was born

thirty years after the death of St Bernard. He not only fed off the fervour of others who had been to the Holy places but actually went there himself. His name was St Francis of Assisi. Unlike St Bernard, he was called to take the new spirituality to ordinary people like himself, founding a new religious order that enabled him to do this on a grand scale. Other mendicant orders began to flourish with the Franciscans, all trying in their own way to respond to the needs of a Christendom which had been sliding back into paganism. The Franciscans originally grew out of a lay movement, the Carmelites out of the eremitical life, and the Dominicans owed much to the monastic life they adapted for the sake of those spiritually languishing in the world.

It was at the Fourth Lateran Council (1215) that these new Orders were encouraged to bring about the reform in the Church that was so long overdue, with the new spirituality developed by St Bernard. These Orders were teeming with saintly men and women who are still household names today: St Francis of Assisi, St Anthony of Padua, St Bonaventure, St Dominic, St Albert the Great, St Thomas Aquinas, St Clare, St Margaret of Cortona, St Angela of Foligno and so many others canonized for their transparent and heroic holiness.

When seeing what seemed to be a freedom denied them by their vow of stability some members of monastic orders began to criticise these new orders suggesting that their place should be in the monastery, not gadding about in the world. It was St Thomas Aquinas who answered them with the words that I have already used to describe the essence of early Christian spirituality. "Our apostolate," he insisted, "is to contemplate and then to share the fruits of contemplation with others."

Chapter 22

The Franciscan Spring

I have already suggested that the arrival of St Bernard should have been announced with drums rolling, cymbals clashing, trumpets sounding and spotlights highlighting him knocking on the door of the Cistercian monastery at Citeaux in 1113, for religious history was about to take one giant step forward. But just under a hundred years later another even greater step was to take place. This time it should have been announced with Bach's B minor Mass, Beethoven's Missa Solemnis, and a dozen or more blasts of Handel's Hallelujah chorus. Why? Because what was about to happen this time was not due to a quirk of history, but to the direct intervention of God. This time the man in question was not a learned and brilliant young aristocrat, but a semi-illiterate draper's son, not knocking on the door of a famous monastery but standing in a tumbledown little church called San Damiano just outside the walls of a small Umbrian town.

When something big is about to happen, and I mean really big and important, God has a habit of choosing the person we would not have thought of; someone remarkable for a lack of fitness for the task in hand, at least to the worldly-wise. It is God's way of teaching a vital truth of the spiritual life, that God's power works best in human weakness. And it was God's power that was about to call this otherwise insignificant little man to change the Church while simultaneously giving him the power of his love to do it.

Like St Augustine before him, St Francis had already experienced God in the beauty of his creation. He not only spent many months turning in prayer to the One in whom this beauty was created, but he had already undergone the beginnings of the purification that would enable God to do what came next. God spoke to him through his Son, still depicted on what we have come to call the Franciscan Cross. Francis not only heard Christ speaking, but he saw his lips moving too, and he experienced Christ's love entering into him to empower him to do what was being asked of him. The task was nothing less than to change the Church, to rebuild it from the bottom up.

After three solitary years living as a hermit for his purification to continue, he set out to do what God had commanded him to do, with the first followers of his new religious Order. Francis wanted it to be written into his rule that it was not he or anyone else for that matter who would lead this Order, but the Holy Spirit. It was the love that Christ sent out on the first Pentecost, the love that he received as he prayed before the Cross in the Church of San Damiano in 1205. It was this Holy Spirit who did for St Francis what was done for the first Christians. He drew him up and into, the one Francis now called Friar Jesus.

It was therefore now through mystical experience rather than through intellectual reasoning that Francis came to see and understand the sublime mystical vision that is at the heart of authentic Franciscan Spirituality. The one St Francis called Friar Jesus, who humbled and emptied himself of his supernatural birthright and entered into him, was the very Word of God who had reigned from eternity, in whom everyone and everything had been created from the beginning. This led St Francis to realize that if everyone and everything had been created in Friar Jesus then all the world must be a friary. The Greek philosopher Plato said that the world is a prison. Shakespeare said that all the world is a stage and the men and women merely players, and a President of the United States said that all the world is a market place and the men and women merely buyers and sellers. But for Francis of Assisi, all the world is a friary and everyone and everything within it are therefore, brothers and sisters to one another. It is not just Brother Francis and Sister Clare, but Brother Sun and Sister Moon, Brother Wolf and Sister Lamb, Brother Fire and Sister Water, for the whole of creation is a brotherhood and sisterhood with a common Father in whose embrace all were created from the beginning. That is why conservationists see St Francis as their inspiration, and that is why he was declared their patron from the outset.

However, this is not the end of the vision of St Francis, but the beginning, the place of departure. For the Masterwork of Creation is Brother Jesus in whom all things were not only created, but in whom they all subsist now, and through whom all things will return to the place where they were first conceived, as to their ultimate destiny. What he saw so clearly was that by coming to know and love Brother Jesus, he could enter into him and with him come to know and love the Father, to taste even in this life something of the bliss to which we have all been called in the next life. Knowing and believing is one thing, taking the next step and dedicating your whole life to pursuing this vision is quite another. This is what St Francis did every day of his life. If you love someone and want to love them more to experience their love in return, you simply must give them your time. This is what Francis did possibly more regularly and for ever greater lengths of time than any before or after him.

Every Lent, Francis spent forty days in solitude and further weeks or months leading up to major feasts like Christmas. He redesigned the structure of his daily life so that both he and his brothers could have the maximum time possible for the prayer and meditation that leads to contemplation. He radically shortened the long monastic Office which could last as long as eight hours and replaced it with a much shorter one. He did not do this because he thought the Office that he loved was unimportant, but because he considered that the contemplation which he wanted all his friars to embrace to be even more important. His friars were called to an apostolate in the world and, as well as everything else, this meant many hours of travelling in those days. That is why he wanted his brothers to learn how to come through meditation on Christ to generate the love that would lead them into contemplation as soon as possible. The reason was simple; it is not easy to travel or work in the world whilst saying or reciting the Divine Office or while practising Lectio Divina or some other method of meditation, but contemplation is quite a different matter. It is by its very nature extremely simple if at times extremely difficult, nor do you need others alongside you to practise it. You do not need anything other than a burning yearning for God and the simplest of prayers to keep your heart at all times attentive to God.

Strange though it may sound, it is contemplation that is the perfect prayer for those working for God in the world. The original hope was that a young person's fervour should be so encouraged that even before the novitiate was over, they could be led into the beginnings of contemplation, and by the time their training was completed it would be their prayer of choice for life. This at least was the ideal, and in those days there were many spiritual directors to guide the young. It was to maintain this ideal that hermitages were set up in solitary places for the friars to go for prolonged periods of time, as did St Francis. The revised timetable for prayer gave far less time for communal liturgical prayer, to maximize time for personal contemplative prayer that St Thomas Aquinas said embodied the very essence of the new contemplative orders. The early sources show how night after night the friars would pray after the midnight office until dawn. The other mendicant orders like the Dominicans and the Carmelites would eventually also use the new shorter office, called the Roman Office, and make more time for personal prayer to contemplation, each according to their own particular charism.

St Augustine, St Gregory the Great and St Bernard, all agreed that although the love experienced in contemplation could not be described, something else could. This was the truth that became clearer to the contemplative the further he or she travelled on the mystic way, enabling the receiver to see with such clarity and ever-deepening detail what they thought they had known before. Seen from the outside, a stained-glass window of the Risen Christ contains all the detail that can be seen within, but when the sun shines through it, it becomes alive and totally engages the viewers, filling them with joy. This is why St Thomas Aquinas defined contemplation as, "A simple vision of the truth accompanied by awe". The further contemplation deepens, the more the contemplative sees God's incredible plan for the world and the part he wants us to play in its implementation. That is why St Thomas insisted that the very *raison d'être* of mendicants was to share the fruits of contemplation with others.

Now perhaps it can be seen how St Francis was able to see, not just with such clarity, but in poetry and in technicolor what St Paul originally called "God's Secret Plan", and to see the way to enter into it by entering through Love into the one who embodied it in his mystical body. I have detailed the mendicant way of prayer as practised by St Francis, because his way is not just for religious, but for all. We are all called to contemplation and to share the fruits of contemplation with others, as the first Christians, who through contemplation came to practise the prayer without ceasing that generated the supernatural love that took the ancient pagan world by storm. Each of us, in our own way, has to find time for having time with the One who continually loves us. The last part of this book is written for those who are prepared to do this, come hell or high water, through prolonged purification, through spiritual deserts, and in dark nights of the soul. This is how we carry our cross daily with Christ and come in, with and through him to the glory of the Resurrection.

Chapter 23

The Primacy of Love

It was thanks to St Bernard and supremely to St Francis that the profound mystical spirituality of the early Church was, at least for those with eyes to see, reborn again in thirteenth-century Europe. When St Francis returned from the Holy Land he built the first Crib in Greccio to burn into the hearts and minds of his fellow countrymen what had happened at the first Christmas in Bethlehem. In subsequent centuries, inspired by St Francis, the practice of building cribs spread all over Christendom and down to the present day. He wanted this moving scene to do for others what it did for him. Now that Christ had returned for ordinary people, at least in a way that was not so evident in the Dark Ages, spirituality could return to do what it was originally meant to do. It could teach people once again how to learn to love Jesus so that the love they would receive from him in return would draw them into his glorified body, thence in, with and through him back to the Father.

St Francis not only longed for but continually prayed for physical martyrdom to complete the union with Christ that he desired above all else. Instead of red martyrdom, however, he was offered a form of white martyrdom that no one had ever received before. On the fourteenth of September 1224, the feast of the Holy Cross, he received the stigmata on Mount La Verna. However, lest St Francis or anyone else for that matter could misunderstand what was about to happen to him, he received a revelation only seconds before he was stigmatized, so that the suffering engendered by this privilege would not be misunderstood. The revelation is told in such a low key way that many people have either failed to notice it or paid scant attention to what is of utmost importance. It should have been heralded by fanfares from on high and with heavenly choirs hitting thunderous crescendos. The revelation was to proclaim loud and clear the "primacy of love", that would become the heart and soul of Franciscan spirituality as it was the heart and soul of the God-given spirituality that formed the first Christians. The revelation that he heard from Christ himself was this. "It is not by suffering that a person is united with God, but by love." The love in question was not our love alone, but our love suffused and surcharged by the love that at all times pours out of the Risen Lord. That is, of course, the Holy Spirit, and that is why Francis wanted him to be named as the General of his Order, leading and guiding them from within.

In the "Dark Ages" the pernicious heresy of Manichaeism mushroomed all over Christendom both in and outside the Church, making people believe that the body was intrinsically evil. It resulted in a rigorous stoical asceticism meant to subjugate the flesh and free the soul from its imprisonment in the body, that was seen as no more than its prison. It was easy to see how it came to be believed that the requisite suffering that this asceticism involved was the way to Union with God. That is why the revelation to St Francis about the primacy of love was of such absolute importance to people emerging from the "Dark Ages". They had forgotten the God-given "spirituality of the heart" that prevailed in the early Church. It was not even the suffering of martyrdom, whether it was "blood martyrdom" or "white martyrdom" that united you with God, but love; the love of God that suffused and surcharged human love that was developed in deep personal prayer, purified and perfected in mystical contemplation. Love was the cause, heroic asceticism was the expression.

The acts of heroism and the eye-catching feats of asceticism in those early days were not the acts of Catholic stoics trying to make themselves perfect. They were outward expressions of men, women and children animated by and inspired with the love of God. Later admirers who were inspired by them and wished to emulate them, made the mistake of thinking they had to copy their acts of superhuman asceticism if they wanted to follow them. What was in fact needed, as the revelation to St Francis underlined, was that they should rather generate the quality of personal prayer that could alone enable them to generate the love that could unite them with the One who makes all things possible even the impossible.

At last, thanks to St Francis, it was not only the effects of Arianism and Macedonianism that were destroyed, but the malicious and pernicious influence of Manichaeism and the heresy of Pelagianism that made people think that everything depended on their own endeavours alone. We were no longer alone, left to make our own way against all odds. The heresy of Pelagianism was put to bed as the Holy Spirit moved in to do what was quite impossible without him. As the Holy Spirit raises a person upward and into Christ, it is to see that all things were created in him from the beginning and that, far from being evil, they are all good, for they are the work of God. Salvation then does not involve the arduous task of trying to free oneself from a world in which all things are evil and imposing on oneself a form of inhuman ascetism that you find nowhere in the teaching of Christ, but everywhere where Manichaeism abounds. On returning to Assisi after receiving the stigmata, St Francis, filled with joy, dealt with Manichaeism in his own unique way.

While St Dominic was trying to put down the latest virulent outbreak of Manichaeism in the form of Albigensianism in southern France, Francis was doing the same in Italy. He did not, however, dispute with the heretics like Dominic, nor did he write a theological treatise; he simply wrote a poem. It was the first poem in the Italian language dedicated to Brother Sun, praising God in the glory of his creation. A little feeble one might think – but far from it. The people loved it and learned and recited it, putting it to music. It was a pop-hit composed by the greatest celebrity of the time and whilst everyone was enjoying listening to it they were being enthralled by the vision of St Francis and relearning the truth of God's goodness and its presence in the works of his creation. What better way to reach ordinary men and women in the market place, and help put to death a heresy that had been making their lives miserable for centuries. St Francis had himself been deceived, so after asking pardon of his own body for wrongfully mistreating it, he stood up at the general chapter to condemn all forms of asceticism that came, not from the Gospels, but from the scourge of Manichaeism that had for centuries been plaguing the Church and most particularly those who believed that subjugating the body was the only way to free the soul from its imprisonment here on earth. The terrible winter of misunderstandings, misapprehensions and mistakes was over.

The Franciscan Spring had arrived, and it was inaugurated by a man who chose to be stripped of everything to imitate the poverty of Brother Jesus. Many, including some of his first brothers misinterpreted the reason why he wanted to be so absolutely poor, arguing that it was not a virtue that Jesus and his disciples embraced – but they missed the point. The absolute poverty of Christ that Francis wished to emulate was the poverty into which Jesus entered when he cast aside the riches of glory in heaven to enter into a weak human nature and subject himself to arrogant human nobodies for us. But the ultimate in poverty for Francis was Christ's decision to continue to humble himself daily to become ordinary homemade bread. Why? So he could enter into our very bodies and there, radiant with the love that he first unleashed on the first Pentecost day, fill every part of our bodies so that we can be taken up into his mystical body where we can contemplate the Father in, with and through him, to all eternity. After he received the stigmata, Francis received a special indult from Rome giving him permission to have Mass in his hermitage. His joy was now complete.

It may sound fine to proclaim a new age in which the primacy of love was to be paramount, as it was in the beginning. But it must not be forgotten that the love Francis was talking about was God's love, the love that can change all things including us. However, as love cannot be forced, only given to those who freely choose to receive it, Francis acted accordingly. He did what was to him so obvious, but which might not occur to us. He went into solitude with ever-increasing regularity and for ever longer periods of time. When you believe that the love that made the world is there, ready to make us into the image and likeness of his Son and fill you with the joy that nothing else on earth can give you, it seems the obvious thing to do; not to us perhaps, but it did to Francis.

As long as the contemplation that St Francis experienced in his prayer life also animated and inspired those who followed him, all would be well. They would not only see the truth with the wisdom that inspired him to show them what to do, but they would be given the power to do it. But take contemplation away and decline and fall would set in until contemplation returned. St Thomas Aquinas defined prayer, and he also defined meditation. He did not say pray, or meditate, and share the fruits of your prayer or meditation with others. He said contemplate and share the fruits of your contemplation with others.

While the Black death in 1349 killed almost half the population of Europe, far more were killed in religious orders because their charity opened them to the pestilence far more than the population at large. This led to religious decline, as in order to maintain all the religious houses that were rapidly emptying due to the plague, all too many new recruits were hastily signed up who were not suitable candidates for contemplation. As a result, decline set in across the board in almost all religious communities. The only hope was, "back to contemplation" and after seventeen years in solitude where he practised the contemplation that was to be his mainstay for the rest of his life,

St Bernadine of Siena was the man who set out to share the fruits of contemplation with others. The new Franciscan reform which he represented was inundated with new recruits.

Next time you are in Franciscan Italy, visit the remote hermitages where St Francis sought solitude. There you will see the caves that he used, and even huts still standing made of wattle and daub. But then you will see the many hermitages still in use today, all built by St Bernadine to accommodate the new members of his reform who stayed there for years, learning to meditate and then contemplate in preparation for the massive spiritual reform they would bring not just to Italy but to Germany, France, and Spain in the fourteenth century. All this was now possible because the Christ who disappeared from view in the Dark Ages had been reborn, thanks to St Bernard and St Francis.

The primacy of love would become central to the mystical theology of the Franciscan theologian Blessed John Duns Scotus and to the reforms of St Bonaventure, St Bernadine of Siena and the other reformers in the years ahead. It was not just the person of Jesus, but his personal love that would henceforth be central to all genuine reforms. It is only when his love is suffused with our own, that together we can contemplate the glory of God, as God intended from the beginning.

Chapter 24

The Primacy of Love in Catholic Reform

If you visit Italy you will see the famous monograms representing the Holy Name of Jesus designed by St Bernadine. These monograms can be seen in churches, but also on public buildings, private houses and on wayside shrines. It was the badge of his new reform with the person of Jesus at its centre. Learning to love him as Bernadine did in his solitude, was the way into the mystic way, into the mystical body and into Christ's loving contemplation of Infinite Love, our ultimate destiny. This is how he tried to convert ordinary people to the principle of the "primacy of love" revealed to St Francis, by leading them to the person in whom that love is generated. If St Francis was called the second Christ by his contemporaries and treated as such, then St Bernadine was treated likewise.

Tens of thousands came to listen to St Bernadine and hundreds of young men moved by his example came to join his reform, hence all the new hermitages that were built to receive them. It was here they were taught the primacy of love by those who travelled before them on the mystic way. Here their love would be purified and refined, enabling their love to mix and merge with the love of Christ, opening them to the fruits of contemplation and preparing them to preach the new reform. St Bernadine was not alone, he was joined by other great saints like St John Capistrano, St James of the Marches and Blessed Albert of Sarteano. The reform that spread all over Europe was not just through the Franciscans but through other orders too. The Benedictines are a good example of monks who were influenced by the reform. One monastery in Spain is of particular interest because it was at the monastery of Montserrat in Catalonia that something destined to have enormous significance for the future took place.

The Abbot Garcias de Cisneros (1455–1510) was not only won over to the new reform but to the latest piece of new technology, the printing press. It was he who conceived the idea of printing what he called spiritual exercises or instructions on how to meditate on Jesus Christ, the centre and inspiration of the new reform. These exercises spread far and wide for two reasons. The first was because Montserrat was one of the most popular places of pilgrimage in Spain as the shrine of Our Lady of Montserrat. Secondly, it was after returning from such a pilgrimage that St Ignatius wrote his own spiritual exercises while living for almost a year in a cave near the town of Manresa, not far from the famous monastery (1523–24). Thanks to the latest technology and St Ignatius of Loyola, the centrality of the person of Christ in Christian spirituality would be assured for centuries to come, not enshrined in a theological treatise, but in a practical method of prayer that taught people how to come to know and love the person of Christ, making his presence pivotal in one's whole life. Not surprisingly, St Ignatius would write in his diary that he wished to emulate St Francis more than any other saint, nor was it therefore surprising that he should call his new Order – the Society of Jesus. Other Orders had also initiated reforms too, like the Dominicans under Raymond of Capua who was led on and inspired by the extraordinary lay-mystic St Catherine of Siena, who, like saint Francis spent years in solitude in her own home, being reformed herself, before she set about reforming others.

Raymond of Capua was not only the spiritual director of St Catherine, and her biographer but a reformer in his own right. When he was Master General of the Dominican Order, he had to deal with the problems cause by the Rhineland Mystics who were deeply affected by the Pseudo-Areopagite and were therefore predominantly speculative and intellectual. If leaders like John Tauler and Blessed Henry Suso were orthodox many others were not, especially those who fell into the sort of heresies for which

Eckhart was condemned by the Church. In order to deal with the many divisive differences of opinion that broke communities apart, Raymond allowed like-minded friars to live in different communities, but all under the umbrella of the Dominican order. Then he let the Gamaliel principle take its course – what is of God will survive and what is not, will not (Acts 5:39). And that is precisely what happened. I will leave the Carmelite reform until later, as the fruits of their contemplation will be pivotal when I detail the journey ahead in the mystic way. Before moving ahead I must mention the reforms that were taking place in the Netherlands.

The name given to the best-known expression of their spirituality was the *Devotio Moderna*. It emphasized a personal piety full of feeling and sentiment that made Jesus a friend and personal saviour. It was particularly associated with a certain Geert Groote and the Brethren of the Common Life. Most of us are familiar with it thanks to a member of that community, Thomas à Kempis, and his book *The Imitation of Christ*, one of the bestselling religious books of all time. While their fellow reformers in the South tended to make use of the spoken word, the northern reformers made good use of the written word too, and of the new printing presses that were coming into use almost everywhere. A new type of literature was beginning to have a deep influence on the faithful, books telling the life story of Jesus. Perhaps the most famous and the most popular was written by Ludolph the Carthusian and published in 1470, the *Vita Christi* (Life of Christ). This book had a lasting effect on St Ignatius and on very many others too.

These reforms sweeping across Europe in the century leading up to the Reformation should put to bed the later Protestant assertion that the Catholic spirituality was in a state of "terminal decline" prior to Martin Luther hammering his 95 articles to the door of the church in Wurttemberg in 1517. In his book *The Stripping of the Altars*, Dr Eamon Duffy has shown how among ordinary people, the faith was alive and well. I hope, from what little I have written, I have been able to show that it was alive and well in most religious Orders too, on whom the laity depended for leadership. The popular devotional prayer known as the *Jesus Psalter* that endlessly repeated the name of Jesus was used perhaps more than any other form of prayer during Penal times by the Recusants in England who remained loyal to the Church. The prayer to Jesus was the last prayer that many of the martyrs made as they were being brutally put to death at Tyburn and elsewhere.

The truth of the matter is that although there was more than enough depravity in high places thanks to the Renaissance Popes, particularly Alexander VI, on ground level the Franciscan reform movement was still bearing fruit. The Council of Trent (1545–1563) was not primarily called to combat spiritual degeneration, but Protestant heresies, and was preceded by great saints like St Catherine of Genoa, St Angela Merici, St Teresa of Ávila, St Peter of Alcantara, St Ignatius, St Philip Neri and so many others. Whilst older Orders were reformed, new Orders were raised up to embody and disseminate the spirit and the teaching of the Council.

Orders like the Jesuits, Barnabites, Theatines, Capuchins, Discalced Carmelites, and Oratorians were theologically and spiritually inspired and guided after the Council by such goliaths as St Robert Bellarmine, St Francis de Sales, St Vincent de Paul, and St John of the Cross. In the hands of such great leaders as these, for more than a hundred years after that Council, spirituality continued to thrive and prosper, surcharged from within by the profound mystical prayer that animated and inspired the Church since the great St Bernard. In his life's work, *Enthusiasm*, Monsignor Ronald Knox makes it quite clear:

The seventeenth century was a century of mystics. The doctrine of the interior life was far better publicized, developed in far greater detail than it had ever been in late-medieval Germany or late-medieval England. Bremond, in his *Histoire littéraire du sentiment religieux en France*, has traced unforgettably the progress of that movement in France. But Spain too, the country of St Teresa and St John of the Cross, had her mystics; Italy also had her mystics who flourished under the aegis of the Vatican. Even the exiled Church in England produced in Father Baker's *Sancta Sophia* a classic of the interior life. (Chapter XI)

In his unique and masterly work, *The Spiritual Life – A Treatise on Ascetical and Mystical Life*, Father Tanquerey admits that he is deeply indebted to the spirituality of the French school of the seventeenth century in which mystical theology reached such an advanced stage of development. Perhaps the best and most detailed exposition of the mystical spirituality that blossomed in this period can be found in *The Religious History of Seventeenth Century France* by the renowned spiritual theologian Dr Louis Cognet.

However, the clouds were beginning to gather. From small beginnings, a pernicious heresy was brewing that was going to do for the mystical life what Arianism did for the Christian life in earlier centuries. The heresy would be called Quietism, the movement that promises the Prayer of Quiet to those who have not been prepared to undergo the inner purification that would enable them to receive it. More on this topic must be said if we are to see and understand why it was put down so vigorously and how it resulted in the demise of true Catholic Mystical spirituality of which so few are aware, with the catastrophic consequences for the Church down to the present day, that we have all witnessed.

Chapter 25

The Curse and Consequences of Quietism

Molinos, the founder of Quietism, was a seventeenth-century Spanish priest stationed in Rome. From there, he presided over the heresy that has deeply undermined authentic mystical theology down to the present day. It has had devastating consequences for the Church that simply cannot be exaggerated. Molinos' heresy was called Quietism because it encouraged a person to do nothing in prayer but remain quiet before God. Here, he or she appeared to do nothing but wait on God's action in total silence. Quietism in all its different manifestations seemed to encourage the reformer's belief that our own efforts are useless and even blasphemous. Everything depends, not on what we do, but only and exclusively on the grace of God alone. It was Quietism that gradually undermined authentic mystical theology and the role of the mystic within the Church.

Its adherents were not only encouraged to do absolutely nothing in prayer, but to do nothing about temptations either, including sexual temptations that could only be overcome with God's grace. While awaiting this grace they had to be endured, or, as it was shown at the court where Molinos was condemned, they were enjoyed on a grand scale. The moral textbooks insisted that with sexual sin there was no "parvity of matter". In other words, all sexual sins were mortal sins, great or small. No wonder Molinos was given a life sentence when Quietism was condemned in 1687, and no wonder that after the trial, gangs of anti-mystical witch-hunters panned out all over Christendom to destroy any form of prayer that had the slightest whiff of Quietism about them.

Forms of prayer like the Exercises of St Ignatius were acceptable because they involved mental activity, but any form of prayer that encouraged inner recollection or quiet was condemned. Even St Teresa of Ávila and St John of the Cross came under suspicion, and henceforth their works could only be found covered with dust on the top shelves of clerical libraries. As a result of the Church's zeal in crushing this heresy and in promoting the Gospel of good works, for fear that Catholics would fall into Protestantism, mystical prayer simply fell into abeyance. The enormity of this and its consequences down to the present day is beyond calculation. In his monumental *History of the Church* Monsignor Philip Hughes states:

> The most mischievous feature of Quietism was the suspicion that it threw on the contemplative life as a whole. At the moment when, more than at any other, the Church needed the strength that only the life of contemplation can give, it was the tragedy of history that this life shrank to very small proportions, and religion, even for holy souls, too often took on the appearance of being no more than a divinely aided effort towards moral perfection.

This moral perfection not only included the moral teaching of the Gospels but the moral teaching of stoicism that had seeped into Christianity in the third and fourth centuries and again at the Renaissance. As we have seen, Monsignor Ronald Knox makes it quite clear that in the century leading up to the condemnation of Quietism, mystical theology was taught and practised more than at any other time before. Moral theology was taught in seminaries, in religious houses and universities side by side with the mystical theology without which nobody could practise the high moral standards demanded by the Gospels. After Quietism, virtually any form of prayer that could be classified as mystical was suppressed. Quietism was not only leading people into Protestantism but into the continual practice of serious sexual sins. That is why such devastating and widespread attacks were made on all forms of prayer that promised to lead people to contemplative prayer.

The devastating attacks on mystical theology set in immediately after the condemnation of Quietism. The anti-mystical witch-hunters first turned their attention to the powerhouses of prayer and the spiritual life: the monasteries, the friaries, the religious houses, convents of every type, seminaries, schools and places of study of every sort, not least the Catholic universities. Any sort of prayer that taught people how to be still and quiet, how to remain recollected and remain quietly open and docile to the Holy Spirit had to be stamped out. In outlawing authentic mystical theology, the anti-mystical witch-hunts also gradually undermined and finally outlawed the spiritual directors who used to lead those who had come to the end of their first fervour into contemplation. The Exercises of St Ignatius survived the onslaught because they were considered safe, firstly because they always involved the use of the inner faculties of the mind, the reason, the imagination and the memory. Secondly, when they did reach one of their main objectives which was to galvanize someone with a nominal or lukewarm faith into a vibrant and heartfelt faith, there was no teaching in the Exercises to lead them on and into the mystic way, but rather into the apostolic way.

At the beginning of the sixteenth century, there was an extremely erudite priest called John Colet. He was the son of the Lord Mayor of London who used his wealth to support good friends like Erasmus, who like him were busily employed trying to reconcile and promote the spirit of the Renaissance within Christianity. He was brought up on the spirituality of the *Devotio Moderna*, but when he visited Italy he not only fell in love with the glories of the Renaissance but with the teachings of Socrates and his "spiritual" descendants, the Stoics. He returned to England full of enthusiasm to share his ideas with his peers and with the younger generation, founding St Paul's school in London. The perfect product of this school would be embodied in a true English gentleman in whom the teachings of Socrates and Christ would be perfectly harmonized. The other eight major public schools modelled themselves on St Paul's and the grammar schools followed suit.

Later, public schools that arose to accommodate the sons of the *nouveau riche* who were born of the industrial revolution and the exploitations of empire, modelled themselves in their turn on the "big nine". The same aims and ideals would eventually be found in more diluted forms in the secondary and comprehensive schools of the twentieth century, including Catholic schools. It has often been argued that apart from Shakespeare, England had not been affected by the Renaissance that is seen in all its glory most particularly in Italy – hence the mandatory grand tours of the gentry and the aristocracy to enjoy the artistic masterworks that could not be found in England. Ironic though it might seem, the very people who felt they had to go abroad to experience the influence of the Renaissance had been personally influenced by it far more deeply than the people who were delighted to show them the artistic masterworks of their forebears. Thanks to John Colet, the inner moral teaching of the Renaissance was merged with the Christian ethic to become the heart and the soul of the English character.

While for some religious, the use of the Scriptures could lead them on to contemplation, this would not be possible in the same way for the laity who were warned to steer clear of them for fear they may do for Catholics what they did for Protestants. Nor should they be consumed by the sort of spirituality that saw Christ as Jesus, their personal saviour, in the way the Protestants saw him. Gradually a change began to take place in Catholic spirituality, re-introducing, albeit in a diluted form, some of the heresies that rampaged in the fourth and subsequent centuries. Even though devotions such as that to the Sacred Heart helped the laity to keep Jesus at the centre of their spirituality, the first witch-hunters did not like too much emphasis on the humanity of Christ. For example, calling Christ Jesus too often as the Protestants did, could sound a little too close to denying his divinity. And so in subsequent centuries down to the present, a sort of Semi-Arianism prevailed that never denied the divinity of Christ but which never properly emphasized his humanity either.

Inevitably a type of Macedonianism returned. It was a sort of semi-Macedonianism that did not deny the divinity of the love of Christ, the Holy Spirit, but it took little, if any, obvious part in the personal spirituality of the laity. I remember in the 1960s searching for a book to read on the Holy Spirit. Sadly, I would find only two. The first was called *The Unknown God*, the second was called *The Forgotten Paraclete*. This was of course before the advent of Charismatic Renewal. Without the Holy Spirit at the centre of the spirituality that prevailed after the condemnation of Quietism, men and women were once more left to themselves and the old heresy of Pelagianism, or more precisely Semi-Pelagianism, reared its ugly head once more. And to make matters worse, the influence of Jansenism, a sort of Catholic Calvinism, reintroduced a type of Manichaeism that was so rampant in the middle ages, with ascetical practices that included painful corporal forms of mortification never taught by Christ and his first followers.

St Bernard and St Francis brought back Jesus as the heart and centre of Catholic theology and spirituality. St Bernadine and his followers would paint the monogram of his Holy Name on homes, in churches and on public buildings where they can still be seen to this day. Devotion to the person of Jesus was taught everywhere. It was central to the teaching of the spirituality of the *Devotio Moderna* as can still be seen in the work of its greatest propagator, Thomas à Kempis in his famous book *The Imitation of Christ*. It was because this spirituality was centred on the person of Christ, and on coming to know and love him, that the pathway back through meditation to contemplation that only seemed to be open to the few in the Dark Ages, was once more open to all.

Even when Jansenism threatened to return Catholic spirituality to a narrow-minded moralism, it was thanks to St Margaret Mary that a new popular devotion began to represent not just Christ as he was, but as he is now, with a glorified body bursting with uncreated love. If devotion to the Sacred Heart has at times been trivialised by bad taste in the cult surrounding it, and the art used to promote it, it should never be forgotten as it proclaims a profound truth that is the central truth of our faith. Jesus is not dead, He has risen and is alive now busting with uncreated life and love that pours out of his heart relentlessly and into the hearts of all who would receive him. For two centuries this devotion counteracted Jansenism with its narrow-minded kill-joy moralism, by proclaiming the love of the Risen Christ in a way that even the simplest could understand. No one should allow their artistic sensibilities to prevent them from appreciating this profound truth that was revealed in a unique way to St Margaret Mary. The Sacred Heart is not just incarnate love but incarnate loving, who will transform all who open their hearts to receive Him.

In the aftermath of Quietism, however, contemplation soon reverted to be seen as the extraordinary way for "a few chosen souls". It is the purpose of this book to return once more to the profound mystical spirituality given to us by Jesus himself in which contemplation in, with and through him is the way back to the place where God first conceived us.

Chapter 26

Devout Humanism

Before going to the Franciscan noviciate to try my vocation, I went on a grand tour of the Swiss Alps instead of giving all my money to the poor, like St Francis. It was there, beneath the grandeur of the vast mountain ranges, that I felt for the first time just how small and insignificant I was. By the time I entered the noviciate I had already discovered what would alone teach me humility: the experience of something, or rather, of Someone whose greatness and grandeur would lead me to the only humility that would become the prelude to all the other virtues. Unfortunately, although the library was full of moral and ascetical masterpieces, I could not find a single book that taught the reader how to pray in such a way that would lead to the contemplation of God's greatness, his grandeur and the glory into which we are all called as our spiritual birth right. And I could only find such books with difficulty in the far larger library at East Bergholt in Suffolk where I went to study Philosophy and Theology.

Between St Bernard and St John of the Cross such books abounded, but between the condemnation of Quietism and the present day, such books have become extremely rare, if they exist at all. Books written in simple modern English by a practitioner could not be found, at least not by me, any more than it was possible to find a spiritual director who knew from experience and not just from books, the journey through the mystic way. There have been many books written on mysticism. It seems intellectuals and academics are fascinated by the subject, but if these books are not positively unsound, they are of little help and even a hindrance to those looking for practical help. This is because they have not been written by practitioners.

One such work which I have used is generally accepted as a classic of its kind: *Western Mysticism* by Dom Cuthbert Butler, which draws together, in an orderly way, texts from the great Western Mystics. But, because it is not written by a practitioner, it can muddle and mislead a reader who is looking for practical guidance. Dom Cuthbert Butler has the humility to admit that he is not a practitioner whereas others do not, and so the reader is not put on their guard. In his Epilogue he writes:

To prevent misconceptions, I say quite simply that I have never had any mystical experiences myself, never had anything that could have been called an experimental perception of God or his presence. The first four Mansions of St Teresa's Interior Castle will always be of practical use to those endeavouring to lead a spiritual life, but the last three Mansions along with the latest and the most mystical treatises of St John of the Cross, and a host of other such writings, would have to be classed in our libraries as outworn ideas of a bygone age, or at best as religious poetry.

If he had only said all this at the beginning of his book instead of in his Epilogue, readers would read with their spiritual antennae alert and at the ready, enabling them to learn from his scholarly work which gathers together the copious quotations from the great mystics, while yet remaining sceptical about his often-erroneous interpretations.

The introduction to the unique masterpiece on mystical prayer, *The Graces of Interior Prayer* by Père Poulain SJ, makes it clear that the author is not a practitioner either, nor does he pretend to be, although his scrupulous research has produced perhaps the greatest and most accurate piece of research into mystical theology ever written. The truth of the matter is, as Poulain's brief autobiographical list of mystical writers since Quietism shows, there have predominantly been non-practitioners trying to write about what was still seen as an extraordinary way for a few "holy souls". That the way back to God was through contemplation in, with and through Christ, was forgotten. There were meditation manuals of all sorts, but no manuals teaching ordinary Catholics how to enter into Christ's contemplation of his Father through travelling along the mystic way.

I first studied Thomistic Theology before I was introduced to what was called the "New Biblical Theology". I was able to compare the two and understand the theology that was taught in universities and seminaries since the Council of Trent, as the theology used by that Council to express its teaching. Although this was the theology that was used by most educational establishments in the years immediately after the Council of Trent, as Monsignor Ronald Knox has established, it was taught when mystical theology was taught and practised like never before. During this period then, when through this teaching the primacy of love was still paramount, there was a perfect balance between the heart and the mind, between the intellect and the will. As the Dominican Reginald Garrigou Lagrange OP shows in his masterwork, *The Three Ages of the Interior Life*, St Thomas Aquinas wrote his brilliant *Summa Theologica* while he was himself travelling in the Mystic Way. Those, therefore, travelling in this Way will be able to see and appreciate this work as it should be understood.

St Augustine, St Gregory the Great and St Bernard were the first to emphasize how it is in contemplation that a person sees the truth ever more clearly as they progress toward the summit of the Mystic Way. Once again I use the metaphor that I used then. With contemplation, a student is able to see and understand more keenly and more deeply than without it, the magnificent masterwork that was St Thomas Aquinas' gift to the Church. Without contemplation, it is seen as a great stained glass window, but from the outside. With contemplation, his masterwork is seen, as if from the inside, iridescent with all the brilliance with which he was able to write, thanks to the Holy Spirit who guided his every word and his every sentence.

The primacy of love would now begin to wane as the primacy of the intellect was seen as paramount in the new "Age of Enlightenment". The decline of the heart and of the will in Catholic theology in general and in Catholic spirituality in particular almost exactly coincided with the decline of mystical theology if it did not also contribute to it. The emphasis on the intellect and on reason as the sole arbiters of what was and was not acceptable seeped into ecclesiastical thinking too. It put the final nails into the coffin of a mystical theology and mystical experiences that could not be put under the microscope of rational thought and intellectual deduction. Henceforth, any attempt at renewal in the Church was almost always purely intellectual, usually by vigorously promoting new initiatives to reinstate and re-emphasize the theology of St Thomas Aquinas into all institutes of learning.

This state of affairs continued until the beginnings of what came to be called the "New Biblical Theology" that enabled the Second Vatican Council to take place. This New Biblical Theology certainly touched hearts, as well as minds and raised hopes. It was, in fact, the very ancient theology that prevailed at the dawn of Christianity but reinterpreted and re-presented thanks to the modern biblical, liturgical and historical research that inspired the Second Vatican Council. The sadness was that the great theologians, scripture scholars, liturgists and historians who promoted this New Theology were influenced by the anti-mystical ethos that has prevailed for the last four hundred years. They were ignorant therefore of mystical prayer and of the vital prayer life that leads up to and into it.

This created in them all a blind spot that prevented them from seeing in their otherwise laudable studies, the absolute importance of the profound mystical theology that prevailed in the early Church. Both the old scholastic and the new biblical theology then were to suffer from both the ignorance of and therefore the failure to practise the mystical theology and the God-given spirituality that I have tried to explain. Sadly therefore, although many genuine attempts have been made to renew the Church in the four hundred years or more since the condemnation of Quietism, what the spiritual theologian Louis Cognet describes as "devout humanism" continues to be the staple diet of Catholic spirituality, although, as we are about to see, even this spirituality is under threat as a new feral liberalism threatens to take over.

However, it is untrue to give the impression that the years following the condemnation of Quietism were spiritually dead. Prayers were said, the Office was recited, the Liturgy was celebrated, but vocal prayer depends on the prayer of the heart. In other words, vocal prayer depends for its power and efficacy on the love that is generated in prayer within the heart of a believer. By vocal prayer, I mean the whole of the Liturgy too. It is this love, practised in deep personal and daily prayer that determines the quality of our relationship with God before we even go into Church, never mind open our mouths.

Chapter 27

The Modern Malaise

When the constitution on the liturgy was promulgated at the end of the Second Vatican Council, many were overjoyed because it did seem to embody a genuine modern representation of the liturgy that was so important to our early Christian forebears. I too was particularly delighted with this excellent document. But sadly, it was not followed by a further constitution detailing a modern representation of the early God-given mystical spirituality that I have tried to develop in this book.

The power and efficacy of the liturgy is the outward expression of the deep and daily prayerful spirituality of those who participate in it. Take this away and we are back in the world that Jesus came to transform, because the love on which it was originally founded is lost to sight. There was, however, one liturgist, the greatest of them all, who had an even deeper influence on liturgical reform than Dom Odo Casel OSB (1886–1948), and my mentor, Pere Louis Bouyer (1913–2004). Let me quote then from perhaps the greatest liturgist of them all, the Jesuit, Josef Jungmann SJ, whose detailed scholarship dwarfed all others and whose words have apparently fallen on deaf ears.

In the present-day liturgical movement, primitive Christianity is often held up before our eyes as a model, an exemplar of liturgical observance. We are to believe that Christians of old, contrary to the tendency of modern individualism, knew no other, or scarcely any other form of prayer than liturgical prayer. Unfortunately, this ideal is not correct. The idea that the life of the primitive Christians revolved exclusively around the liturgy is not correct. And it cannot be correct, simply because it would be unnatural and in contradiction to the Gospels. How could the Christian life exclude private and personal prayer? It is a gross exaggeration to restrict the prayer of Christian antiquity to liturgical prayer alone.

In his many books on early Christian spirituality he goes on to explain how the early Christians like Christ himself, prayed at least five times a day. They prayed in the morning and evening and then at nine, twelve, and three o'clock, and even rose to pray at midnight. This was not just for vocal prayer, but for meditation too, on the life, death, and Resurrection of Christ, as he states quite clearly in his writings. This was of particular importance when later Christians who had never seen Christ personally, came to know and love him spiritually, and with the love developed there, to enter into him mystically, into his mystical body, thence into his mystical contemplation of God his Father.

We have seen how, in the sweep of history, secular ideas and ideals have tended to infiltrate the spiritual ideals of Christianity. In the early Church it was the ideas of the Hellenistic world that were to blame. At the Renaissance, those same ideas were once again at fault, as we have seen instanced by stoicism seeping into Catholic education thanks to John Colet. At the Enlightenment it was the enthronement of reason and reason alone, as the arbiter and measure of all things that were at fault, not just for its peremptory dismissal of mystical theology, but for inculcating the mindset that only an intellectual renewal could reform the Church. After the French Revolution it was communistic ideas and ideals that were thought to be the only bulwark against rampant authoritarianism and absolutism in its many forms. In this milieux the needs of the individual, of the personal, and of self-sought advancement were dubbed "bourgeois" and unworthy of a right-minded human being who should be totally dedicated to the common good, to the development of socialism or even communism.

Fr Jungmann refers to these ideas and "ideals" that had seeped into Catholicism in his time, through many of his "progressive" peers, many of whom like him, were so influential at the second Vatican Council. Although they were great intellectuals, theologians, scripture scholars, and liturgists, their antipathy to mystical theology received a further shot in the arm from the social idealism that had been understandably aggravated by their reaction to Fascism that flourished, both before and after the Second World War. They could not therefore be expected to see the necessity of, or emphasize, the importance of personal piety, or individual personal spiritual advancement, let alone the mystical prayer, which was still seen as an extraordinary way for the few, if it was a way at all. In short, although they were eager to reintroduce the ancient Catholic liturgy which was the "communal" expression of the whole, they were hardly likely to see the importance of, let alone introduce another document that for them seemed to emphasize the importance of the individual, the personal, and the mystical prayer, that was absent from their own spiritual education. The new liturgy was therefore doomed to fail as an instrument of renewal, without the inner dynamism that fired it in the early Church.

The early Christian liturgy was deeply inspiring, vibrant and spiritually re-energizing, not because it was rubrically correct in every detail, or verbally faultless, but because it depended on the daily personal prayer of the faithful. The early Christian sources like Fr. Joseph Jungmann SJ, make it quite clear that it was the practice of all Christians to pray, just as Jesus prayed with his disciples. And they would pray for more prolonged periods of time, just as Jesus did whenever and wherever he was able.

The omission of the Second Vatican Council to provide us all with a detailed modern presentation of the early spirituality of the first Christians, comparable to what they did for the liturgy, is quite simply the greatest ecclesiastical tragedy of modern times. A tragedy is when a good person or a great person, or even a good and great achievement is ruined by what might seem to be a small human failure or omission. This is what happened when an otherwise laudable Second Vatican Council that promised, and in fact gave so much, was sadly undermined by this serious omission. It was hardly noticeable at the time, for a whole Catholic population had come to believe that mystical prayer, if they had in fact heard about it, was an odd exceptional and eccentric way for a minority of "holy souls". The truth of the matter is that it is the very essence of God's great plan, called by St Paul the *Mysterion*. In this plan *all* are called to contemplation, as to their final destiny, conceived by God as their ultimate happiness, from all eternity.

It is not an eccentric idea to believe that God has called all to contemplate and then to enter into his glory to all eternity. That we should believe that it is, is to show just how far we have come from knowing and trying to live out in our daily lives the God-given spirituality that was the meat and drink of our first Christian forebears. The fact that the Council did not produce a document reinstating the profound mystical spirituality that prevailed at the dawn of the Christian era, left a gap that has in the intervening years been filled by secular forms of "spirituality", if they can be called that. They have been drawn from the latest liberal pop-psychological and sociological fashions that are becoming more and more extreme with each passing day. Some of their frightening agendas from infanticide to sexual depravity, and even with theological agendas that seem more protestant than Catholic, have been taken up, not just by some of the laity, but among and between Priests, Bishops, and Cardinals from top to bottom in the Church.

This must alert us to the catastrophes that have already begun to afflict the barque of Peter. We must follow the teachings and the example of the great saints, mystics, and reformers to whom I have referred, who have kept the barque of Peter on course. If we wish to be guided by the Wisdom of God, then we will find it in Jesus Christ to whom we must turn in prayer, else we will be lost. External and visible reform in the Church must begin here and now with the clergy, most particularly in the seminaries and houses of religious education. If young men and women are asked to make a vow of chastity, without at the same time being taught how to come to know and experience the love of God, then disasters will follow because no one can live fully without love. If a person has had to forgo the experience of God's love reaching out to them through another human being in the sacrament of love, then it is an obligation on those who insist on this sacrifice, to teach them how to come to know and experience God's love in prayer, the prayer that leads to contemplation, or the disasters to which I have already referred will simply continue and become more and more widespread.

By prayer, I do not just mean saying prayers or performing prayers of obligation but practising the deep prayer that leads onward beyond first beginnings into the mystic way. It is only here that we will come to know and experience the love that surpasses the understanding. This is the love that was the making of the great saints, mystics, and prophets who we need today like never before. Mystical theology, as the foundation and completion of spiritual theology, must be taught by practitioners to all young men and women in seminaries and houses of further education. This is their right that must be granted to them by those who have placed on them the obligation to forfeit their natural desire to seek God's love in and through the sacrament of marriage. If it is their right, then it is also the obligation of their superiors to teach them how to come to know and experience the love of God through profound mystical prayer. Failure to do this means that they, their superiors, are guilty of leaving them in a state in which they are perpetually in danger of serious sin, and traditional moral theology would call this a serious sin in itself.

Moral theology also teaches that those who place someone in that position are morally culpable, a culpability for which they will one day have to answer. Nor are they just culpable of failing the young priests and religious themselves, but for the terrible and almost unthinkable physical, psychological and spiritual sufferings that they may go on to inflict on others, when failure to find love leads them to seek the "satisfaction" of lust that will destroy them and those others whose lives they will destroy.

What I have written and most particularly, in the final part of this book, is the traditional Catholic teaching on how we who are drawn into the mystical body of Christ can generate the love that will prepare us to be united with him, to experience with him his contemplation of the Father, and how the fruits of this contemplation will first change us, then the Church to which we belong and then the world we are committed to serve.

Chapter 28

When a Historian Becomes His-story

Many of us have not known or experienced, except perhaps for brief transitory moments, what it is like to belong to a Church founded by Jesus Christ, and to be inspired by and animated with the same love that excited, enlivened and exhilarated our first Catholic forebears. The great spiritual writers of the Church liken the relationship of Christ to his Church as that of a bride, and the Holy Spirit as the love that bonds this marriage together. As we have seen, the Fathers of the Church and many of the great mystical writers in subsequent centuries, use the beautiful love poem from the Old Testament known as the "Song of Songs", as a spiritual paradigm with which to describe the love of Christ with his Church and our ascent into God.

Just as in any marriage, when love is taken out of a once deep and exhilarating union, everything simply descends into an unholy chaos. What was once a haven of peace and security is destroyed, reaping havoc on the physical and psychological well-being of the children. Transfer what you can picture in your imaginations when secular marriages collapse to what happens to the Church when its spiritual marriage with Christ, and the myriad millions of individual marriages with him within that Church, break down because love has been extracted from them.

If you can do this, you may begin to see for yourself what has happened to our beloved Church, when in the aftermath of Quietism, the mystical theology that teaches people how to love, was taken out of Catholic spirituality. This is not the superficial sort of love that never lasts for long, but the quality of love that led Jesus Christ to live for others throughout his life and then die for them. This is the selfless other-considering, self-sacrificial quality of love we need to learn if we wish to take up our daily cross and follow him. This is the love that can change our lives and the lives of those whom we love irrevocably for the better, and the life of the Church that is languishing without it. If you want to learn how this sort of love can be generated within you, then read on. The last part of this book is for you.

T.S. Elliot said, "I have only one thing to say, and I have spent my whole life trying to say it, in as many different ways as possible." I can only say "Amen" to that. So, for the last time let me say again what I have spent my whole life trying to say, but this time in a story from my own life. I am in danger of falling into a literary mortal sin, which is self-indulgence, but it is worth the risk for the clarity it may bring to those still not sure of what I keep emphasizing.

In the mid-1950s I was privileged to be present in Rome for the re-introduction of the new Easter Liturgy at the Rosminian Church of St John at the Latin Gate. According to St Jerome, it was there that St John is believed to have survived being thrown into a vat of boiling oil in AD 92 before being exiled to Patmos. The liturgy began with a massive bonfire in the courtyard from which the Paschal candle was lit to symbolise Christ, then our candles were lit from the Paschal Candle to represent Christ's life that was communicated to us. Thanks to Pope Pius XII this was the first time the ancient Easter liturgy had been celebrated in a parish church, albeit in Latin. The way the vigil was celebrated so inspired me that I decided to major in liturgy and spirituality.

Ten years later, after graduation, I spent several years introducing the new liturgy instigated by the second Vatican Council into local parishes. It was in fact the ancient Catholic liturgy inspired by Christ himself and spread by the first apostles, albeit adapted to suit our contemporary world. Then in 1969 Bishop Casey of Brentwood asked me to become the director of Walsingham House, his retreat and conference centre in Chingford, London. He asked me to put special emphasis on teaching the new liturgy to both clergy and laity alike, that was then seen as the main instrument of renewal in the Church. In order to do this effectively I also arranged for speakers in what was then called the New Biblical Theology, Scripture, and the History of the Early Church.

Halfway through my twelve-year tenure I came to realize that the hoped-for renewal simply had not happened. In fact, by 1975 not hundreds, but thousands of priests and religious men and women left their vocations on both sides of the Atlantic. Droves of laity voted with their feet and churches that were once crammed full were more than half empty. What, oh what, was wrong and what, oh what, was to be done. It was at this point that a friend, Fr Anthony Rickards, a Franciscan priest, asked me to join him for a retreat at a remote Franciscan hermitage in the Rieti Valley in Italy called Fonte Columbo. When I discovered that Fr Angelo, the hermit who was guiding me through the retreat had lectured at the Antonianum, the Franciscan University, in Rome before retiring into solitude, I put my problem to him. Why, I asked, did the introduction of the new liturgy not bring about the long-anticipated renewal for which we were all longing?

The hermit took me into the church and turned on the lights. He then drew my attention to the words of St Bernadine of Siena written in the sanctuary behind the main altar. The words were these: *Si Cor non orat, in vanum lingua laborat.* "If the heart does not pray then the tongue labours in vain." It was, for me, something of a revelation. "You may have the best possible liturgy," he said, "but if your heart has not learned to pray before you even come into the Church to celebrate the liturgy, whether it is the Mass, the divine office or the Easter mysteries, or whatever, then you will not have generated the love that can alone unite you with the love of Christ, who is at the heart and centre of every liturgical celebration."

He then went on to say something that I have never forgotten: "I firmly believe that the Second Vatican Council was, not only good, but a blessing on the Church, but its influence could have been deeper and more effective if it had only reintroduced with the 'new liturgy' the spirituality that once prevailed in the early Church that underpinned and inspired it. I am referring to the God-given spirituality infused by love, that was originally introduced into the Church by Our Lord Jesus Christ himself. When I say infused by love I do not mean by our love, but by the Spirit of God's love which is the Holy Spirit. Then in the document that would have introduced it, the faithful should have been taught how to receive this divine love by explaining to them how to generate pure selfless loving in the deep personal prayer that was practised everywhere in the early Church. I mean the sort of daily prayer that characterized the life of Jesus and his apostles, showing how God's love can suffuse and surcharge human love with divine love. This is not only the quality of love that gave life and vitality to the early liturgy, but which enabled God to set the first Christians afire with a quality of selfless self-sacrificial loving that transformed a pagan Roman world into a loving Christian world in such a short time.

"It is time that we came to see and understand that renewal in the Church does not primarily depend on a perfectly designed liturgy, but on the quality of the personal prayer life of those who participate in it. Let us suppose that I had a magic wand, and I could wave it to give everyone the liturgy of their choice each time they went to Mass. It may be the new liturgy as introduced by the Second Vatican Council, with a perfect translation of the text and with all the rites and rituals perfectly designed to satisfy everyone. On the other hand, it may be the old Tridentine Mass in Latin that so many of us were brought up on, or a grand sung high Mass with music by Perosi, Palestrina or Purcell, or the mediaeval Mass that was so loved by some of the greatest saints that have ever lived, or the ancient Mass known to the Fathers of the Church which was said in Greek long before the introduction of Latin. Or what about Mass according to the Chaldean rite said in Aramaic, the language that Jesus himself would have used at the Last Supper.

"The introduction of any or all of these rites in themselves would do nothing to change us personally and permanently for the better, or the Church to which we belong, unless they are animated and inspired by the same profound daily liturgy of selfless giving and sacrifice as practised by the first Christians in imitation of how Jesus prayed and served the neighbour in need throughout his life on earth."

Fr Angelo told me that the most unforgettable Mass that he ever attended was in a prison camp during the Second World War. He said that the altar was a wooden bench, the priest had no vestments other than a homemade stole, the wine was begged from a Catholic guard contained in a thimble, and the host was made from a crust of bread. But he said they prepared for that Mass for weeks in personal prayer, sacrifice and suffering, and spent weeks after the celebration trying to assimilate and absorb slowly and ever more deeply what they had received. That Mass changed his life and convinced him that he wanted to become a priest, to do for others what that Mass did for him.

I personally have never met another priest before or since who said Mass with such devotion, as did Fr Angelo, nor have I ever experienced before or since the almost hypnotic pull to share in what he was celebrating. But what he did at the altar was already determined by his prayer before he started to say his Mass. His tongue never laboured in vain when he said Mass or chanted the divine office, because it expressed the prayer that his heart had been praying long before he began to say Mass. My friend Fr Anthony told me that he had the same experience when he was a Chaplain in the British army, billeted for a time at the friary at San Giovanni Rotundo in Southern Italy when attending the Mass of St Padre Pio. The retreat with Fr Angelo became for me one of the major turning points in my life.

When I returned from my retreat, I gave questionnaires to the priests and religious who came to the Residential Centre and

I was horrified to find how very few of them had been taught the importance of personal prayer and how to practise it, thanks to the anti-mystical ethos that still prevailed in the wake of Quietism. Hardly any of them appreciated that without the deep personal relationship with Christ that develops and grows in personal prayer, the liturgy can soon become ineffective, not in itself, but in those who are not prepared to receive it.

Chapter 29

St John Henry Newman's New Spring

Thanks to the words of St Bernadine of Siena and the Franciscan hermit who inspired me, I was able to see with clarity why the introduction of the new liturgy had not had the impact that was expected. Now, in addition to lectures on the liturgy with the help and inspiration that I received from Fr Angelo, I began to re-double my efforts in my own personal prayer life. I wrote my first book on prayer and began to give talks on prayer to those who participated in the courses on Biblical Theology, Liturgy and Church history. Job done you might think, as I thought myself, but I was wrong. What I was trying to do was being undermined by an extremely powerful "spiritual" trend that received a shot in the arm immediately after the condemnation of Quietism. It was a trend that had been slumbering in the wings for generations, but in the aftermath of the anti-mystical witch-hunts it began to take centre stage and to dominate Catholic Spirituality so effectively that the witch-hunters could retire sure in the knowledge that the fruits of their labours would be guaranteed to remain intact.

In order to explain myself, remember that in the early Church the Philosophical religions that thrived in parallel with the Christian spirituality of love, like Gnosticism in its many forms, Neoplatonism, and Stoicism, all had one thing in common. For them all the pathways to perfection depended on their own personal endeavours alone, and that is why they never succeeded. Unfortunately, this attitude of heart and mind continued to live on like a parasite when some new converts brought it with them after their conversion to Christianity. This was especially true when the consequences of Arianism and Macedonianism meant that Christ and his love was no longer at the centre, nor the heart and soul of Christianity, as it was in the earliest centuries. One of the greatest promoters of this do-it-yourself attitude who began to infiltrate Catholic spirituality with his ideas was the British monk Morgan, given the name Pelagius, with his Catholic stoicism, Pelagianism. Although St Augustine spent the latter part of his life trying to combat Pelagius' teaching, he could do no more that force it to retreat backstage, from where it continued to make centre stage appearances in subsequent centuries, and no more blatantly than in modern times, as I was about to discover.

It was at the Renaissance that these ideas began to make their way into the spotlights once again in what I can only describe as Catholic Stoicism. It was the Catholic Stoicism that we have seen entering into the Christian educational system thanks to John Colet whom I mentioned earlier, from the schools this insidious form of Pelagianism seeped into noviciates, seminaries and other houses of religious education. When, after the demise of Catholic mystical theology that put all its emphasis on God and his action as the major agent in remaking and transforming a human being, and prayer as the means of receiving that love, Pelagianism or semi-pelagianism returned thanks to the Renaissance. It has been with us to the present day, unbeknown to me, at least until what happened next in my personal story. The older religious orders such as the Benedictines, the Dominicans, the Franciscans and the Carmelites, for instance, whose foundations preceded the Renaissance, emphasized the action of God in their theology in general and in their spirituality in particular. Whilst congregations founded after the Renaissance, and the rise therefore of humanism, tended to emphasize human action in their spirituality. However, since the condemnation of Quietism most religious orders have been infiltrated with semi-Pelagianism too, although its influence is usually seen as more pronounced in the activity-centred congregations founded during and after the Council of Trent.

When in the 1970s the Dominican order decided to do something to renew themselves, they started a course in Rome for Dominicans from all over the world. After attending some of my talks the director of this renewal course invited me to Rome to lecture at the Angelicum on mystical theology. This enabled me to see that what I discovered from my questionnaires was echoed throughout the world. The problem was that the response to Quietism went so deep and was so widespread that virtually all monks, friars, nuns religious and priests were gradually weaned from any form of prayer that could lead them to mystical contemplation. And those few who, despite the anti-mystical ethos that was against them, did get through and progressed alone into the mystic way, had no one to help guide or support them, and as my inquiries enabled me to see, many sadly drifted off course. Those effected included even the great scholars, the biblical theologians, the scripture scholars, the liturgist and the spiritual historians whose presence was so influential at the Second Vatican Council. No wonder there was no special document on the spirituality which was the source of the inspiration that animated the liturgy with the profound mystical prayer as practised by our earliest Spiritual ancestors. This was not true of other great reforming councils that dramatically renewed our Church in the past. It is time for us to learn from the past and particularly from successful renewals in the Church in previous centuries. The great reforming councils of the past owed their very existence and their success to myriad mystics and saints who were steeped in prayer, as were the new orders that they founded.

One of the most successful of all Councils called to reform the Church, the Fourth Lateran Council (1215) was so successful, that its moral and spiritual ethos successfully spread all over Christendom and beyond. It was through the new mendicant orders like the Franciscans, Dominicans, Carmelites and the

Austin friars founded by great saints and mystics that was imbued with the moving theology of St Bernard that was founded on the humanity of Christ. These Orders were teeming with saintly men and women who are still household names today, like St Francis of Assisi, St Anthony of Padua, St Bonaventure, St Dominic, St Albert the Great, St Thomas Aquinas, St Clare, St Margaret of Cortona, St Angela of Foligno and so many others canonized for their transparent and heroic holiness.

The other great reforming Council of the last millennium was the Council of Trent (1545–1563). This too was preceded by great saints, like St Angela Merici, St Teresa of Ávila, St Peter of Alcantara, St Philip Neri and so many others. While older orders were reformed, new orders were raised up to embody and disseminate the spirit and the teaching of the Council. Orders like the Jesuits, Barnabites, Theatines, Capuchins, Discalced Carmelites and Oratorians, and myriad congregations of men and women were filled with apostolic zeal. After the Council there was ongoing theological and spiritual guidance by such goliaths as St Robert Bellarmine, St Francis de Sales, St Vincent de Paul, and St John of the Cross, as I have already explained. It was in the hands of such great leaders as these that for more than a hundred years after that Council, the Church continued to thrive and prosper, surcharged from within by the profound mystical prayer that had animated and inspired the Church since the great St Bernard. After the Second Vatican Council, not only were similar mystics and saints all but absent, but so also were the sort of new and vital religious orders to help spread and disseminate the teachings of the Council, and the existing religious orders diminished in personnel on a scale not experienced before since the Black Death in 1348.

As subsequent years passed by the problem simply exacerbated, as fewer and fewer were left to minister to the needs of the faithful. The quality of preaching the faith diminished and more and more people voted with their feet. Without the inner mystical life developed in the deep and prolonged prayer that inspired and animated their first Christian forebears, their spiritual lives gradually declined, not just to their own spiritual impairment, but to that of others too, who looked to them for leadership. Without the same inner life and love that animated Jesus, they were unable to generate the infused virtues and moral standards that shone through everything that he said and did. Nobody can acquire these virtues merely by desiring them. They are the gifts of the Holy Spirit, given during and after deep mystical purification.

However, as history has shown, pendulums do swing. St John Henry Newman's "New Spring" is at last on the horizon; of this I am absolutely certain.

Chapter 30

An Unexpected Personal Climax

Following the lectures I gave each year at the Angelicum in Rome, I received many invitations from all over the world to repeat these lectures from Dominicans who could not travel to Rome. One invitation was to prove my downfall. It began with an invitation to lecture to Dominican nuns in South Africa, the same nuns who owned and helped me run the diocesan retreat and conference centre in London. All went well, or so I thought, but a problem was brewing. The mother general was influenced by a Dominican sister from another Dominican congregation, who had been trained as a depth psychologist in Rome under the Jesuit Professor Rulla SJ. She believed that psychology could do what spirituality did in the past more quickly and she persuaded the mother general to send a group of sisters to participate in therapy groups. Once trained, they would be equipped to change others by introducing the latest pop-psychological techniques using group therapy sessions and sociological methods into their communities.

There were four factions that disrupted each community. There were modern stoics, those who wanted the classical Dominican tradition, those who wanted no change at all, and those who followed a strange Angel cult. I therefore wrote a paper for them detailing the Dominican Raymond of Capua's methods of reform. I called it the Umbrella Approach with the Gamaliel principle using the principle of Acts 5:39, that what is of God will survive, and what is not, will not. It was duly admired but not taken up, so the split between the modern Stoics and those who wanted to live the classical Dominican Tradition was only a matter of time. When a new mother general exclusively supported the new stoics with their modern methods of renewal, and insisted on all participating in it, the writing was on the wall. All were encouraged regardless of expense, to go on as many of the current self-help, self-discovery and self-awareness courses as possible. On returning from their training, two totally different approaches to renewing the congregation were clearly evident and the two groups clashed. Prayer and spirituality, was out, mystical theology was openly derided whilst modern depth psychology, group therapy and other pop-psychological techniques were in, and the dunces cap was made for me.

The final catalyst came in the person of a Jesuit priest, Fr John Carroll Futrell, who was at the behest of the sisters seeking socio-psychological renewal at the Jesuit spirituality centre in Denver, Colorado, sent to give the annual retreat to the Dominican Sisters at Chingford. With his permission I attended that retreat and was appalled to see how a modernised version of Jesuit spirituality was being used to replace the Dominican Spirituality to which they aspired. In the exercises of St Ignatius, the relationship between human action and divine action is totally orthodox. But sadly not so in subsequent centuries when many of his followers so emphasize human endeavour and human wisdom that God's action is minimized, if mentioned at all. Once again semi-pelagianism reared its ugly head. When challenged, as I challenged Fr Futrell after the retreat, they say that grace is important, but in fact all the practical importance is placed on human endeavour. In a letter to Sr Dominic the superior of the community, which she showed me, he warned her of me and how if she listened to me I would lead them astray. She did listen to me and I did lead them, but not astray, but rather back into the Dominican tradition to which they aspired to return.

The break came when I was away lecturing on Mystical theology in Rome for the renewal course for Dominicans from all over the world. However, they were not alone as a Dominican priest from the USA, Fr Gabriel O'Donnell OP, was staying at the Chingford Convent in North London at the time completing his doctoral thesis. The Sisters sent to the Jesuit centre in Denver were being instructed in a spirituality that was all but the opposite to that being taught by contemporary Dominicans in Rome and elsewhere. But sadly, the new mother general sided with those who wanted to transform their congregation with the modern man-made socio-psychological methods that were being taught in both Denver, Colorado, and in Rome. When the seven sisters who would break away refused to submit to, what was in effect semi-pelagian anthropocentric means of reform, they received a letter from their Mother General cutting them off from the congregation over which she presided. It was a grace that Fr Gabriel O'Donnell OP was there, not just to help them to move out of the convent and into what was originally a stable block that I had renovated for the use of the conference centre, but with the brotherly support and spirituality of a fellow Dominican.

The Mother General was summoned to Rome where she was severely sanctioned. Her letter to the seven sisters referred to them as a "cut off branch". She was told in no uncertain terms that only Rome can do what she had just done on her own initiative. However, the two factions stayed separate while the legal niceties were worked out. Having first only offered his services as a "facilitator", Fr Lachy Hughes SJ became the advocate for the "Magnificent Seven" when the mother general's advocate arrived from South Africa and embezzled the deeds to the properties held by the Chingford Dominicans. The seven remained silent while their semi-Pelagian Sisters did all in their power to undermine them, particularly with a new method of discerning God's will, learnt at Denver called "discernment". Rather like a Ouija board, the method they used had an uncanny and infallible way of getting the answers that you want, proving that you were, not only right and being guided by God, while those who opposed you were wrong and in the hands of an evil spirit or bad angel who was an agent of the "Enemy". That what you had discerned was God's will was always proved by an inner feeling of peace, given by God himself, when the truth had been discerned. Not surprisingly they discerned that the "breakaway sisters" were wrong and in the hands of the devil, while the evil genius who had incited them, the cause of their disobedience, was the very devil incarnate, and so I was sacked without further ado. Such people could only be dealt with by "exorcism", but none of them, including me, seemed inclined to seek the ministrations of an exorcist.

Simultaneously with the psychological and pseudo-religious methods employed by the "Denver" group, another perhaps even more frightening attack on authentic spirituality was coming from Rome from the Professor of psychology at the Gregorian University, the Jesuit Fr Rulla. A Dominican Sister who had studied under him was busily plying her trade when I was giving a retreat to Dominican Sisters in South Africa. The then previous mother general who had helped set up the Dominican renewal course in Rome recommended me as the main lecturer on prayer. Fr Rulla's thesis was that what had been done in the past to change a person from their ordinary sinful selves to their ideal selves, could now be done far better and far more quickly by his methods of depth psychology. The Dominican Sister who was implementing his travesty of the truth, was also used as an enforcer, whose techniques were employed to psychologically undermine and destroy anyone who stood for prayer and traditional spirituality, and who opposed the implementation of Rulla's methods. In short, she was being used as psychiatrists are used in totalitarian systems to smash all opposition and declare those who oppose them as psychologically unsound. It is easy to break a person psychologically, but it takes years if not decades to help them to spiritual and psychological rehabilitation. I know, because that is what I found myself doing all those years ago and am still doing today. If there is a devil who is trying to destroy the Church, you will not find him in the mystical and glorified Body of Christ and in those who try to live and grow there, but in those who try to undermine and destroy them with the psychological torture that they use to discredit and destroy them. However, I have said enough here to make my point, but I will return to this subject elsewhere and in detail, to unmask the "real demons" who are hell bent on turning the Church into an Orwellian nightmare. This nightmare has already begun, with devastating attacks on contemplative orders and their "pointless" way of life, when they should be outside preaching, teaching, and evangelizing. Have they forgotten the old Latin saying *Nemo dat quod non habet* – You cannot give what you do not have? The great saints were so effective in their apostolic work because they had first received in prayer the love that they communicated to others. Take away Contemplative prayer that is the heart and soul of the spiritual life and you are left with neo-Arians, neo-Pelagians, and neo-Macedonians, bent on changing the Church with the latest "here today and gone tomorrow fads and fashions" that often pander to and try to legitimatise some of the basest of human instincts.

As the evil genius who was propagating authentic Dominican renewal, I was sacked almost overnight, and the order was split. Thanks to the help of two good friends of mine, the brilliant canon lawyer Fr Lachy Hughes SJ of the English Province, and a secular lawyer, John Ashurst, Barrister and General Manager of the then Midland Bank and others, the new Dominican congregation was formed in 1981 to follow the classical Dominican Tradition. The semi-Pelagians quickly disintegrated and are no more. I felt part-father, part-midwife, and part-bereaved mother, for the newborn aspired to live the classical Dominican tradition which I had studied, admired, but never lived, so I gave way to their Dominican foster-father, Fr Gabriel O'Donnell OP who took over. Today they are flourishing in the New Forest in the South of England. Fr Gabriel OP continues to look after them making regular visits from Washington where he is at present stationed. It has to be said that their movement was initially away from the new psycho-sociological methods for renewal that were being imposed upon them, rather than a movement to new beginnings, where the development of personal prayer would be in pride of place. However, that has now changed. Since then, other renewals formed through the selflessness and the self-sacrificial loving that is taught by and practised in mystical theology have all flourished. However, endless different forms of renewal based on myriad types of modern, so called "spiritualities" of one form or another have continued to rise and fall like a roller coaster. Some have presented themselves as almost acceptable, but when you put the microscope on them, they are predominantly anthropocentric not theocentric, and the main emphasis is on the renewal that comes through human and not divine endeavour.

In the business of sanctification both human and divine endeavour are deeply involved and intertwined. It is, however, all a matter of emphasis, and if that is wrong then everything is wrong. If the emphasis is any other than that seen in the God-given spirituality that Christ gave to the early Church and as practised by the first Christians, then you are being deceived. Remember again that St Teresa of Ávila said that there is only one way to perfection and that is to pray, and if anyone points in a different direction then they are deceiving you. If in any new spirituality that is being offered to you, prayer, and how to pray is not paramount and not just assumed but taught above all else, then you are being deceived, and so is your teacher no matter how sincere that teacher may be. Change, renewal, individual transformation, call it what you will, comes from God and only from his love.

A genuinely Catholic spirituality is merely the expression that we use to describe how we re-order our lives in such a way that we can be open to receive that love, not do for ourselves what only God can do, no matter how the techniques proposed are dressed up in traditional religious language. Is this person who is teaching me, teaching me above all else how to love God in prayer? Is this the main emphasis or is prayer simply assumed and in practice ancillary to myriad methods of self-sanctification or transformation systems to which I am being introduced? If so, we will remain little more than Catholic stoics continually failing to live up to the moral imperatives demanded of us, just like the pagan stoics before us. No real progress will be made until we realize that the God-given spirituality of the heart that Christ introduced is essentially so simple, that it is for all, and does not depend on following and mastering myriad methods and techniques that have to be learned and put into practice, primarily depending on you and your endeavour, not God's. Despite the use of words like prayer and the grace of God, if in practice a method depends, not so much on what God does, but on what we do, it is our old friend Pelagianism, or at least semi-Pelagianism that has once again taken centre stage, and all time and energy is dissipated trying to make ourselves holy. Any truly Catholic Spirituality is for all and depends on personal prayer because the person who brings about authentic renewal in individuals and through them the Church, is none other than the Holy Spirit. Although this love is continually being poured out through the sacraments and at all times through Christ, this love can only be received as we turn and open ourselves to receive it, in the love that is generated in personal prayer. This is where the repentance that St Peter told his listeners to perform in order to receive the Holy Spirit, is practised every day of our lives, else we cannot receive it.

In the early Church one of the greatest and most virulent critics of Christianity was the Alexandrian philosopher Celsus. He mocked the first Christians because, unlike him and his disciples, they were in his opinion, and in the words used by the Duke of Wellington to describe his troops, the "scum of the earth". Although this was not quite true, they were predominantly drawn from what used to be called the "lower orders". They were not so well educated, not great intellectuals, at least with the wisdom of the world, but with another form of

God-given wisdom that is given with the reception of his love in prayer as simply everyone can love. Personal Prayer in Catholic tradition is where we try to return Christ's love in kind, first by practising the "asceticism of the heart" by finding quality space and time in which to pray. Then in that time by continually trying to raise our hearts to him by using whatever traditional ways of prayer are best suited to do this, at whatever particular point we are in our spiritual journey. It is essentially so simple but I do not say easy, as acting selflessly never is, although this is essentially what is happening in any authentic act of prayer. As the love of God, his Holy Spirit, draws a person up into his Son and into his mystical body, it also draws out of them all the sinfulness and all the selfishness that prevents them from being taken up into Christ's mystical contemplation of the Father. It does this slowly and gradually, simultaneously giving the grace to both see the hell that is within them, that prevents them coming to know and experience heaven, beginning even in this life. Human man-made methods of uncovering the hell that is within us can break a person, sometimes permanently. Just keep praying using the traditional methods of Catholic prayer as your guide, and God will do the rest. The work of a true Catholic Spiritual director is not to direct you to their methods that purport to change you for the better, but to the Holy Spirit, and to support you in doing this.

When I lost my job, I also lost my position and the platform that it gave me to spread the teaching that I have developed in this book. For several years I took to the road in answer to many invitations to give lectures and retreats. It was then that I realized that for twelve years, as director of Walsingham House, I had been living in a bubble. Yes, I had seen the terrible way deep personal prayer had been all but discarded by the majority, but I had not seen its frightening consequences. Now on the road I was shattered to hear disgusting and degrading stories of the sexual abuse of both women and children by priests, religious, friars and monks, perpetrated by the very people who should have respected and protected them. Take love out of secular marriages and they implode with disastrous consequences. Take love out of spiritual marriages and the same happens, but the consequences are usually even more disastrous and certainly more scandalous as we have all seen. What I am trying to do is to insure against such disasters in the future, by introducing people to the teaching and practice of mystical theology. This explains the true meaning of love, selfless other-considering and ever-giving love and how to practise it long before marriages are finalized. It involves the dying to self that we promised at baptism and a lifetime living out the call to take up our daily cross in order to follow Christ. This love that is embodied in him can be embodied in us too, in our families and in the family of mankind who he has chosen to carry on loving through us.

I had many sleepless nights before deciding what to do about the sexual abuse in the Church that seemed to be practised on an industrial scale. When in your talks you continually emphasize prayer, your listeners, rightly or wrongly believe you to be a holy man, one therefore in whom you can confide in a way that you cannot confide to others. In my case the assumption was wrong, but nevertheless they did confide, and everywhere I went I was horrified with what I heard. Then I made the mistake of believing that it was the right thing to do to draw these abuses to the attention of those who could best deal with them. It was the mistake of proclaiming a truth too soon before those in authority were prepared to admit what they found inadmissible at the time. While at Fonte Columbo I heard of the Franciscan scripture scholar who wrote a book in the 1920s that challenged the view that King David had composed all the psalms. His books were banned, and he was censured and lost his position as head of the scripture department. Although he was proved right and all subsequent scholars agreed with him, he remained for the rest of his life the whistle-blower who blew too soon and suffered the consequences of it. Like him, I blew the whistle too soon.

There was therefore, as it seemed to me, only one way forward and that was to write, not about the abuses because nobody would believe me let alone publish me, but about the root cause – the demise of personal prayer. My friend Fr Anthony told me that if that was my future, and if my writing was to bear fruit, then I would have to find more solitude to practise what I wanted to communicate to others. So in the intervening years that has been my vocation. Meanwhile, without returning to the prayer and the spirituality of our forefathers, the Church has seemed to have gradually deteriorated at every level. However, I am now witnessing the many, mainly laity and some religious, who are beginning to see the truth. They are beginning to see and do what can alone bring personal renewal, and Church renewal, by generating and receiving the only love that can change the world as God originally planned. If you want to join them, then read on and learn from the teaching of the great saints and mystics whose wisdom I have gathered together in one place to help you seek and find the only love that can transform you. But if you seek any other way than the way of the cross, this book is not for you.

Part 4

Christian Mystical Contemplation

Chapter 31 When Two Histories Meet

Chapter 32 Spiritual Weightlifting

Chapter 33 Love Is All You Need

Chapter 34 The Beginning of Contemplation

Chapter 35 Sweetness and Light

Chapter 36 From Light to Darkness

Chapter 37 From Darkness to Light

Chapter 38 The Interior Castle

Chapter 39 The Dark Night of the Soul

Chapter 40 Union with the Three in One

Chapter 41 Confirmatory Signs of the Mystic Way

Chapter 42 True Imitation of Christ

Chapter 43 The Language of Love

Chapter 44 The White Martyrdom that Leads to Union

Chapter 45 How to Pray in Mystical Contemplation I

Chapter 46 How to Pray in Mystical Contemplation II

Chapter 47 How to Pray in Mystical Contemplation III

Chapter 48 How to Pray in Mystical Contemplation IV

Chapter 49 God's Holy Angel

Chapter 50 Death to the Demons Within

Chapter 51 The Fruits of Contemplation – The Infused Virtues

Chapter 52 Renewal and Family Love

Chapter 53 To Contemplate and Share the Fruits of

Contemplation

Chapter 54 Traditionalism and Tradition

Chapter 55 Contemplation Made Simple

Chapter 56 Obedient Men

Chapter 57 Humanism Rides Again

Chapter 58 Not by Suffering but by Love

Chapter 59 Marcus Aurelius Rides Again

Chapter 60 The Last Minute of Extra Time

Chapter 61 The Father of Counterfeit Mysticism

Chapter 62 Followers of the Counterfeit Mystic

Chapter 63 Contemplation Is for Children Too

Chapter 64 Practising the Prayer of the Heart

Chapter 65 The Ascetism of the Heart

Chapter 66 From Stumbling Blocks to Stepping Stones

Chapter 67 In the Trying Is the Dying

Chapter 68 Into the Redeeming Christ

Chapter 31

When Two Histories Meet

In this book I am not just trying to view God's Plan, but our personal and unique part in it. God can only enable us to participate in his plan to the degree to which we are prepared to respond to his call as the Apostles did, and those who radically chose to follow him later. If we are prepared to give our all, so is God. Just as I had no idea what God's plan was for me at the beginning of my journey, nor have you. All you must do is to love him in such a way that your love becomes so purified as you journey on in the mystic way, that it is able to rise to him and his love descend into you. Then the rest will be history, your history, that you could never have envisaged at the beginning of your journey. If you are prepared to go onward in an adventure of a lifetime and are not only prepared to read on but give your total attention to what is the wisdom of the great saints and mystics who have gone before you, then the future is yours. You will come to know and experience what it means and even what it feels like, when divine loving and human loving meet and mingle together as one. Only then will you be able to attain the destiny of which you have never even dreamt. As this journey deepens to admit the love of God ever more fully, you will continually rise to become your true self, the real self that only God's love can make of you. Then, what you never thought possible will become possible, because with God all things are possible, even the impossible. Begin your journey now by learning from the Apostles.

The first apostles were converted almost immediately when they met Jesus, but that was but the beginning of a lifetime of repentance that would redeem them permanently from the world of sin and from the self-centredness that had made sinners out of them. Re-read the Gospels and the Acts of the Apostles and you will see that even the privilege of encountering the love of God in Jesus did not instantly sanctify them or absolve them from a commitment to a permanent and ongoing life of repentance. It is this ongoing and daily repentance that would gradually make them into saints. If we do not learn this then we can condemn ourselves to a life of superficiality, of nominal Catholics nodding our head to every article of the creed but never entering deeply into the One who has inspired it. I believe in everything from instant coffee to instant resurrection, instant emotions, instant miracles, instant ecstasies if you like, but instant sanctity – never. It is a long journey as it was for the first apostles despite their privileged calling. They were called by Christ and called personally just as many of us have been called, but the call and the instant conversion that we may experience does not make instant saints of us.

All committed Catholics are brought up to say their morning and evening prayers, to make their Morning Offering, to use the prayers handed down like the Lord's own prayer, and many other prayers and devotional practices, and above all to take part in the Mass with all our hearts and minds. However, the time always comes when Christ reaches out to us personally and calls us to a deep personal relationship with him that can change our lives. It may be through a book that is read, a Christ-like person who is met, a sermon that is heard, or even through a direct spiritual touch that is felt. Then, a new and personal relationship with Christ can begin. But beware, these special moments when God "touches" us are a call to deepen our own spiritual lives, so that one day he can use us. They are not a reward because we have been living a holy life but a call to holiness. They are not a prize for living a virtuous life but a call to live a virtuous life.

Pride can wrongly convince believers that his or her call to deepen their own personal spiritual lives is a call to start leading, guiding, and lecturing others, when they are in fact only beginners themselves. It is sad to see such people who have had an authentic conversion experience but misunderstand it. They tell the world of their privileged calling, as if they were called because of their perfect life, rather than that they have been called to live a perfect life. There are all too many self-serving self-appointed prophets today and not enough God serving sinners who seek forgiveness through repentance, in solitude and in the purification in prayer where true prophets are made. They can misguide others with the Pelagianism that is always the favoured heresy of those who think and act as if they can do for themselves, and for others what only the Holy Spirit can do. In his famous history of the early Church, Monsignor Philip Hughes shows how the first apostles continued to live in Jerusalem to deepen their spiritual lives as a preparation for the apostolic life that was to come. He further tells us that the new apostle St Paul, spent ten years, that he used as his "noviciate", learning to practise for himself the repentance that he was going to preach to others. The time was spent in Arabia, Cilicia and his hometown of Tarsus before he set out as the apostle to the Gentiles, and even then, it was only on the insistence of Barnabas that his ten-year "noviciate" came to an end abruptly.

There are two main types of conversion. The first is the conversion of an outsider who for one reason or another, although reason may have little to do with it, feels impelled to join the Church. It is the love of Christ that calls them. These are the conversions that were naturally commonest in the early Church. Such people were therefore shown by both word and example, how to come to know and love the Christ who called them by being introduced to a new aid to prayer that came to be called meditation. As the years passed by a second type of conversion became common, the conversion of insiders, who although they were born into the Church of Catholic parents, had no deep personal relationship with Christ, but rather a general allegiance to and love for the teachings and practices of the Church. Some, however, may even have lapsed from this when a call to conversion came. They too feel called to a deeper personal relationship with Christ and if they are fortunate enough to find the spiritual help they need, they too are taught the same aid to prayer, meditation.

In order to practise this new aid to prayer which leads to mystical contemplation, the need is felt for some sort of solitude in their own homes, inside their local church or elsewhere. St Francis of Assisi spent years living as a hermit practising the repentance that he then began to preach to others whilst endlessly retiring into solitude to allow the Holy Spirit to guide him. St Catherine of Siena too, retired into a room in her own home for years until Christ summoned her. St Bernadine of Siena spent seventeen years in his hermitage before his preaching was to have a decisive effect on the world of fifteenth-century Italy and beyond. The hermitage of Fonte Colombo was but one of many built by him for his disciples. When God called St Antony into the Desert it was to spend twenty years allowing God to change him, before he was fit to lead and guide others. Even then he did not set himself up to teach others, it was others who sought him out to teach them. The wisdom contained in the New Testament could not have been imparted, except to those like St Paul who were purified by the Holy Spirit to receive it. The same could be said for the wisdom contained in the writings of the great Fathers of the Church, and for the exemplary lives and deaths of hundreds of thousands of the ordinary faithful who have taken up their daily cross to follow Christ, as seen in the way they lived and died, as read in the Acts of the Apostles and the Acts of the Martyrs.

In what follows in the final part of my book I will explain in more detail what is happening when you are being led into the crèche where saints are made, and how to continue in prayer when, as St Teresa of Ávila says, "the well runs dry". If you put your faith in the Holy Spirit and continue, come hell or high water, then you will eventually arrive at planet Paradise. But, as this planet comes ever nearer, the gravitational pull that draws you to itself, simultaneously draws out of you all the evil that can prevent you "walking and talking with God in the cool of the evening" like Adam before you. The analogy of the spaceship that was raised off the ground through the earth's atmosphere and out of its powerful gravitational force by powerful surges of energy from its supercharged engines, represents the first part of the journey. Sometimes called first fervour or first enthusiasm, it is hardly five per cent of the journey to planet Paradise. Once the beginning of the journey is over, then the real and longest part of the journey begins. Once the fuel tanks that supplied the engines for the initial thrust have been cast away, the journey suddenly become smoother, quieter, less exciting, even monotonous. When this goes on for weeks, months or years that are still given to prayer as before, travellers are tempted to pack up prayer because they do not seem to be going anywhere. Further to this, distractions and temptations seem more powerful and more frustrating. The temptations to give up the journey become all but irresistible, most particularly because no one to whom they turn seems to know what is happening. It is for this reason that St John of the Cross said that ninety per cent of those who have come this far give up, and myriad saints, prophets and mystics are lost to the Church. What follows is a travel guide drawn from the experiences of many thousands of Catholic mystics and saints who have preceded you. It is not my guide, but I have spent a lifetime putting it together to help you come to the place and to the person whose love, like the gravitational pull of an infinite planet, is relentlessly drawing you to your final destiny.

Most readers will have understood what I have written so far but may have difficulty understanding what I am now writing about – the practice of mystical contemplation. The reason for this is the deplorable lack of teaching on this subject in the last few centuries, for the reasons I have explained and will explain further. However, I beg those who have tried to put into practice what I have already written to press on regardless. The truth of the matter is that after initial success, what seems to be a dead end in your prayer life will tempt you to give up serious mental prayer permanently, like so many others before you. What follows will explain why this happens and will give the traditional Catholic teaching, so long neglected, that will lead to the heights of mystical contemplation, in, with and through Christ, and to a deep experience of happiness you did not believe possible on this earth. But what is even more important is that it will prepare you to become one of the prophets, the saints and the mystics that the Church so desperately needs to bring about the radical reform that is long overdue.

It would be a terrible mistake to wait for such reform to come from the top down when history shows that it usually comes from the bottom up. It will only come about, as in the past, through ordinary lay people who give their lives over to doing extraordinary things for God. This will infallibly happen in your life, if you decide to develop an ever-deepening prayer life that will enable his love, the Holy Spirit, to renew the world through you, by renewing the Church first. This is the challenge for the reader for what follows.

Is this journey to and through contemplation absolutely necessary for our salvation in this life? To answer this question let me quote from an article by Father Alexander Rozwadowski SJ, in *La Vie Spirituelle* (January 1936), shortly after St John of the Cross was made a Doctor of the Church:

We do not affirm that mystical contemplation in this life is necessary for salvation, but the question is, is it necessary for sanctity. By sanctity we mean a great love of God and neighbour. The sanctity in question here is the normal prelude to life in heaven; a prelude which is either realized here on earth or in purgatory which pre-supposes that the soul is fully purified and so capable of receiving the beatific vision immediately. Finally, we say that according to St John of the Cross, infused contemplation is indeed necessary for sanctity and we even add that the perfection of the Christian life will not be possible without it, because it implies the eminent exercise of the theological virtues and the gifts of the Holy Spirit which accompany them.

Now it is time to learn how, after meditation, we are to journey on in the mystical contemplation that will enable us to receive the love of Christ more deeply than ever before, together with the infused virtues and the gifts of the Holy Spirit. May they blossom in us as they blossomed in Christ to the glory of God and for the glorification of his Church on earth "that seeing they may come to believe".

Chapter 32

Spiritual Weightlifting

The difference between conversion and repentance is so important that it needs further explanation. I hope to do this by putting the microscope on one of the greatest of all saints from the moment of his conversion to the moment when he was perfectly identified with Christ, at least as far as this is possible in this world. The saint to whom I am referring is St Paul. His conversion on the Damascus road when he heard Christ asking why he had been persecuting him, was instant. It was an instant conversion, but it was only the beginning. Before he was baptised a few days later, he was convinced that Jesus Christ was indeed the Messiah and had risen from the dead, and the very people he was persecuting had been taken up into his risen life. Here they lived and moved in a new world that was constituted within Christ's Risen Body that would come to be called his Mystical Body, the Kingdom of God or the Kingdom of Love on earth. Paul came to realize that the same love that was released on the first Pentecost had drawn him up too and into Christ's mystical body. As a well-educated Jew the significance of what was happening would not have been lost on him.

For a devout Jew, the feast of Pentecost was the celebration of God's law that had been given to his people through Moses many hundreds of years ago. It was on this feast day that God had aptly chosen to give his new people the new law – the law of love. This new law was not inscribed on stone tablets as before, but embodied in a person, the person of Jesus Christ, now Risen and Glorified. When St Paul turned and opened himself to receive this love at his Baptism, this love drew him up, not just into Christ's mystical body, but into Christ's mystical loving of his Father. Although love is the greatest power for good in heaven and on earth, it differs from all other sorts of power because it cannot be forced on anyone. It has to be freely received, not once but over and over again. However, the human heart is so fickle that, what is chosen one minute can be taken back the next, what is accepted one day can be rejected the next and what has been possessed for years can be lost after many years too. This is sadly the salary of original sin. Thankfully, the fountain of love to which new Christians are exposed at Baptism, continues to pour out and into them for the rest of their lives and at every moment of their lives.

Realizing this, St Paul like so many who followed him, sought out solitude to learn how to practise turning and opening himself to the fountain of Christ's love, to receive it into him, and to be drawn by it into the community of all other Christians. Then, he would be drawn with them into the love that Christ offered to his father, and the love that he received from the father, to bring about the communion of all humankind in the love of the Three in One. I need to emphasize something that can be overlooked so easily. Paul went into solitude for at least three years. With his background, as a devote Jew, it should not surprise us that he went, not just into the desert, but into the Arabian desert. Then he spent seven more years in what Monsignor Philip Hughes calls his "noviciate", learning to practise what he was going to preach to others.

We receive love in the secular world as well as in the spiritual life, by loving the one who loves us in return. In the spiritual world the One who loves us is God, whose love reaches out to possess us through Christ. When on the first Pentecost, everyone who heard about the new outpouring of God's love asked what had to be done to receive it, the answer was simple, they had to repent. There is no word in Hebrew or Aramaic for someone who has repented but only for someone who is repenting. It is the word used to describe our ongoing and never-ending turning and opening to God to receive his loving of us. His love never stops, but when our love stops, when we stop turning and opening ourselves to receive his love, then his love stops, not loving us, but entering into us to draw us up and into himself. This loving has to be learned and all the great saints spent years learning to love God in what St Angela of Foligno called the school of Divine love which is prayer. That is what St Paul was doing in his "noviciate" as the other apostles were doing the same in their "noviciate" in Jerusalem.

The other Apostles had more than a head start for they came to know and love Christ personally. St Paul would have been introduced to the new form of meditation and the love generated there would lead him into contemplative prayer where like every serious searcher in mystical prayer, his love would be refined and purified for the union for which he yearned. After his conversion in AD 34 and after initial first fervour, he would have spent the majority of his time in solitude in what later came to be called the Dark Night of the Soul where in prayer he would have to learn to carry his daily cross as he underwent a profound spiritual purification, as would the other Apostles. This intensive period of purification when he also received the spiritual help and strength to share the wisdom in contemplation with others lasted until about AD 45. His first apostolic journey for which he had now been prepared began in AD 47.

What must have happened in those crucial formative years for St Paul, is confirmed by St Paul himself ten years later when he writes in his second letter to the Corinthians (2 Corinthians 12:2) of visions, revelations, and ecstasies that he received fourteen years before. He was referring to his purification in which God had been preparing him in his "noviciate" for the apostolic life upon which he had more recently embarked. The graces he referred to could not have been received, nor could he have received the wisdom that he imparted to others, without a long sojourn in the profound mystical purification that some people have wrongly thought was an invention of later medieval mystics.

Because they do not speak in the language later developed by future mystics, they think that mystical theology was unknown to the first Christians, when in fact it reached its high point in the mystical body of Christ in whose contemplation they shared. This is the very essence of true mystical contemplation. Tragically it subsequently receded, never to rise to such heights again.

The wisdom contained in the New Testament could not have been imparted, except to those who had been purified to receive it by the Holy Spirit, like St Paul. The same could be said for the wisdom contained in the writings of the great Fathers of the Church, and for the exemplary lives and deaths of hundreds of thousands of the ordinary faithful who took up their daily cross to follow Christ. It was from Christ that they received in return a quality of supra human loving that first amazed and then awestruck their pagan contemporaries, especially in the way they lived and died. Read and reread the Acts of the Apostles and the Acts of the Martyrs to see what I mean. They converted hundreds of thousands from a pagan Roman world to the world over which Christ ruled.

The importance of preparation to receive and to continually receive God's love both before and after baptism, soon inspired the first apostles to insist that in future a period of at least two years "noviciate" for spiritual preparation should precede baptism. In this period of preparation for baptism and in its immediate aftermath, personal daily prayer would have pride of place. Converts and those responsible for receiving them into the Church, must realize that conversion involves, not just a change of minds or *metanoia*, as the Greek word suggests, but a change of minds and hearts and of one's whole being by a continual and ongoing repentance. It was only here that the first converts could learn to practise the first commandment which was "to love God with your whole heart and mind and with your whole body and soul, and with your whole strength". In doing this they would be given the help and strength, not just to love God in return, but to love others as Christ loves them. That is why this book is called *The Primacy of Loving*. And that is why it is subtitled *The Spirituality of the Heart*. The word asceticism is derived from the Greek word for an athlete. Athletes spend their whole time developing the muscles of their bodies to attain their deepest desire. Spiritual Athletes spend their whole time developing the muscles of their hearts to attain their deepest desire too.

In every athlete worth their salt there is a certain impatience that induces them to speed up the journey to achieve their objective by developing the requisite muscles of their bodies. For those spiritual athletes, who are also possessed by a certain holy impatience, the Holy Spirit leads them to the spiritual gymnasium which is to contemplative prayer where the spiritual muscles of their hearts are developed, enabling them to receive the only love that can lead them to the profound Transforming Union which they desire above all else.

As my dyslexia guaranteed that I would never be remembered at school as a scholar, I decided to be remembered as an athlete instead. The coach at the local gymnasium introduced me to an infallible method of training that would guarantee my objective. It was so simple because it only depended on performing one single action, continually raising weights above my head time and time again. This single action developed all the muscles in my body simultaneously. It was only later that I came to realize that what happens to the muscles of our bodies can happen to the muscles of our hearts too. This can happen with ever greater intensity when spiritual weightlifting is practised in prayer, in the mystic way. As distractions, and temptations become stronger, they act like spiritual weights that prevent us, or at least make it more and more difficult, to keep raising our hearts to God in what St John of the Cross calls the Dark Night of the Senses. Far from hindering a person's progress toward spiritual perfection, what appears to a novice as spiritual encumbrances, are actually as necessary to spiritual advancement, as lifting weights is to physical advancement.

St John of the Cross goes on to describe the Dark Night of the Spirit, when an even deeper purification adds to the spiritual weights that conspire to prevent mystics trying to raise and open their heart to God. Before this particular testing purification begins, God usually fortifies spiritual searchers with profound experiences of his love, as described by St Teresa of Ávila in her masterwork *Interior Castle*. Love has a magnetic quality that draws us toward the one who is loving us. When that person is God, his love is so powerful that it not only fills the receiver with his magnetic love, but simultaneously draws out of the one who is loved, what are called in common parlance, the demons that lurk deep down within every flawed human being. Seeing what we have never seen before rising from within the nether regions of our personalities and having to face and come to terms with the truth of what we have tried to hide from before, is far more testing than the more superficial distractions and temptations that previously weighed us down. Gradually we begin to see the sinfulness that drags us down, rising from below the surface to prevent us from continually trying to raise our hearts to God. Although the journey becomes ever more difficult, it becomes ever more rewarding if we persevere. This spiritual weightlifting not only develops the muscles of the heart but enables them to open what was once a heart of stone to the heart of God. This is how our loving enables God's loving that endlessly pours out of his heart, to enter into our hearts and through them to be disseminated to every part of our personality.

In his famous letter written less than eighty years after Christ died, the Bishop and Martyr St Ignatius was the first to use the expression, the "Catholic Church". This expression does not just mean that our faith can be found universally in every country on earth, but that it is universal because it is for all. It is for all because all human beings have a heart and are capable of loving.

Further, St Augustine insists that our loving ultimately desires union with the source of all love, which is God, and our hearts will be restless until they come to rest in him. This is fundamental to the whole Christian Spiritual tradition. If our hearts are full of selfishness and sin we can never receive the pure selfless loving of God, in this world or in the next. A purification or a purgatory has to take place, or the union for which every human being ultimately desires simply cannot take place. The good news is that the journey onward, into, and through the mystic way, is for all. It can be undertaken by all, because there are no intellectual qualifications that could restrict this journey to a few highly intelligent members of the intelligentsia. Love and the capacity to love is open to all human beings. Aristotle may well have defined human beings as rational animals, but he then describes a human being as having a capacity for love. It is this capacity for love that will determine our degree of happiness in this world and in the next. The place where this capacity for love is filled to overflowing is in the mystic way where everything that reduces that capacity is removed from the human heart, as rubble is removed from a bucket before it can be filled with spring water.

Although the ability to attain high intellectual achievement, or any form of secular achievement is not an obstacle to developing what Christ calls the "one thing necessary", it can seriously divert the best of us. Enough has now been said to encourage the reader to press on beyond first enthusiasm into the way of purification. If the spiritual journey could be depicted in a graph, first enthusiasm would be but five per cent of the journey, while ninety-five per cent is taken up with the simple, I did not say easy, task of being purified in the Dark Night. This is the place where the great saints, the mystics and the prophets were formed in the past as they will be once again in the present. The Catholic metaphysical poet Francis Thompson said that we are all called to become geniuses, because spiritual geniuses are saints who are formed by the Holy Spirit in the mystic way. Here, their work, which is nothing other than the re-creation of themselves into the image and likeness of Christ, involves five per cent inspiration and ninety-five per cent perspiration.

Chapter 33

Love Is All You Need

I once attended a conference titled "The Moral Malaise" during which the speakers examined the virtues necessary to regain the new paradise from paradise lost. It was then that a naive novice spoke for the first time, asking, "But how do we get the wherewithal to generate all these wonderful virtues?" Mayhem ensued as everyone tried to explain what no one seemed to know. Eventually, an elderly priest who entertained us the previous evening with his mellifluous tenor voice began to sing the words to the song "All you need is love". He received a standing ovation and everyone left with a beautiful idea, a platitude gift-wrapped by the tenor's sonorous voice. But, like most platitudes, it was not sufficiently unwrapped to be seen for what it is, the principle that could change our lives, the principle of the "primacy of love". But love has to be learned.

Love may begin like lightning, or with a spark that gradually flickers into a flame. But if it is to burn ever brighter and bond people together it must be learned over very many years, if not decades or rather over a lifetime. If you wish to become a pianist, an athlete, a lawyer, or a teacher, you must learn over many years of study and practice, the profession, the science or the art that you wish to perfect. But learning to love is more important than anything else because it guarantees the happiness that nothing else can. That is why the whole of the spiritual life and the mystic way is dedicated to teaching how love can be learned, sustained and perfected. Everything else should be directed to this end and everything that is worth having flows out of it.

St John said that "God is love", and if we are created in his image and likeness then what is deepest within us is the love of God. It is from this Presence that the love arises that St Augustine said is always restless until it rests in God. It rises from our own human desire for the fullness of love, and when suffused with the divine love that is deepest in us, the journey upon which love is about to embark is made possible. Wherever this journey begins, a person is led, like St Augustine, to God's love embodied in the person of Jesus Christ.

Remember William of Saint-Thierry's words, "You will never love someone unless you know them, but you will never know them unless you love them." In the prayer journey, we first come to love God in Jesus Christ. In order to do this we must begin by using our mind, our intellect, our powers of reasoning as well as our imaginations and our memory, to come to know and love the Christ of history. However, when that love is fully ignited, like all love it wishes to be united with the One who is loved. It is at this point that the direction of our love changes to focus not so much on the Christ of history, but on the Christ who in his mystical body now encompasses the whole of God's created glory on earth, while simultaneously embracing his uncreated glory in heaven.

We can love someone who died many years ago, but we cannot be united with them. Whereas we can be united with the Jesus whom we have come to know and love through meditating on all he said and did; because meditating on him as he once was, leads us on to the contemplation that unites us with him, risen and alive and loving us now. For obvious reasons, the mind and all its faculties with the imagination and the memory that enabled us to learn to love Christ in his physical body, can be of no help when God calls us to enter into Christ in his mystical contemplation. Love, love and only love, can do this; only love can lead us to the union that we have yearned for from the very beginning. That is what is meant by the primacy of love, and the meaning of the revelation that St Francis received moments before he received the stigmata. Meditation is the way Christians have come to know and love Christ from earliest times, just as from earliest times contemplation has been the way Christians have come to enter into him, to experience the union that will alone satisfy their primeval craving for love without measure.

When contemplation begins, it is because God has led us into contemplation where love and only love can lead us on to the union that we desire. It should go without saying that our love has to be purified, refined and brought to perfection for this purpose. Self-centred, self-seeking and sinful human beings will have all and everything that prevents their love from entering into the divine stripped away. This is what happens in the dark contemplation that everyone experiences to begin with. The fact that this is unpleasant, to say the least, is the reason why in the words of St John of the Cross, the vast majority who have come so far give up seriously giving regular quality space and time for prayer as before. Forms of meditation that helped them come to love the Christ of history before, must be cast away. They can no longer be of any use. It is not in months or even years, but more usually in decades for most of us that our hearts are purified sufficiently to be united with Christ in his contemplation of God. This union with Christ is ultimately brought about not only in our hearts or our wills but in our whole person, our minds and hearts, our bodies and our souls, united with his heart and mind and body and soul.

In their comic opera *Iolanthe*, Gilbert and Sullivan's hero, Strephon, half mortal and half fairy, is always complaining that he is unable to escape back to fairyland because of his earthly body. If he tries to pass through a keyhole or a crack in the door, or even through the eye of a needle, his spiritual self has no problem but his human body holds him back. In a sense, it is the same with us. However, when our love remains open to God and for long enough, then his Holy Spirit uses our love as a "spiritual lightning conductor", not just to purify our hearts, but our bodies too, that are gradually "spiritualised" so we can return to our true home. This home is in the Risen and glorified body of Christ. What happened to him and to his body after the Resurrection will eventually happen to our bodies too.

That is why genuine Christian mystics call the high point of the mystic way the Mystical or the Spiritual Marriage. One day our bodies will be "spiritualised" as Peter, James, and John saw Christ's body "spiritualised" at the Transfiguration on Mount Tabor. This does not mean that he no longer had a true body. The Apostles were to see after his Resurrection that although he was "spiritualised" by the same Holy Spirit who penetrated every part of him on Mount Tabor, he could not only eat and drink to show that he was still a complete human being, but pass through bolted doors, be in two places at the same time, levitate, and be present at any time, at any place, and at any point in history simultaneously. Eventually, we will be "spiritualised" too. Our heart's desire, our will becomes the medium, the go-between or the lightning conductor that directs the love of God, his Holy Spirit down and into us to prepare us, body and soul, for union with him, in, with and through the glorified body of his Son. Notice once again how everything depends on love; our love suffused with the divine, to bring about God's Plan which St Paul called his *Mysterion*. Everything depends then on the primacy of love, above and beyond everything else.

The purification through both light and darkness must take place before union with God, either in this world or in the next. But if you choose to become a radical Christian and not just another nominal Christian by taking up your daily cross, you will find it easier, happier and far more joyful to pass through your purgatory on earth. It is the way to help others and the Church that is in such need of the saints, the mystics and the prophets who are formed in the Dark Night. The fruits of Contemplation that await you are far more spiritually nourishing and delightful than any other fruits known to man. Because the contemplative way is the way of love, it is uniquely Catholic. By that, I mean open to all, not just to academics or intellectuals or those gifted with great human talents and abilities. Everyone can love precisely because God has put his love within us, and that is the only qualification needed to enter into what St Angela of Foligno called the "School of Divine love". If meditation is the primary school then contemplation is the secondary school that teaches only one subject and that is how to love and how to love perfectly. This, Jesus told Martha, is the one thing necessary.

Chapter 34

The Beginning of Contemplation

From the very beginning, the faithful have been taught that the Church is the bride and Christ is the bridegroom. The Fathers of the Church used the "Song of Solomon" to show how this relationship extends to every single member of the Church as they detailed their journey along the mystic way toward the ultimate mystical marriage in heaven. However, St Bernard was even more specific: it is in and through contemplation itself, that this marriage first finds its completion as we are bonded to Christ. Then, in, with and through him we are led into the ultimate marriage with the Three in One, to all eternity. It is of paramount importance, therefore, to realize precisely what constitutes this contemplation. I began by using the metaphor of the spaceship destined for Mars to show how it is necessary to use canisters of fuel or boosters to lift the spaceship off the ground and through the earth's atmosphere. This is the role of meditation when we are first filled with the love of Christ on earth that concentrates our heart's desire and raises it up to be united with Christ as he is now in heaven.

Once this primeval desire for God has been directed towards Christ who will take us into Infinite Love, then contemplation has begun in earnest. However, to begin with and for a long time, we feel nothing. Only the desire for Love keeps drawing us to prayer where nothing apart from distractions and temptations seem to engage us – including the biggest temptation of all, which is to pack up the obscure prayer and do something "meaningful". Let me insist that there is nothing a person can do who is searching for Love, other than to persevere in the selfless giving that can alone finally open them to this Love. This is the whole point and purpose of what some have called confused or dark contemplation. It is to teach us the selfless giving through daily practice that will eventually make us a sufficiently selfless person who can be united with the perfect selfless One. There is no other way to union with Christ. The demise of mystical theology has meant that this indispensable truth has been forgotten, and therefore never taught to celibates who stop serious daily prayer the moment the feeling and fervour of first enthusiasm leaves them, with disastrous results. First enthusiasm might have left them, but, if they only knew it, it has propelled them forward into the mystic way where they are asked to carry their daily cross and die to self as they embrace the white martyrdom that involves acting selflessly day after day. This is the school of love where gradually our love mixes and merges with the divine love, that enables us to be united with God, even beginning in this life.

I do not like to emphasize high mystical states, as it can instil in a person a desire for pleasurable states of mystical experience. Our sole concern should be to give ourselves to God and God alone, whether we receive something or nothing in return. If we do come to experience mystical touches from God, not just briefly but more regularly, then they are only given to those who seek him for himself alone and not for what we receive from him. This is the whole point of the beginning of contemplation. Until the attitude of mind of the cupboard lover has been changed, our desire to experience the love of God will remain unfulfilled, and the desire to give up the prayer that seems to be going nowhere will become almost irresistible. However, when we have committed ourselves to God come hell or high water, continually giving the same time for prayer when all is dark and dismal as we did when all was sweetness and light, then in God's good time, not ours, the light of his love will indeed touch us. It will lead us on to experience that love to ever greater degrees of intensity that will be commensurate with our selfless loving. These moments of delight when God makes his presence felt do not last forever, nor are they a reward for perseverance, but rather they are strength for further perseverance as the mystic way continues, sometimes in light but most times in darkness as the purification for union continues.

One very important point is that God is not only present in moments of light, bestowing the fruits of contemplation on the traveller. He is present in the more prolonged periods of darkness too, as long as we are persevering in the selfless giving that enables him to enter into us. The first time that any intimation is given that God is present in what seems to be a pointless occupation, happens when we feel that although we seem to be receiving nothing from contemplation, we also feel we can no longer do without it. We still feel drawn to it despite the darkness and the endless turning away from distractions and temptations in which selfless loving is learned. As we have seen from St Augustine, St Gregory and St Bernard, the further they travelled in contemplation, mostly in darkness, the more they were able to see the truth of God's plan. They saw what God wished of them while simultaneously receiving the power to do it. The vast majority of people who take their journey in the mystic way seriously can spend their whole lives in the Dark Night where for most of the time they experience darkness. But it is in this darkness as they continually give themselves to selflessly loving God that they are given his truth, his wisdom, and the strength to do the truth simultaneously. Moments of mystical presence are comparatively rare to begin with that encourage the traveller along the way. The selflessness learned in darkness prepares us for the Presence that is experienced in light.

I am purposely not stressing these moments of presence for fear of encouraging "bounty hunters". But still, something must be said, not only for the sake of the truth but also for the sake of encouragement. When God first makes his presence felt, travellers are astonished and overwhelmed by the power of God which strengthens and fortifies their belief that God exists. They can never again doubt that this power is love and loving them deeply and personally, spurring them on when the darkness returns to enable their love to be purified further for ultimate union.

The priest or religious who takes a vow of Chastity, binding them to Christ as to their spiritual married partner, will be lost without daily access to the contemplation that is for them the indispensable means of uniting them with him. In the aftermath of Quietism, so many of the clergy have been afflicted in one way or another and to a greater or a lesser degree by lovelessness, as what St Bernard calls their "marital act of contemplation" has been taken from them. It is the laity who must now take the lead. In the sacrament of love the laity have for years been learning the selflessness that opens them to receive the love of God that they minister to each other and to their children. Here is the hope for the future for the Holy Spirit who cannot work through those who have no or little access to him but can work through the laity who have learned selfless loving in their marriages.

I do not want to give the impression that prayer is unimportant in marriage, for without it married couples will not receive the grace to persevere in the selfless loving, giving, and forgiving upon which all successful marriages depend. It is this selfless loving that enables the Holy Spirit to do through the laity what the clergy can fail to do if they neglect to practise selflessness in prayer. This is what will enable them to experience the love of the one to whom they made their vow of chastity. The great Jesuit mystic Père Lallemant said that a person can do more in a month with contemplation, than in ten years without it. Now is the time to listen to him and to act on what he said. If priests only take him seriously and begin again, then the renewal that is long overdue will be underway.

I am trying to draw together the ancient mystical tradition of the Catholic Church to show once more the way to loving contemplation, long since forgotten in the aftermath of Quietism that has robbed us of our most cherished birthright. When the faithful, and in particular the clergy begin to do what can alone bring renewal to themselves and through them to others, then I hope that the essential teaching of Catholic Mystical Theology that I have been able to assemble here, will help them go forward without delay.

Chapter 35

Sweetness and Light

It is all but impossible to determine with any accuracy when mystical contemplation begins, as everyone is different and so are individual circumstances. The best I can do therefore, is to detail my own unique experience of how this happened to me in the hope that together with the signs given in the Catholic mystical tradition, and in the regrettable absence of a good and trustworthy spiritual director who understands the mystic way, you will be able to discover the way forward for yourself.

My own journey into the mystic way was comparatively swift because I thankfully found the ideal conditions. Firstly, my desperate need for God was heightened by my very serious dyslexia which was not understood in those days. When at a retreat I was told that God knew everything, I realized that he might not only be able to understand me but also help me. The school that I went to also served as a junior seminary, so each week the spiritual director taught us how to meditate. My need was far greater than the others so I gave more daily time for meditation than they did. It was there that I decided to try my vocation as a Franciscan to continue the prayer that became so easy for me. Never before had I experienced such misery as during that year as a novice. My dyslexia meant that my Latin was virtually non-existent making the Latin of the Divine Office, the Franciscan constitutions and books on liturgy and spirituality virtually unreadable. However, I found my personal heaven in the two hours we had to ourselves after Compline each evening. I spent the time lost in the meditation that was my greatest joy. I learned a way of meditation from St Ignatius' Exercises that involved visualizing individual scenes from the Gospels that I found helpful. This not only involved picturing the Gospel scenes but listening to the words that Christ said or that were said to him. I loved it. I had a good imagination so I could easily leave the space and time world where I was so unhappy to go back into the past to the Holy Land to visit the place where Christ was born and lived, suffered and died. It was not just my mind that was involved in this form of visualization, but my memory, my imagination and my emotions too that ignited my heart and began to react, drawing my whole self into the experience. After Easter, everything came to a head when I was moved more deeply than at any other time as I was visualizing the sending of the Holy Spirit on the first Pentecost day.

The more I read and reflected on the Acts of the Apostles and in particular on the conversion of St Paul, a new dimension in my spiritual understanding awoke within me. I understood something that I never understood before. The Jesus whom I had come to know and love more than ever before, was still alive and loving me now. His love, the Holy Spirit was drawing me up into his mystical body where all other Christians who love him "live and move and have their being". It is here that I would one day be reunited with all whom I love: my parents, my brothers, my close friends and relatives. All the sin and selfishness that prevented us from being as close as we would have wished on earth would be purified by the Holy Spirit. Then we would all be ready to continue our journey together into infinite love whilst being drawn ever more closely to each other in Christ, in whom and with whom we first glimpsed and then gazed upon the glory of God. My whole prayer experience was so thrilling and moving, that I could not wait for Compline to end so that my personal prayer could begin. I was so moved by success at prayer and how that prayer enabled me to be moved in every part of my being that I began to believe that I was about to enter the Mystical Marriage. I even believed that I might, sooner rather than later, begin to develop mystical powers like levitation and bilocation!

Then one evening when I came to pray as usual, I found myself in a black hole. I had not heard of St John of the Cross or the Dark Night. I thought it was a temporary blip and "normal service" would resume as soon as possible, but it did not, nor has it ever returned in quite the same way. I asked my confessor at the time and other priests and theologians later, but the only answer I received was, "Oh, we all go through first fervour at the beginning." When I asked what happens next, they all seemed to say the same: "You just get on with your life." But for me, prayer was my life and for a dyslexic like me, it was my only hope on which I had pinned everything. Perhaps that is why I nevertheless continued to give the same time for prayer each evening despite the fact that "sweetness and light" had deserted me for "darkness and depression". I could not have been easy to live with at the time, but I came to realize that the other novices preferred "brother misery" to "brother sweetness and light", about whom I heard one novice say to another, "He is just too good to be true!"

Because I had the perfect conditions in which to pray and because therefore my prayer was so vibrant, the end of first fervour and the beginning of the Dark Night seemed to take place suddenly, almost at a particular moment in time. However, because the majority do not have these perfect conditions, the change from meditation to contemplation is not so immediately apparent. A person just notices that over a period of time the meditation that was once so helpful simply dries up. Mystical writers often use such phrases as, "Then God leads a person into contemplation." or "At this point in their spiritual journey God takes the initiative by leading them into the Dark Night." What does in fact happen is that the love that developed in meditation or first fervour reaches a certain intensity and sensitivity that enables it to suddenly become aware of and reach out to God. Although he has been close to us at all times, we have failed to recognize him because our love was not sufficiently sensitized to become aware of his presence. St John of the Cross calls this strange new world that we have been drawn into the Dark Night of the Soul, but he also calls it Contemplation.

The longing for God's presence that originally drew me to meditation was so intensified there, that it now drew me out of meditation and onwards into mystical contemplation. For it was here alone that my desire to love God would be so purified that it would be able to reach out to and enter into union with him; not as I had been picturing him in my imagination, but as he is in himself. Nevertheless, it seemed to lead me into a dull and dreary world compared to the world of sweetness and light that so delighted me before.

This desire is not only there in prayer, no matter how dark it might seem, but it is there outside of prayer too. I remember this happening to my brother, Peter, and he spent hours just mooning around doing nothing in particular and not particularly wanting to do anything. My mother said, "Oh, he is in love with love," and she was right. When he later applied to join the Cistercians, it became evident that he wanted to follow his heart's desire to a place where his contemplation could reach out to and touch the One he desired more than any other. At first, contemplation is called dark or confused contemplation because our heart's desire needs to be purified and refined in many months, if not years, before the Love of God becomes tangible. That it eventually does is certain for those who persevere, but as St John of the Cross says, very few remain on course because of ignorance. When many more do, then renewal is on the way as the Holy Spirit comes to those whose patience and perseverance in adversity enables them to receive him.

Chapter 36

From Light to Darkness

Without any human help, it was my own desperate need to find God that enabled me to persevere in the Dark Night in which I found myself when first fervour left me flat. However, in case I give the impression that first fervour is of little consequence and can easily be bypassed, this is not the case. First fervour is essential, for it is where that primordial desire to love and be loved is set ablaze to support and urge the would-be mystic onwards when, as St Teresa of Ávila put it, "the well runs dry".

In order to drive home my point, let me give a brief synopsis. God's glory is the expression of his inner self, which is, according to St John, Love. Here the Three in One endlessly give their all to each other. When we say that we are all created in the image and likeness of God, we mean that deep down beneath all the dross God's love resides in us, inspiring and suffusing our weak human love with his. This is what I am referring to when I speak about a deep primordial yearning to love and to be loved that can only be ultimately satisfied in the Three in One. This primordial yearning might find a brief satisfaction in experiencing God's glory made matter and form in the works of his creation, or in the artistic masterpieces of those who try to portray it in their works. Most people can reach out to and experience God's love in the love they have for another human being in whom his presence resides. True human love is the flashpoint when the primordial love that has been suffused by the divine in both partners, draws and then bonds them together. However, all are called to union with the love of God, for that is our final destiny.

The powerful and all-absorbing love that gripped me in my first enthusiasm was not just an emotional extra that could be bypassed, but a vital part of the rite of passage. Here, the primordial yearning for God is brought to a fever pitch and strengthens the traveller for the journey ahead where selflessness has to be learned if the fullest and deepest possible union is to be attained. For married couples too, the early emotions and passions that bond them together are of great importance to strengthen and support them when they subside. The selfishness that is in both of them has to be overcome in the years ahead if they are to find the fullest and deepest possible union with each other. In the last eighteen months of their lives together my father told me that he was more deeply in love with my mother than ever before, even more than in those early days when the fires of first love burnt so intensely. But it was evident to me and others who knew them that it was the strength they also received from seeking another Love, too, that made possible something that would be impossible without it. There is another aspect of first fervour that St Teresa of Ávila mentions. She suggests that it is in a sense a sort of premonition of the Mystical Marriage when after purification in the dark night, the emotions and the feelings have been sufficiently purified and refined, they can take us up into the glorified body of Christ, in, whom and through whom we come to contemplate the glory of God.

When I found myself in a spiritual desert with no oasis on the horizon, I had never heard of St John of the Cross or St Teresa of Ávila or any other mystic for that matter with the exception of St Francis of Assisi whose life I was reading. What impressed me was his simple but compelling logic that he received from the Gospels that he knew by heart. When he read that St John, his favourite evangelist, said that God is love and realized that this love was at all times ready and available to all who would receive it, he simply gave up everything else to seek it. It seemed the obvious thing to do. Jesus said that when you find a pearl of great price or a treasure hidden in a field you would sell and give up everything to obtain it. Is there any pearl greater than its creator or any treasure more precious than his love? The radical logic that seems to be lost on us galvanized St Francis into action, and that action was to give up all and seek out the solitude for the prayer that would enable him to receive the love that continually pours out of God. What moved me next was that although he initially experienced the excitement of first fervour as I had, he also was plunged into darkness.

After several months of praying daily in local churches, his endeavours took such a toll on him that his friends did not recognize him. So it was thanks to St Francis that I was persuaded to keep giving the same time to prayer as I did before. That is all the help I had, and in retrospect, it was all the help I needed if I could not find a spiritual director to help me. If a well-wisher had advised me not to worry and that resurrection would be coming soon and had given me St Teresa's *Interior Castle* it would have been a hindrance rather than a help. Why? Because it might have encouraged me to journey on, not for God's sake and for him alone, but for what I hoped to get out of him in the way of profound mystical experiences. I would not become a selfless lover but a cupboard lover.

When writing about mystical experiences in the early Church I said they were never emphasized, nor were they by later mystics, most especially St Francis. Even though we know St Paul experienced them he never boasted about them or set them up as the rewards that are given to those who pray. He endlessly preached "Christ and him Crucified". It was the same Christ for whom St Francis gave his all and wept so copiously that it damaged his health. Whatever graces we do receive in prayer are received not because they are sought, but because they are the consequence or byproduct of giving our all to God, for his honour and glory, not our own. Emphasizing spiritual goodies can be counterproductive, nor was this the reason why St Teresa detailed them in her great masterwork *Interior Castle*. There were so many heresies similar to Quietism in her day and so many ignorant spiritual directors that St Teresa decided to detail the psychological experiences that were the genuine action of the Holy Spirit. When she was not there, or after her death, her sisters would not be frightened by what they came to experience or think it was the work of the devil or become the pretext for ill-educated confessors to condemn them. *Interior Castle* was not written for everyone then, but only for her own sisters in Carmel and this should be borne in mind when recommending it to people at the beginning of their journey along the mystic way. I am grateful that I only read this masterly work later, and that it was St Francis who inspired and encouraged me to journey on when I first entered the dark night.

Someone in me encouraged me to keep giving the same time for prayer that I gave before, despite the fact that I felt nothing and experienced nothing but distractions and temptations. The most powerful temptation of all was to give up this black and barren prayer and return to the prayer that had so exhilarated and excited me before, but I simply could not. Then another temptation began to engage me and that was not just to give up this empty form of prayer that seemed to be going nowhere, but give up the whole enterprise, leave the noviciate as several had done already, and go back to "normality" in the "real" world. It was quite evident that just as nobody understood me at school because of my dyslexia, nobody understood me in the noviciate because of the new incomprehensible prayer that had engulfed me. I had to decide and I did. I would not leave but take my simple vows at the end of the year and then move to our student house at East Bergholt in Suffolk. This would give me three years in which to make a more mature decision and give God time to decide whether he wanted me or not, at least that is what I thought. So, in the middle of September in that year I moved to the student house, full of apprehension.

Chapter 37

From Darkness to Light

The whole atmosphere at the student house was refreshingly pleasant after the claustrophobic intensity of the noviciate. There were over forty other students all full of life and genuinely delighted to welcome the new intake. However, in time I noticed that no one stayed on after Compline for personal prayer. The liturgy was paramount and they "performed" it well, but no one seemed too interested in private prayer. Perhaps like me, they had also experienced first fervour and when it all disappeared they took the advice on offer and simply moved on with their lives.

There was no change at all in the misery that I had to endure inside of prayer. However, it has to be said that outside of prayer I was continually drawn, as if by some undefinable magnetic force to solitude and to the prayer that was rather my hell than my heaven on earth as before. I remembered my brother and what my mother said about him. "He has fallen in love with love." But you would be as likely to meet a girl in the friary as a Martian, so it was not human romance for which I was yearning. The church that remained empty for hours after Compline made me feel I would receive no more help here than I did at the noviciate, either from other students or our teachers. The effects of Quietism had done its work in the Franciscan Order and, as I was later to discover, in all the other Orders and Congregations, but I did not know it at the time. How sad that the nicest community of men who I had, or would ever live with, were blissfully unaware that the effects of a hideous heresy had been visited on them without them even realizing it. One thing, however, was in my favour. There was an excellent library that had not been denuded of the classical mystical writers, but they were all either covered with dust or the older ones still had "uncut pages" making it plain that although they had not been weeded out, neither had they been read.

I had no idea what books I should read, but the very title of *The Dark Night of the Soul* seemed to describe what I experienced each time I went to pray. No other book before or since has had such a dramatic effect on me. This Spanish Carmelite who I had never heard of before, died four hundred years before I was born, understood exactly what I was experiencing and detailed it with such precision that I could be in no doubt that I was on the right path. It encouraged me to press on come what may, although his words did nothing to alleviate the darkness that he insisted was God-given and even deserved the name contemplation, even though it was a dark form of contemplation that could not see through the gloom that enveloped me. I did not even have a "kindly light amidst the encircling gloom" to lead me on, except the faith of the saint whom I believed would in time lead me on "to see the distant scene".

Far from cheering me up, the beginning of his book made for depressing reading although I did not doubt a word of it. His explanation of why the dark night had fallen on me did make sense, but it did nothing for the ego that was riding high before my well ran dry. I was too busy enjoying the delights of first fervour and preparing for sainthood that I failed to notice the sinner beneath the sweetness and light that blinded my understanding. But now I understood. I did not like facing the truth: the self-centred young man who so recently believed he was about to scale the heights of Mount Carmel was in fact hardly in the foothills and would never make much headway on his ascent until he was relieved of all the baggage weighing him down. With relentless accuracy St John of the Cross detailed all my faults and failings, all the sins and the selfishness that first fervour had done nothing to purify away. In fact, it actually encouraged the biggest sin of all, the pride that led me to believe that I was about to reach the mystic heights and that levitation, bilocation and other esoteric gifts were only a matter of months away. What he said made sense, even if I did not like it at the time. How could a seriously flawed human being like me be united with the most perfect human being who ever lived, in his transformed, transfigured and glorified body, and then share with him in his pure and perfect loving of his Father in mystical contemplation?

That the deep purification in what St John of the Cross called the Dark Night of the Senses and the Dark Night of the Spirit was necessary could not be doubted. Whether or not I could make it – that could be in doubt. I now understood that this purification was simply the purgatory that we all must go through before union with Christ would enable us to be united with his Father to enjoy the delights of eternal life and love to eternity. The question is not whether or not we have to go through it, but whether we go through it in this life or in the next, for perfect union is impossible for imperfect human beings. Those who go through it in this life, even if they are only half or a quarter way through it, will be able to see, understand and express their faith so much better than anyone else, even if they are no good with words.

It must have been over six months praying at the student house before I began to notice a change. It was not anything dramatic, far from it. Despite the fact that there was no change in the daily, dreary monotony of prayer, I still felt drawn to it, but I became aware that I was receiving something from it that I could not put into words. Without this darkness where I battled against distractions and temptations, I somehow felt diminished and morally weakened. It was as if through this dark contemplation I was nevertheless receiving strength, although I felt nothing to confirm that I was receiving anything at all. Then three or four months later I began to be aware of a presence. I knew the experience because I first experienced it for myself as a boy whilst gazing for hours at the kestrel searching for his supper on the Yorkshire Moors where we had a summer cottage. Sometimes this presence was there in prayer, sometimes it was not, but what was always there were the temptations and the distractions, the strongest of which was to think that I was wasting my time doing nothing and that I would be better employed attending to my studies.

It was after about eighteen months of perseverance that something quite dramatic happened. So far there had been an occasional sense of presence similar to the natural mystical experiences I had on the moors and later in other places of unusual scenic splendour. These had not only enthralled my outer senses but my inner spiritual senses too, in such a way that even when I closed my eyes the experience of the "numinous" remained with me. However, this new and dramatic sense of presence was far more striking and arresting. It was not actually of a different order to the rather gentle and capricious sense of the "numinous" that I hitherto experienced in the beauty of creation. It was that experience, but it was far more vibrant and far more powerful. Not only that but it was quite evident to me that it was not the "numinous" that I was experiencing, but it was God, at least the experience of his love that was enveloping me. Nor did it depend on any external event or scenic beauty to induce it. It was quite clearly a gift that was in my power to receive but quite out of my power to produce, because quite apart from anything else it came and went when least expected, and I had no power to generate it nor any power to sustain it.

After continually experiencing the presence of God's love in this way, something even more dramatic took place. It was essentially the same experience, but after experiencing a lifting sensation in the higher part of the head, the lifting sensation suddenly spiralled upwards with such force that I knew if it continued I would experience oblivion, which mercifully I did not. If I never had such an experience again for the rest of my life, which I did, then nothing would shake my conviction, not just that God existed but that he was Love and that I had experienced that love in my life in such a way that I could never be the same again. However, I needed help. I needed confirmation and I needed to be assured that all was well and I was not being deceived. I found that help in the library. The book was called *The Interior Castle* by St Teresa of Ávila.

Chapter 38

The Interior Castle

The new, sudden and dramatic experiences that had all but overwhelmed me in my prayer life needed an explanation. Deep down I knew I was experiencing God's love enveloping me, but I still needed some sort of assurance that I was on the right road. I discovered that like St John of the Cross, St Teresa of Ávila was a Doctor of the Church and while he excelled in describing mystical darkness, she excelled in describing mystical light in her masterwork *Interior Castle*. I had been staggered to discover how St John of the Cross understood the darkness through which my inner soul had been travelling. This time I was staggered to discover how St Teresa of Ávila understood the experiences of light that had raised me up above myself to experience something of God's love reaching out to touch me.

However, I still felt the need to express myself to a living human being who could reassure me too. St Teresa of Ávila said that she would rather seek advice from a learned man than from a pious one, so I approached the most learned man in the Province who taught us Theology. While assuring me that my experiences were genuine, Fr Gabriel also insisted that he had never experienced them himself. When I protested that I was no better than the other students, and no more virtuous than my peers, he answered that such graces that I had received were not given as a reward for my virtuous life, but to give me the grace to live a virtuous life in the future. I came away feeling chastened as the words of the Gospel came to me. "To whom much is given, much will be required." For the first time in my life, I was totally and transparently honest when I expressed my unworthiness. True humility comes, not from being humiliated for a year by a novice master, but from the experience of He who is mighty doing great things in you and realizing that you are totally unworthy of it. My experience in the Swiss Alps was right after all.

If I was in danger of becoming arrogant at the thought that God had singled me out for these mystical graces, then I would have to think again, when in little less than a month they were taken away from me and I was left where I started for several years. The purification went on whether I liked it or not, but now I had the assurance that I was on the right way, and the way ahead was the deep mystical purification towards union with the only One who would lead and guide me along that way. The way ahead for the saints took many years, but for me it would take many decades. The sort of experiences that I had, come and go in such a way that the receiver is left in no doubt who is in control of their spiritual purification that takes place sometimes in darkness, sometimes in light. Later I will explain the psychological reasons why one follows the other in this way. However, I have no intention of detailing any further my spiritual journey because it is private and personal. I have only described what happens at the beginning for the same reason that St Teresa wrote her *Interior Castle*. She bared her soul far more completely than I intend to do. And then it was only for her sisters in Carmel, for fear they should be misled by the sort of ignorant spiritual directors whom she said she had to endure.

St Teresa calls the first gentle feeling of God's love as the Prayer of Recollection and the far more powerful experience of his love that follows, as the Prayer of Quiet. For St Teresa this is the first stage of experiential mystical contemplation and the recipient soon realizes it is a pure gift of God, as it comes and goes without anything we can do to generate or prolong it. In both the Prayer of Recollection and the Prayer of Quiet there are distractions and temptations that are always there beneath the surface. Their strength depends on the power of the mystical experience. In the Prayer of Quiet for instance, sometimes the experience is fairly weak but sometimes there is a lifting sensation in the head and the receiver is raised to experience this prayer to a higher degree of consciousness. Although there are always temptations and distractions beneath the surface, their strength becomes weaker and weaker as the mystical experience becomes stronger and stronger.

However, when a person is taken up into the Prayer of Full Union the experience is so powerful that for the first time there are no distractions of any kind. The intensity of the power that captivates is so utterly enthralling and captivating that the receiver cannot move from the spot where they are praying, or at least not without a great effort. Unlike the Prayer of Quiet, this prayer only lasts for a brief time – ten to twenty minutes, before it subsides leaving a person back in the Prayer of Quiet. As the high point of the Prayer of Quiet, Full Union, begins with a lifting sensation, but this sensation not only becomes far more powerful but begins to spiral upwards at great speed. The receiver is seized with a fear that the power of this experience might be too much for them and they may be taken out of themselves into some sort of ecstasy. This fear is not without foundation because this can, and sometimes does happen when the power of God's love becomes so great that ecstasy does take place to the dismay of the receiver. This experience is not just a faint because the person who experiences it remains exactly how they were. They do not fall to the ground but remain standing, sitting, or kneeling, totally lost in God until he withdraws the power of love that was enthralling them in such a dramatic way.

St Philip Neri, who was often swept up into an ecstasy, did not so much see it as a grace but as an embarrassment and he continually prayed to God to relieve him of the "privilege". He would be mortified when he was taken up into an ecstasy at Mass which was a regular occurrence, or even when preaching or walking down the street. All these mystical experiences are not in essence completely different but the same experience of

God's Love, but with ever-increasing power and magnitude and therefore with a corresponding effect on the receiver. Imagine them if you like as a colour – the colour yellow. Initially, this colour is so pale that it can hardly be distinguished from white, but then it can become ever-deeper and richer until it becomes a deeply rich and dazzling gold. As different names are given to the different degrees of intensity of the colour, the same happens to different degrees of intensity with which the love of God is experienced in the mystic way.

All these experiences take place in the higher part of the head, but for a Christian, this is not the summit of the mystic way because the Holy Spirit has been sent not just to purify and penetrate our heads but our whole human being. This is so that we can come to be transformed and transfigured as the body of Jesus was transformed before Peter, James, and John. The Transfiguration on Mount Tabor was a pre-enactment of what would happen to Jesus after the Resurrection when he was glorified. The event not only pre-enacts what happened to Christ at his glorification but what will happen to us too when the Holy Spirit penetrates us as Jesus was penetrated by the glory of God. When this purification is complete, the Holy Spirit can pour his love into us to penetrate and possess the whole person, mind and heart, body and spirit, in what is called the Mystical Marriage or the Transforming Union. This takes place as the preceding experiences of light and darkness in the Mystical Body of Christ, finally enabling a person to participate more fully than ever before in Christ's mystical contemplation of his Father. While all previous experiences would come and go, including what St Teresa calls the Spiritual Betrothals, the Mystical Marriage becomes permanent, enabling the recipient to be aware of their continual union with Christ at all times.

As would be expected, the Spiritual Betrothals precede the Mystical Marriage but unlike secular betrothals, they can take place many years, even decades before the marriage itself. Many more people experience the Spiritual Betrothals in this life than go on to enjoy the Mystical Marriage before they die. The Spiritual Betrothals usually begin while a person is experiencing the Prayer of Quiet and are characterized by a tingling feeling in the body that is usually triggered by a sudden spiritual thought or realization. This may come from a scriptural text that strikes you like never before or the realization of what gifts God is giving you, and the counter realization of your total unworthiness. However, I would like to make it clear that this does not happen at the beginning, but towards the very end of the Dark Night of the Spirit and after very many years if not decades of penetrating purification.

This is the beginning of the spiritual re-sensitization of the body and the reopening of the feelings and the emotions that have been rendered inactive and unresponsive during the long Dark Night of the Soul. It is for this reason that St Teresa said first fervour is, in a sense, a premonition of the Mystical Marriage. There is one thing above all else that grows, even in the darkest moments of purification, and that is the understanding and appreciation of the faith and how God wishes us to implement it, giving us the power to do it. The continual contemplation that Christ experienced while he was on earth enabled him to see the truth that God wanted him to proclaim with ever-increasing understanding and to proclaim it despite knowing the consequences. "And Jesus increased in wisdom, in stature and in favour with God and men" (Luke 2:52). What was true for Christ would be true for all who follow him. The suffering of purification inside of prayer is always compounded by the suffering experienced outside of prayer by those who try to proclaim the same truth for which their Lord was crucified. That is why St Paul said that he preached Christ and Christ Crucified and was crucified for doing it.

Chapter 39

The Dark Night of the Soul

When studying Philosophy, I had a brief flirtation with Existentialism. My hero was Sartre who said that "hell is other people" and essentially, that this is the trouble with the world. However, my own experience in prayer soon led me to agree with someone else whose dialogues I was reading at the time: St Catherine of Siena, who said that the trouble with the world is not other people, but ourselves. "The trouble with the world is me." In saying this she was summing up the realization that led so many men and women in the first centuries to flee into the desert to seek the solitude where they would come face to face with the "demons" within, to defeat them before they were free to contemplate the One who had drawn them into the wilderness.

The same happens in the spiritual desert that a beginner finds within them when they are led into the Dark Night of the Soul. Here, they soon become dissatisfied with the sparse spiritual food they have to survive on, day after monotonous day. Inevitably they begin to remember the delights of first fervour that not only gave them pleasure in God but strengthened them to resist other pleasures, illicit pleasures too that would draw them away from him. Now, finding themselves in a place of sensual deprivation like never before, they begin to yearn not only for licit spiritual pleasures but for the illicit pleasures too, that with God's help they were able to resist before. But where is God's help to be found in this inner wilderness where they now languish? It is now in the Dark Night of the Senses that sensual desires of every sort rise up and demand to be gratified. The more the traveller tries to journey on in the seemingly soulless solitude, the stronger these desires become and the more difficult they are to resist. Nor are they always resisted, for, truth to tell, we fall time and time again, and so experience our utter need of God.

Perhaps there have never been so many enticing sensual pleasures today than ever before. It is not only every kind of food and drink that could not even be imagined by our spiritual forebears but diversions like the radio, the television, the cinema, smartphones, smart speakers and so many other smart distractions; from pubs and clubs to sports of every sort to watch or take part in. How can we give up all these things to follow an obscure pull that appears to be leading us to God, although God is nowhere to be seen nor experienced? The answer is we cannot, nor is it necessary or even prudent to try to give them all up. What should we do then? Follow this little dictum and the Holy Spirit will gradually do for you what you cannot do for yourself: "Do not give up anything you like or enjoy except when it prevents you from having daily quality time for prayer, come hell or high water, whether you feel like it or whether you do not." This principle is so important that I will return to it later and explain it in far greater detail. But for the present let me just insist that true Christian ascetism means doing all we can each day to enable the Holy Spirit to make us perfect, trying to do the best we can by observing this little principle. I will return to how to pray in this night later, but first I want to introduce you to another and far more testing night that St John of the Cross calls the Dark Night of the Spirit, that purifies us more deeply than anything we have experienced so far.

Because this night comes later, do not think that the first night has to run its course before the second can begin. They continue together, both preparing us through purification for union with God. If, as the gospels insist, God is perfect and we must, therefore, become perfect to be made one with him, then we must be purified for this union in both nights. The first Christians did not speak of dark nights but of daily carrying one's cross of white martyrdom, and of giving everything up for the pearl of great price. They were speaking of the same journey that came to be called the mystic way, taking place unseen inside the mystical body of Christ. Here the way to union with God would take place for those sufficiently purified in, with and through the loving contemplation of Christ. St Padre Pio said "Pray, trust and do not worry", because the more we allow the Holy Spirit to purify us then the more his love suffuses and surcharges our love to enable us to do what is quite impossible without him.

In the Night of the Senses, we are gradually purified from all illicit sensual desires that lurk in the subconscious part of our minds. But in the Night of the Spirit, we are purified of the source of these temptations and even deeper and more ingrained evil inclinations and habits that lurk deep down in what Freud called the Unconscious or the "Id". It is from here that powerful forces that we rarely even know about determine how we behave. What has been called a Freudian Slip may from time to time enable us to glimpse what is down there and what has to be purified before we can be united to Christ who can alone lead us on to union with God. One happened to me almost fifty years ago when my brother told me he was about to marry a black African. In those days many were horrified and said so, while I, the great white liberal said nothing. The truth was, I felt exactly the same as they did but could not say so.

I did not sleep that night. It was not just the realization that I was prejudiced against black Africans, but that I had deceived myself into believing that there was not a shred of such prejudice in me. And if I was able to deceive myself about my prejudice against one particular race, what about all the other races on earth? I deceived myself into believing that I was not prejudiced against anyone, neither race, class, gender, or any ideals or other religion. I did not sleep because I was horrified to face the truth about myself and the deep-seated pride and prejudice that lurked deep down within me, determining how I behaved in the world where I thought myself an enlightened liberal, at least in all matters of irrational prejudice.

There is, however, a ray of hope. When I came to know my sister-in-law and experienced her love for me, that enabled me to love her in return. I found I was no longer prejudiced against black Africans, although I am sure all my other prejudices were still intact. This is the ray of hope, because as a person progresses in the Dark Night of the Soul, gradually in many years, the ray of God's love does for all the pride and prejudice within us, what my sister-in-law's love did for one particular type of racial prejudice that was within me. Let me try to explain how the transformation that this brings about within us takes place.

Every time the love of God envelops us, our love or our will is so absorbed in him that it loses control of what Freud called the censor in us. This censor redacts the truth that we cannot or do not want to face, or others to see, rising from our unconscious. The experience of God's love so enthrals our will that it is totally absorbed in his love and is, therefore, unable to do anything else than lovingly gaze upon him. The will is no longer able to censor all we hide which rises into the conscious mind where it shames us and scandalizes others. That is why, as the Dark Night continues, the love that we experience in such prayer as the Prayer of Quiet or Full Union is followed by darkness, as we then have to face the evil in us that rises from the deep. Just as a hot poultice draws all the infection out of a boil, the heat of God's love gradually draws out all the evil that infects the nether regions of our personalities. As this happens, it is the time to confront them, confess them and make reparation for them as best we can, and then continue to journey on, come what may, to allow God's love, his Holy Spirit, to continue the only purification that can prepare us for Union.

All must go through this purification to attain union with God. In this life it is called the Dark Night of the Soul; in the next life, it is called Purgatory. No one can avoid it, any more than we can avoid having a cancer removed before returning to full health. Mystical theology teaches how this purification is brought about in this life. Without it, spiritual theology has no inner dynamism, depth or ultimate meaning.

Chapter 40

Union with the Three in One

I began by using the analogy of a spaceship destined for planet Mars to show how the prayer of first fervour generates the power to raise the primeval desire for God off the ground. There is another more ancient aeronautical analogy that can explain our journey back to our maker: the analogy of the balloon. Earlier ascetical writers used it to explain that our desire for God would never rise heavenward unless the ropes that tethered it to the ground were severed. Each and every one must be cut before the balloon can rise and even one rope would be sufficient to keep it earthbound. Each rope represents an ingrained habit of selfishness and sin. Some of the more obvious sins of sensuality are encountered at their most testing in the Dark Night of the Senses, while the deeper sins with their insidious ingrained habits are encountered in the Dark Night of the Soul.

The Active Night involves giving time daily, no matter how dark the night, to employ a new form of prayer that I will describe later. The strength given by the Holy Spirit in this prayer assists us in severing each and everything in our lives that can prevent our purified love rising to God. However, from the Fathers of the Church onwards, the ascent involves passing through formidable barriers often depicted as contained within a dark and forbidding cloud. The Fathers of the Church see Moses as the archetypal mystic. He, like those who would follow him had to pass through a dark and forbidding cloud before he reached the top of Mount Sinai to receive God's Commandments. The idea of a cloud through which a mystic has to pass to reach a spiritual summit where the new law of love can be received is used by many later mystical writers.

While this cloud is usually visualized as high up above

us, blocking our way to our ultimate destination it should be visualized rather as located within us. It rises from the powers of evil that reside deep down in our unconscious mind that influence all we say and do in our conscious mind, without us hardly realizing it. Most of all it affects our minds and the powers of reasoning that philosophers have agreed distinguish us from the animal world. But the real truth is that we are not primarily rational animals as the philosophers would define us, but loving animals as the theologians would define us because we are made in the image and likeness of a loving God. Only love can rescue reason from what perverts it – not our love, but the love that is received in divine contemplation. That is why it is Jesus Christ who is our Saviour, not Socrates or Marcus Aurelius.

God's love is deepest in us, as the very ground of our being. It is here in our deepest self that our desire to love and be loved that will only ultimately be satisfied in God, rises to enter into him. Inspired by and supported with as much of God's love that our weakness can contain, our love must try to pierce and pass through the cloud that stands between us and God; the cloud that arises from evil powers residing deep down in our unconscious mind. It is here that powerful, unruly and unacceptable urges, impulses and drives rise from what Freud called the Id, to disturb, disrupt and distort pure rational thought and action. Apart from occasional "Freudian slips", they remain hidden from view. They most usually rise from the unconscious like a "malign miasma" to hover over our conscious mind to seep into it surreptitiously to influence all we say and do without us being aware of what is happening. These perverted urges that lurk deep down within our unconscious do not have their ultimate origin in "nature" or "nurture", but they do influence them. They influence them by determining their strength and the way in which each person is individually controlled by them. However, I do not intend to delve any further into depth psychology, for salvation, sanctification and mystical transformation do not come from psychology, but from the knowledge and practice of mystical theology that details the power of divine love and how to receive it.

With perseverance in prayer, our desire for the fullness of love suffused by the divine, can alone gradually penetrate through the cloud that would stop and stifle it. Eventually, in many years of inspired endeavour, our desire reaches an otherworldly mystical meeting point when the sparks of God's love from within us on earth meet to be engulfed in the furnace of God's love in heaven. It is then that our love, and the desire that directed it Godward, becomes like a spiritual lightning conductor, to which I referred before, that enables the fullness of God's love to be drawn down to do what is impossible without it. If we believe that we alone can combat, confound and conquer the powers of evil within us then we would not only fail but more often than not be conquered by them ourselves. However, after the mystical meeting point in which the divine and the human are united, the very love that enabled us to rise to God enables his love to descend into us, gradually dispelling and destroying the powers of evil within. These are the powers that prevent the fulness of God's indwelling from possessing every part of us in the Transforming Union. This is the union in which a sinner is transformed into a saint.

Whereas I have used the analogy of a lightning conductor, ancient writers use the analogy of Jacob's ladder, or the ladder of perfection to signify the vehicle by which our love rises with God's angelic help into God and his love descends into us. This enables God's love to come down and enter into us, gradually dispersing the clouds that have been hiding his presence. This finally leads to the profound union, often called the Spiritual or the Mystical Marriage which begins to take place. This is indeed heaven on earth, Paradise regained and a foretaste of the perfect Paradise to come. This whole journey has been taking place in the mystical body of Christ, ultimately brought about by God in what has been called the Passive Night, when after we have done all we can, God's love does the rest, because we have chosen to admit him in the Active Night, in other words by what we have tried to do.

Just before he died on the Cross, Jesus promised the good thief, "Today you will be with me in Paradise" (Luke 23:43). When St Paul experienced the rapture that raised him to the heavens, he was "caught up into Paradise" (2 Corinthians 12:4). The Fathers of the Church continually used the idea of Paradise regained to depict our ultimate destiny. The earliest baptistries are festooned with frescoes depicting paradisal scenes so that the new Christians would be in no doubt about their ultimate destination. This whole mystical ascent would take place in Christ, the New Adam. It would be in, with and through him that the Paradise lost, the Paradise postponed through sin, would become the Paradise regained through love. Just as the old Adam was said to have "walked and talked with God in the cool of the evening", so we will be able to do likewise in the New Adam in whom we have been living and moving ever since we were baptised into his Mystical Body. The Fathers of the Church tried to describe the completion of the mystic way as encountering and entering into the life of the Three in One in a beautiful paradisal garden. Later mystics emphasized the psychological dimensions of our ultimate destiny. In his work *The Spiritual Canticle*, St John of the Cross visualizes the soul as Adam who is led into Paradise to celebrate his mystical marriage with God.

When we first encounter the joy of the Mystical Marriage, or the brief foretastes of this encounter in what St Teresa calls the Spiritual Betrothals, the feelings and the emotions that were so unresponsive in the darkest moments of the Dark Night are suddenly reawakened by Love. We begin to respond to the scriptures as we did before. Profound thoughts are ignited by psalms, hymns, sermons and so many other expressions of the faith that once moved the emotions, that were all but dead in the deepest and darkest moments of the night of purification. It is for this reason that St Teresa said that what is experienced in first fervour foreshadows in some way what is to be experienced in the Mystical Marriage. This does not mean that there is a return to the sort of detailed meditation that was so helpful before. However, the love that has been purified in the night needs just a few moments to stir us, considering what Christ did for us while he was on earth, most particularly his birth, passion, death and Resurrection. Now, with arms wide open he draws us into himself to contemplate the Father and experience the infinite love that passes back-and-forth between the Three in One.

It is in this joyous contemplation where all we want to do is worship, praise, give thanks and adoration to God, that our thoughts soon begin to tell us that it is not enough. It is not enough to enjoy what we have been given and continually receive, because it is time to express our gratitude for the fruits that we receive in contemplation by sharing them with others, as Christ did throughout his life on earth. We may have been observing the first commandment, but now it is time to observe more fully and formally the second commandment. The temptation to remain and enjoy what we are receiving in prayer may induce us to forget our calling. When St Francis came to enjoy the first fruits of contemplation that filled him with God's love, he was tempted to be selfish. But when he consulted St Clare in her monastery and Brother Rufino in his hermitage, they both gave him the same message: he must go out to share the fruits of contemplation with others. Without hesitation, he left his solitude. Now he was called, like Antony before him, to Spiritual Paternity.

Chapter 41

Confirmatory Signs of the Mystic Way

It is essential that, at a time when it is so difficult to find a competent spiritual director, people are taught how to make a diagnosis for themselves. It might not be ideal, but reality may dictate that we have to make the decision for ourselves as to when meditation has come to an end and when, therefore, we have been led into contemplation. Although fraught with dangers, sometimes there is no alternative. I never found a competent spiritual director when I needed one. I had to make a diagnosis for myself from reading books. Thankfully, the first book I read was *The Dark Night of the Soul* by St John of the Cross. In order to help my readers make a diagnosis for themselves and to avoid the dangers that I referred to, I will summarize the teaching of St John of the Cross and then add the teaching of other mystics to make myself as clear as possible.

There are two places in the writings of St John of the Cross where he enumerates the signs by which a person can determine whether or not the desert in which they find themselves is the beginning of Contemplation or the Dark Night of the Soul. St John uses both terms to describe this place of purification. The first place is in his book *The Dark Night of the Soul*, book one, chapter nine. The second is in *The Ascent of Mount Carmel*, book two, chapter thirteen. He gives three or four signs, but there are others that he assumes, and still others that you can find in the writings of other mystics. I have gathered ten together.

The first sign is that a person has already been through first enthusiasm or first fervour, when meditation or some other forms of devotion has led to what some have called Acquired Contemplation, when prayer becomes relatively easy. Then, after enjoying a sort of emotional climax for a relatively short time, everything suddenly flops into an anticlimax when all the feelings of fervour disappear and do not return despite all the efforts to revive them. This can happen to a person in their private prayer, or in forms of group prayer such as that experienced in Charismatic Renewal. However, I would emphasize that people who do not pray daily and consistently will not pass through their first fervour and into the mystic way, whether they pray mainly in private or whether they pray as members of a particular prayer group.

The second sign which is mentioned by St John is that despite the relentless dryness and aridity, there is still the deep desire for God, which grows if they press on. The desire expresses itself in a pull to be alone that draws them aside into solitude for the contemplative prayer they want above all else but which always seems to elude them.

The third sign is that, despite the desire that regularly draws them to prayer, they find it all but impossible to concentrate as they did before. The reason is quite simple. As the heart's desire or the will is drawn to God alone, it loses its power over the mind, the memory and the imagination that was so essential for meditation, so that it now becomes quite impossible.

The fourth sign is, as their inner sensual faculties cannot function as they could before, they cannot picture the Jesus who was the centre of their meditation, so their desire is directed towards God and God alone. Henceforward he is the only One who gradually becomes the object of their deepest desires and longings, although the experience of his presence seems to have totally left them.

The fifth sign is that the lack of concentration that afflicts them inside prayer begins to affect them outside prayer also. They moon around like lost souls, not knowing where to go or where to look for the love they have lost. Like anyone who is in love with love, they become vague, woolly, dreamy and forgetful. Their pleasures, pastimes, interests, hobbies, as well as their work, leave them flat. They find it difficult to concentrate on anything except this strange desire for God. The paradox is they no longer have the interest they had in the Sacraments or the Liturgy, or in reading the Scriptures that meant so much to them before, or in devotional exercises or the hymns that helped them in the past. It is not surprising, then, that at times they begin to doubt that this strange new world in which they find themselves has anything to do with God after all.

The sixth sign is that they appear to be suffering from a moral decline that they cannot stem. They seem to be getting worse rather than better. The truth of the matter is that the spiritual fervour they were able to generate before no longer sustains their moral behaviour, and they seem to be going backward and unable to do anything about it. But the situation is not as serious as it seems. It is not that there is any serious moral degeneration. It is just that the sweet vapours of first fervour hid from view what was always lurking beneath the surface.

The seventh sign is that certain temptations always tend to predominate at the beginning of the Night of the Senses. The temptation to pack up prayer permanently becomes at times almost irresistible because it seems they are going nowhere at all. It all seems to be a waste of time, doing nothing day after day in the time that used to be full of wonderful feelings and fervour. The vast majority usually succumb, and never go any further in their prayer life. As they cannot return to meditation, they can only return to vocal prayer if they pray much at all. If, however, a person does persevere, the temptations only increase and their failure to find any sort of pleasure where it was found once before leads a person to seek it elsewhere. So they are beset with sensual temptations, inside and outside prayer, to which they often succumb regularly, making it even more difficult for them to believe they can be on any sort of spiritual journey.

These temptations become worse as the Night of the Senses gives way to the Night of the Spirit. It is no wonder that the eighth sign is depression. Who would not get depressed when it seems you are unable to pray anymore, and the Scriptures that meant so much before move you no more, and your moral behaviour seems to be deteriorating with each passing day? What is worse, other people seem to be noticing it too, and they see yesterday's happy, smiling, budding saint making a mockery of his or her perseverance in prayer by persevering in behaviour that seems to belie a genuine spiritual journey. But worse still, it seems that nothing can be done about it. When asked what he found most difficult about the spiritual life the *Curé d'Ars* said it was depression. Anyone who claims to have passed through the Dark Night without having experienced depression has been deceiving themselves.

The ninth sign is that if, despite everything, a person does persevere in prayer, come what may, all the negative features that have been outlined above will become progressively worse, at least for a time. It is not surprising, therefore, that the final sign is that they will eventually be totally convinced that they are on the wrong path. And if they are ever fortunate enough to find a spiritual director who does understand them, then they will spend much of their time trying to convince this director that they are indeed on the wrong path.

If despite all I have said, it is still impossible to make a diagnosis with certainty, a person should be encouraged to practise the way of prayer that I will shortly describe for those at the beginning of mystical contemplation.

However, I may have given the impression that when the Dark Night begins, you do not use the Scriptures anymore and the humanity of Jesus no longer seems to have the importance it had before. It is not that the humanity of Jesus has disappeared, but it seems to have disappeared. Before, the Scriptures were a window through which to see Jesus Christ and study everything that he said and did. He was the fulfillment of all hopes and dreams, but the gaze upon him was from the outside like an onlooker or a bystander. All that has changed now. Once an outsider is touched by love, he or she wants to be an insider. Love wants to reach out, to take hold of, to possess, to enter into and have at-one-ment with the one who is loved.

Let me remind you of the story of the astronaut that I used before because the point it makes is so important. Every morning, he woke to see the spaceship that was going to carry him to his destination. Then one morning he awoke feeling dreadful. His mouth was dry, his body cramped and he could see nothing. "It's gone. It's gone, the spaceship has gone," he shouted. Then he heard the voice of his superior through the intercom. "No it has not. You cannot see it because you are in it." And he was in it, and he was travelling more quickly than ever before towards the destination for which he was born.

Although you can no longer see Jesus as you used to in prayer and meditation, it is because you are within him and you are in fact being fitted into him more perfectly in your prayer than ever before. However, this state of affairs does not persist forever because as dawn approaches, and the emotions and feelings have been purified, they reopen and enable a relationship with Jesus and the Persons of the Holy Trinity as never before. The Mystical Marriage is on the horizon.

Chapter 42

True Imitation of Christ

As I once explained, a brief appearance on stage at the end of my school days enabled me to understand the spiritual life as I never understood it before. I was playing Henry V in Shakespeare's play about England's greatest warrior king. The dress rehearsal was a disaster, or should I say, I was a disaster. But moments before I stepped back on stage for the scene in which Henry makes his famous speech; "Once more unto the breach dear friends, once more," the English master took me by the arm and said, "Now listen here, Torkington, forget about that pathetic little performance last night; this is the real thing. This is not a stage, it's a battlefield. These are your men who are tired and exhausted. They have been storming the breach in the city wall all day. They have seen their friends falling at their side. They have heard the cries of the wounded, the screeching of the horses and they are all but defeated. Get out there, rouse them up, and rally them for one more attack before it's too late." Then, with those words he pushed me onto the stage with one hand and pulled back the curtains with the other. Everyone seemed to think it was a great performance, but it was not a performance at all. I was not acting, it was for real. Somehow the English master had managed to inspire me with the spirit of the man who trounced the French at Agincourt. I was famous for fifteen minutes, not because I was a good actor, but because for fifteen minutes I became a living reincarnation of the greatest warrior king in English history.

That performance was a key moment in my life as it gave me my most important spiritual insight. Thanks to the English master, I was able to see that you can only really become like someone else, act and behave as they do by being inspired by the same spirit that inspired them. There is only one way to copy Christ and that is not by trying to copy his outward behaviour, but by trying to allow the same love that continually animated him to flow into us to animate and inspire us in all we say and do. Throughout his life on earth, Christ continually opened himself to be inspired by his Father's Love, the Holy Spirit, who conceived him in the first place, inspiring everything he said and did while he was on earth and filling him to overflowing when he returned to heaven. The love that continually flows out of the Risen Lord to fill us now, is the same love that flowed into him throughout his life on earth. It is the same love that was brought to perfection after his death, and the same love that reunited him with his Father, enabling his Father to send that love out through him onto and into us to transform us into Christlike people.

The spiritual life is the expression used to describe a new way of life in which we start turning towards God regularly to receive his love that comes to us through Jesus, to make us like him in every possible way. I began to study the spirituality of the first Christians to learn from them how to change my daily life by practising the God-given spirituality that Jesus bestowed upon them. I wanted to learn from them how I could at all times be open to receive the love unleashed by Christ on the first Pentecost Day, taking us up into his mystical body. I knew that it was here alone, praying in, with and through him that I would receive and be animated and inspired by the same love from God that had inspired and animated him throughout his life on earth. I learned from my memorable theatrical "performance" that this was the only way to imitate him, so that the same Holy Spirit who inspired all that he said and did would inspire me too and make me into the Christ-like person I desired to become.

Although at our baptism we are taken up into Christ's Mystical Body, we are not instantly united fully with him, body and blood, mind, heart and soul, because of the sin and selfishness that separates us from the total union that is our deepest desire.

Nevertheless, we are in him, and so when we pray, we pray in, with and through him. It is his love that suffuses and surcharges our love in such a way that it can pass through the "cloud of evil" that has arisen from our sinfulness which prevents our love from freely rising to God as we would wish. It is now, as long as our love remains fixed upon God, that his love uses our love as a lightning conductor to be directed to the place where it can burn away the evil that separates us from him at source, deep down within us.

As this purification progresses in the Dark Night we are gradually filled with the love of God, the Holy Spirit, who animated and inspired everything that Christ said and did on earth and continues to do now that he is in heaven. It is only when the Holy Spirit has sufficiently purified us that the real and total union with Christ that we have always desired can take place. To believe that a union can take place and can be achieved in mere minutes by learning to recite mantras before our love has been purified, is to believe in magic. Christianity introduces a new age in which salvation comes not through magic as of old, but through love.

My Father owned a special portrait camera designed to take perfect pictures. When focussing on the subject, two images came into view. The first was an exact image and the second was transparent, see-through, wraith-like. On turning a dial the two pictures would draw closer together until the two pictures became as one. This is what happens when we keep turning to God to receive his love that purifies us, sometimes in darkness, sometimes in light. Gradually we are made sufficiently like Christ to be united with him more effectively, more completely, more perfectly than ever before. When this happens we not only enter into the mystical marriage with Christ, but simultaneously with God the Father. Remember the words that Christ used in answer to Philip at the Last Supper. "On that day you will understand that I am in my Father and you in me and I in you"

(John 14:20). In this sublime union we are not just united with the Father and the Son but with the Love who unites them together as One, in the mystery of the Three in One. My short theatrical performance enabled me to see that only the same Spirit who animated and inspired Jesus could make me into a Christ-like person. I was right, but also so ignorant of what this would involve in the years ahead!

After telling Philip that he and the Father are one, Jesus went on to state with absolute clarity what would be necessary for union with them to take place: "Anybody who receives my commandments and keeps them will be the one who loves me; and anybody who loves me will be loved by my Father, and I shall love him and show myself to him.... and we shall come to him and make our home with him" (John 14: 21–24). There are two "new commandments" and together they sum up and incorporate all the others. The first is to love God with your whole mind and heart, with your whole body and soul, and with your whole strength. The second, most usually quoted as stated in the Old Testament, is to love our neighbour as ourselves. However, in the New Testament and at the Last Supper it is now far more exacting, for we must now learn to love our neighbour as Christ himself loves us. This is impossible unless we have allowed the same Spirit who animated Christ to animate us too so that his love can do for others through us, what we can never do alone.

But this takes many years trudging on in the Dark Night where true selfless loving is learned in many years for those who have the courage to persevere. In the words of St Ignatius we have to learn "to fight and not to heed the wounds, to toil and not to seek for rest, to labour and not to ask for rewards, except to know that I am doing your will". These words perhaps better than any others sum up the whole attitude of mind and heart that must determine how we travel on in the Night despite all that would try to draw our heart's desire from reaching out to God. I have often wondered what would have happened if that callow young thespian had known from the start where his inspiration would lead him? But the best advice is taken from the hymn of St John Henry Newman: "I do not ask to see the distant scene; one step enough for me." The distant scene cannot be seen because we are enveloped by the Dark Night, and we travel on in faith. But moments of light do penetrate the darkness, sometimes like moonlight, sometimes like dawn light, sometimes like sunlight, sometimes like lightning, to give us hope that the One who dwells in light inaccessible is guiding us to the place where God our Father is waiting to enfold us in his infinite loving.

Chapter 43

The Language of Love

The great astronomer, physicist and polymath from Pisa Galileo Galilei, said that the only language with which you can explain and understand the physical relationships in the universe is the language of mathematics. However, the greatest human being who ever lived Jesus Christ from Nazareth, said the only language with which you can explain and understand the spiritual relationships in that universe, is the language of love.

It was God who uttered the first word ever spoken in this language. That word was simply *love*. It was later called the "Word" by St John because it was the most important word ever spoken. However, because it was spoken by God it did not just disappear into thin air like human words but took form and was transformed into a person who was the mirror image of God. For this reason, St John also called the "Word" the "Son of God". It was in and through God's Son, his Word, that the greatest and most sublime plan ever dreamed of was to be put into action. This plan was to share with other beings who would be created for that purpose, the height, the depth, the length and breadth of God's own love that surpasses the understanding, and to experience it with and in him, to all eternity.

The crowning glory of this plan was, "the Word, in whom all things were created" was made flesh to dwell among those destined to share in his glory, to be their King and deliverer. He would be called the Saviour for he would deliver to all who were open to receive it the same life and love that animated him, drawing all into his kingdom of Love. St Paul called this divine plan the *Mysterion* because it was a mystery, a secret plan that was unknown to all but those who accept the call to enter into it. Those who enter into this mystical kingdom, called

Christ's mystical body, would be gradually prepared to enter into Christ's own loving contemplation of God. This preparation would involve a prolonged purification. It would be by living, loving and praying in this mystical body that we would be able to reach out to God through our Risen and glorified Lord and come to know and experience God's plan from all eternity.

God's love was not only personified in the Word, but this love continually flowed to and fro between the two without ever diminishing. As a mark of reverence and respect we call this loving the Holy Spirit. It was by the power of the Holy Spirit that the Word in whom all things were created was made flesh, made man, on the first Christmas day by being conceived within Mary's womb, for she was made Immaculate for this purpose. Because he had a human as well as a divine nature, the Son of God, Jesus Christ, could draw other human beings to him while he was on earth. After his death and glorification, however, he would not only draw people to him, but into him, through the love of the Holy Spirit. This was the same love that united him at all times to the Father which he sent after his ascension, as he promised when he was alive for "there was no Spirit as yet because Jesus had not yet been glorified" (John 7:37–39). This enables us to come to know, experience and enjoy God's love to the end of time and beyond, for there is no end to the ecstatic bliss of experiencing God's love to all eternity.

The journey onwards into "love without measure" will be undertaken in union with all those we have lived with and loved in this life, with whom we will be united to embark upon the journey of all journeys in the next life. When our joy is shared with another whom we love it is doubled. When it is shared with many others whom we love it is doubled again and again and many times over. When it is shared with the vast new family whom we meet within the mystical and glorified body of Christ, then it will be multiplied beyond what human words can ever describe. Further to all this the love that we continue to receive without the distractions and temptations that hindered us on earth, enables something that we have so far never imagined. It enables us to continue growing into our true selves as Love possesses us in ever increasing measure. When the sun shines on a rose bud it grows and expands until it opens sufficiently to let a shaft of sunlight into its heart. As the sunlight penetrates the bud it gradually expands until it finally opens to reveal its glory, inspiring all who gaze upon its beauty, and intoxicating them with its sublime scent. This is what happens to us in heaven.

On earth our true self, originally created in the image and likeness of God, remains nevertheless hidden beneath the sin and selfishness that stunts our growth. It is only when the requisite purification begins that the sun of God's love is able to begin preparing us to allow him in, to make us what he created us to become from the beginning. In heaven our growth continues, and we continue to become ever more perfect expressions of God's glory. When this happens simultaneously to all with whom we are travelling, dispelling all the imperfections that kept us apart on earth, then something special happens. We not only come to share in God's glory in itself, but in that of all of our fellow travellers too as they are becoming what God has destined them to become, enhancing the ecstatic bliss to which we have all been destined. This endless, ongoing, ever-expanding bliss planned for us by God from the beginning, is the measure of the "height and depth, the length and breadth" of his love for us that surpasses the understanding.

It is only in heaven that the first of the great commandments is practised to perfection together with the second commandment, to love one another with the same love with which Christ loves us. This enables the Trinity of love that flowed between the Father and the Son from eternity, to overflow in such a way that it can now circulate as the life blood of the mystical body of Christ. In this way the mystical body of Christ becomes the most perfect expression of God's glory. And further to this, for those who receive it, the enjoyment of this love is the most perfect experience of heavenly bliss for all who abide in Christ's glorified body. Writing what I have just written is one thing, understanding it not just with the mind but with the heart, is quite another. Fortunately for all of us, it cannot be understood effectively with the mind, but only with the heart. This is the beauty of our Catholic Faith because it is for all; for all who through purification have a pure and humble heart. For such believers, just intuiting a fraction of what I have been trying to say about what God has created us for is enough to transport us into utterly enthralling raptures.

Love and love alone will enable us to come to know and experience God's love, not human academic learning, no matter how profound. Yet, since the love learned in mystical theology has been lost sight of many years ago, so too has the spiritual renewal that is long overdue. Over the last four centuries many intellectual revivals have failed to bring about the renewal that can only be brought about through the love generated in personal holiness. Intellectual renewals alone have always failed because true renewal is the work of the Holy Spirit. It is he alone, working through those who choose to receive him in prayer, who can bring about authentic Christian renewal. When his love mixes, mingles and merges with our love, the union with God that we all desire can be brought about.

When a renowned theologian was asked what he considered necessary for us to come to know and love God as we should, he answered by quoting a verse from an old evangelical hymn: "Jesus loves me this I know, 'cos the Bible tells me so." All we need to know, believe, and act upon is the simple truth that our Risen Lord loves us here and now, and then to turn to him in daily personal prayer. Then his love, the Holy Spirit, will suffuse our weak human love in such a way that we can be drawn up into Christ's mystical body to prepare us for the only loving union that will enable us to glimpse his glory before being drawn ever more fully into it as to our final destiny. But as this is happening he will use us to do something else. As we are being transformed, beginning here on earth, we will be used as spiritual prisms, enabling us to receive, reflect and refract the light of the Holy Spirit onto others, reflecting on earth something of the love, the goodness and the peace that prevails in heaven.

"Come, Holy Spirit, fill the hearts of your faithful and enkindle in them the fire of your love. Send forth through them your Holy Spirit that the world may be recreated."

Chapter 44

The White Martyrdom that Leads to Union

My parish priest was an expert on the Holy Shroud of Turin. He was always talking, writing and speaking about it in his sermons, as well as his favourite subject, the Mystical Body of Christ. I became confused as a child and came to think that the mystical body was the image of Christ's crucified body on the Holy Shroud. It took me years before I came to understand that although the image on the shroud is the holiest relic of Christ that we possess, his Mystical Body is so much more. The Holy Shroud can inspire us deeply and help to strengthen our faith, as it is the risen body of Christ's image on the shroud. But those who love him do not only see this image, but they can also enter into his glorified body in heaven and participate in his action – his loving contemplation of God his Father.

Although it took me years to understand this, it was the very first thing that St Paul understood at his conversion on the Damascus road. The very moment that Christ said to him, "Why are you persecuting me?" St Paul understood firstly that Jesus had indeed risen from the dead, and that all his followers were somehow in him, within his new glorified body, later called his Mystical Body. This would have been made even clearer at St Paul's baptism in Damascus a short time later. The very moment after he was baptised, he would have been clothed in a shining white garment, just like Christ when he rose from the tomb on the first Easter Day. By this sacred liturgical symbolism, the first Christians would be taught that henceforth all they said and did would take place in their risen Lord, within his Mystical Body, in whom and through whom they would offer their love to God the Father. Although it is not mentioned in the Acts of the Apostles, we know that as soon as possible after he was baptised he would join the members of his new family to celebrate what was then called the "breaking of the bread". As Christ was made present in the Eucharist, their communion with him enabled them to offer themselves, in, with and through him to God. They would then receive the outpouring of his love to the measure of the love they had been offering him in their daily prayer, and love of each other.

This offering would be made whilst Christ was sacramentally present, not just to all of them, but within all of them. Every day would begin with a Morning Offering in which they would commit to put into practice the offering of themselves made that Sunday, and every subsequent day. In this way they would gradually transform their whole lives into the Mass, so that it would become the place where everything they said and did would be offered up through Christ to God the Father. This would lead them on and into true imitation of Christ, because when he celebrated the first Mass at the Last Supper, the offering that he made was in fact the offering of his whole life from the moment he was born to the moment he died. In addition to this they would give further quality space and time each day to private personal prayer. In this prayer, from first beginnings to the heights of mystical prayer, they would in essence be trying to do one and the same thing: trying at all times to turn away from temptations and distractions to act selflessly. In this way they continually endeavoured to attain White Martyrdom as they died daily to self, endlessly trying to raise their hearts and minds to God, in, with and through the love of Christ.

Perhaps it can now be seen that the temptations and the distractions that we thought prevented us from praying actually help us to pray. The very essence of prayer consists in acting selflessly by turning away from what we would love to think about, or what our imaginations would love to revel in, in order to turn to love God. That is why St Teresa of Ávila said that you cannot pray without them, but neither, of course, can you pray if you continually give way to them. Personal prayer is the place where the selfless loving is learned that opens us to receive the perfect loving of God. That is why St Angelo of Foligno called prayer time, "school time", because it is the place where loving is learned by endlessly practising it in what she called the School of Divine Love. It is because all our prayer takes place in Christ's Mystical Body that in one sense all Christian prayer is mystical and we are all therefore on the mystic way. However, in the course of time, only that form of prayer in which we begin to experience God's love tangibly working in us, sometimes through darkness, sometimes through light, as it begins to purify us came to be called mystical. The word mystical is taken from the Greek and merely means hidden, unseen or secret. In time this word has been incorrectly used, predominantly by "bounty hunters", to mean seeking and benefiting from exotic or esoteric experiences. Sadly, they fail to see that their endeavour is not for God's pleasure, but for their own. Inevitably, self-seeking prevails and prevents them receiving what they desire more than anything else.

True love that we all desire is always experienced as the result or the byproduct of selfless loving. Those who set out to seek physical pleasure for their own self-gratification from other human beings are called Lotharios, philanderers or seducers, never coming to know true love, only lust, destroying lives in their pursuit of it. It is the same for those who only seek God for their own self-satisfaction. Receiving nothing in return they soon give up their search or turn to counterfeit forms of man-made mysticism instead. These at best offer little more than the psychological palliatives that have sadly deceived so many, even good people, into believing they have achieved what only relentless selfless giving can obtain. The biblical word for relentless selfless giving to God is "repenting" and that is what St Peter told the crowds to do who wanted to receive the love that was poured out on the first Pentecost. And it is this that we try to do as we endeavour to put our Morning Offering into practice every day, and what we try to do inside the time we give to personal prayer. These endless acts of selfless loving that are practised in prayer gradually develop into a habit, creating an inner disposition of selflessness that makes us at all times porous to the love of God, both inside and outside of prayer. This means that we are not only taken up into the love that prevails within Christ's Mystical Body but that his love penetrates us to the very marrow of our being.

St Augustine uses a striking analogy to describe the new world in which we find ourselves. He likens the life that abides in Christ's Mystical body to an all-encompassing ocean of love. Likening us to living sponges, we are at all times surrounded by that love that simultaneously penetrates every part of those who through selfless loving are open to receive it. However, if we choose to resist the spiritual energy of Christ's love then our human love will remain self-centred and self-absorbed so the love of Christ cannot penetrate it. This sadly means that the divine and human energy of love cannot mix and merge together to become as one, to rise to contemplate the Father. Although we are taken up into Christ's Mystical Body at Baptism, the dying to self, symbolized in this rite of Christian initiation, must be practised day after day. This will teach us to carry our daily cross most especially when we are led into the Dark Night. Here we will be sufficiently purified to enable our inadequate human love to receive, share and then be surcharged by the divine.

Repeating the analogy that St Teresa of Ávila makes, she likens those who go into the night to a caterpillar who, if they persevere enter into the state of a chrysalis. The caterpillar that was at all times earthbound is gradually transformed into a beautiful butterfly that can rise into the heavens to be united with the One who created it. For those who have been, or are in the state of a spiritual chrysalis, will know only too well how apt this analogy is. How often before coming into this state have we sung or prayed "that God would melt us, remould us and make us new". However, when he takes us at our word, we find that the melting and remoulding that goes on under the direction of the Holy Spirit is all too much for us, especially as the way we prayed before is no longer of any help.

This is especially testing when, due to the current antipathy to mystical theology in the Church, there seems no one at hand to help us. At best, the Mystic Way is seen as an eccentric way for a few, not a way to be encouraged for the "ordinary faithful". There are few, therefore, to lead and guide us onwards and through the painful, penetrating, and purifying transformation that can alone enable us to be united as fully as possible to our risen and glorified Lord.

For myself, I have never found anyone in the whole of my life to turn to. Nor have I ever found any modern books that deal with this subject as fully as I would wish. That is why I have spent my long life trying to write the books that I could never find to help me, in the hope that I might help others who are in my predicament. I would be delighted to find that my hope has not been in vain!

Chapter 45

How to Pray in Mystical Contemplation I

In a Jewish world it was easy enough for the daily timetable of the people to revolve around the religious practices of Judaism. But after the siege and fall of Jerusalem and the destruction of the Temple in AD 70 the Jewish people, as well as Christians, became a minority in a much bigger pagan world whose daily timetable did not revolve around religious practices. The early Christians followed the example of Jesus, praying three times a day in the Synagogue, dedicating their day to God, until they were no longer welcome there, or because it became dangerous to go there. It became all too easy for their persecutors, like Saul of Tarsus, to find them there at the third, the sixth and the ninth hour of the day. St Paul confesses, "Lord, I used to go from synagogue to synagogue, imprisoning and flogging those who believed in you" (Acts 22:19–20). The Morning Offering used by the first Christians could not so easily be repeated in the Synagogue several times a day, according to the Jewish custom, so it came to be said early in the morning to consecrate the whole day to God before work began.

It was then that in the new Temple, "not made by human hands", which was Christ's Mystical body, they would offer themselves to God, offering him their love "with all their heart, with all their soul, with all their mind and with all their strength" (Mark 12:30). The first Christians may not have been able to visit the Synagogue to renew and reinforce this Morning Offering as Christ did, during their busy days at work, but they could and did pause to do this at the third, the sixth, and the ninth hour as before, as the early sources make quite clear. In many towns it would often be the sound of a drum, a horn or a trumpet used to mark off the main sections of the day that Christians would use to remind themselves to renew their Morning Offering.

In the old Temple it was a physical offering of something precious that was made to God, but in the new Temple it was something even more precious that was offered. Just as Jesus, the New High Priest had offered himself from the moment he was born in a wooden crib to the day he died on a wooden cross, his followers wished to do likewise. Jesus called this a new worship in "spirit and in truth" as it would no longer consist in offering a physical offering to God to represent ourselves, but it would be a spiritual or mystical offering of ourselves, our love and our entire being. We often sign letters, emails, birthday or Christmas cards to friends and even acquaintances using the word "love" with which to sign off. But in doing this we are all too often devaluing a sacred word. To love someone means to go out to them with your whole heart and soul and with your whole being. It means that you would not only be prepared to live for them but to die for them too. Repeating the words of the first commandment again, it means to offer yourself to someone "with all your heart, with all your soul, with all your mind and with all your strength". As only we ourselves can make this offering, we become priests, because nobody else can make it for us. That is why St Peter called the first Christians a royal priesthood (1Peter 2:9), because although they made their offerings themselves, they made it in Christ the King, the only true High Priest through whom alone human offerings could be effectively offered to God like never before.

The offering of ourselves that we make is a "true" and therefore acceptable offering when it is made with a "pure and humble heart". When we learn to thank, praise, adore and glorify him for who he is and for what his love has done for us, then we are learning the meaning of true selfless loving. It is for this reason that God leads us into the Dark Night of the Soul. It is here we are asked to keep giving over and over again until our impure motives, our cupboard loving and our desire to obtain spiritual "goodies" to satisfy our desire for self-satisfaction are purified out of us. This alone is where the same Holy Spirit who conceived Christ in Mary's womb conceives a "humble heart" within us. Now it can be seen how important contemplative prayer is as it is practised in the Dark Night. This is the crèche where Christians born of the Holy Spirit are nurtured by him to become the saints and mystics without which no authentic reform or renewal of the Church can take place. This is why I have tried to develop a brief history of Christian mystical spirituality to show how and why the mystical spirituality that took place within the Mystical Body of Christ in the early Church has been taken away from us in the last few hundred years. It must be resurrected amongst us once more, and without delay.

After making our Morning Offering we must spend the rest of our day transposing what we have expressed in words into actions in the real world in which we live. This real world means doing a hundred and one little things such as dressing the children, making their breakfast and taking them to school. It means doing an honest day's work, often amongst and for dishonest people who hate you for your honesty. It means doing the washing, the shopping, the cooking and working in the garden. It means facing up to big things too, like the loss of your job or the curse of cancer, or some other malicious malady that has been diagnosed, if not in oneself then in others who are dear to you and coping with the consequences. It means standing up for the truth, not just in a pagan world but in the Church too when it loses its way, and even being prepared to die for it, as were the early martyrs. Multiply these examples from your own daily life to see the reality of daily living in a world that is becoming more and more self-centred.

The Morning Offering, together with a brief review of the day ahead, will help you make what might appear to be a series of spiritual stumbling blocks into stepping stones, that with God's help can enable you to surmount the tide of evil that might otherwise engulf you. This sadly is the truth in the world we have been called to transform. This transformation, as St Catherine of Siena insisted, begins with us. The sincere way we make our Morning Offering and the sincere way we try to put it into practice in the day ahead is a perfect beginning. It gradually enables us to learn and practise what came to be called the "prayer without ceasing", as everything we say and do becomes a prayer. It will involve the daily dying to self that we will experience as we try to take up our daily cross and follow Christ. Just as selfishness is porous to evil, the selflessness learned in the Night, becomes porous to the goodness that brings the same joy to us that Christ said he experienced and wanted to share with us.

Instead of a few brief moments at the beginning of the day praying for those we love, whether alive or dead, our prayer for them should correspond with the "prayer without ceasing" as every moment of our day is taken up with turning to God in formal prayer and turning to him in the neighbour in need. We can do the same for those who ask us to pray for them. Instead of just giving them a moment of our time, we give them every moment of our day. In this way they not only benefit from our selfless giving, but from what we receive in return from the God who can use us as a prism to direct his love through us to others. Practising this daily offering to God and dying to self in the Dark Night is so very much harder than before. But no matter what stage you are passing through in your spiritual journey, you must never fail to say your Morning Offering, and if possible short prayers of the heart throughout the day. This will help you to transform your day into the Mass, making it into the place where you continually offer all you say and do to God, in, with and through Jesus Christ Our Lord.

The good news is that those who persevere will travel more swiftly towards the selflessness that leads to union, thanks to the Holy Spirit who guides and supports us. While you are still travelling in darkness, he teaches you how to seek God alone and nothing for yourself, while in moments of light he begins to give you the sublime fruits of contemplation that will enable you to become a Christ-like human being.

Chapter 46

How to Pray in Mystical Contemplation II

All good parents hope their children will be successful at school, at work and in their marriage, living fulfilled and happy lives. This is why they temper their desire to overindulge their children by teaching them how to act selflessly, to become conscious of the needs of others and to share and care for others as they have been cared for. Catholic parents have an advantage as they have the example of Jesus to inspire their children. Teaching them to pray can inspire them to receive his love into their hearts, as they learn about his life on earth before his Resurrection, and how he is alive and loving us now. In this way their hearts can be opened to receive his love, enabling his divine love to suffuse and surcharge their human loving making it possible to generate the only form of selfless loving that can unite them with God. This profound mystical union between divine and human loving is brought to perfection in the Dark Night.

The purification then that takes place in the Dark Night is the only place where self-centred human beings can be transformed into selfless people, reformed through love into the image and likeness of Christ. The reason why so many give up, who were once happy to pray when all was sweetness and light, is because the daily drudgery of learning to be selfless simply grinds them down and there is no one to support them by telling them what is happening and how to continue. I cannot pretend that it is easy because it is not. Everything that is worth attaining demands time and effort and learning to love is the most important lesson of all because our whole life, our whole happiness in this world and the next depends on it.

One of the main problems and great ironies for those who first come to contemplative prayer in the Night is that their heart yearns for God like never before, but they find it all but impossible to pray, at least as they used to. All previous prayer that was successful before has done one thing; it has inspired and fortified the primeval desire for God with no other objective than union with God. The only form of prayer that can now help is a form of prayer that can keep that desire on course and in so doing remain at all times open to God's love. Some months ago I had a rather sad email from a genuine spiritual searcher trying to navigate the mystic way. He said he had read St Teresa of Ávila and St John of the Cross from cover to cover and found no systematic teaching on how to pray in mystical contemplation. Let me make it clear that neither St John of the Cross nor St Teresa of Ávila wrote their works for the general public, but only for their own brothers and sisters in the new reform of the Carmelite Order. Nor did they need to detail how they should pray when they were led into contemplation because the prayer pattern open to them was all part of their monastic way of life.

The Carmelite Order began as an eremitical community of hermits living on Mount Carmel in the Holy Land, hence their name. When they became integrated into the religious life of the Western Church they began to live in communities where they lived their particular interpretation of the monastic life which was signified by wearing the scapula, the insignia of traditional monasticism. They also adopted forms of prayer that were traditionally used by Western monks. I am not only referring to their daily recitation of the divine office, but a practice that naturally flowed out of the Divine Office that would enable them to generate the "prayer without ceasing" throughout their day. Like monks before them, they learned to choose a verse from the liturgy, from a prayer, a psalm or canticle that seemed to them to encapsulate the way in which they were relating to God at the particular point of development in their spiritual journey. They did not need to be told what verse to use as a prayer because it was personal to the spiritual needs of each individual. While reciting, chanting or singing the Divine Office they prayed as one in Christ, but throughout the subsequent day, they prayed individually and differently, as each chose and fashioned their own short prayers from the liturgy, each to their own personal needs.

When my father tried to do this, as we shall see later, he was following the monastic way of trying to practise the prayer without ceasing as taught by Abbot John Cassian. The prayer my father took was from the daily monastic liturgy, "Oh God, come to my aid. Oh Lord, make haste to help me." I am sure he is pleased to know that he has inspired his son to follow his example by using this short prayer, perhaps more than any other, to support him in his daily life. This method of monastic prayer was so taken for granted that it was not thought necessary to teach a person how to pray in any other form of prayer outside the daily liturgy. The Holy Spirit who inspired that liturgy would surely inspire them to choose what they needed each day at every point of need during their spiritual advancement. That explains why we find no detailed explanation from the great Mystical Doctors on how to pray in the Night.

What we have to do is follow their example by choosing for ourselves a short prayer as they did. It can be taken from the liturgy, from the psalms, from the hymnal, the scriptures or from the popular prayers or devotional practices that once helped us so much before. Begin by choosing what can be used as a short prayer; one that somehow sums up how you feel at the time – how you genuinely feel you relate to the God who seems to have taken his leave of you.

Let me explain what I did so that you can do the same, but in your way, to express how you feel. I chose the prayer Jesus himself made upon the Cross, most especially when everything seemed too much for me. "My God, my God, why have you forsaken me?" Or choose the prayer he made in Gethsemane, particularly when temptations come thick and fast. "Father may this chalice be taken away from me." When I felt really in the pits I turned to the *De Profundis*. "Out of the depths I cried to thee, O Lord. Lord, hear my prayer", or the prayer from Cardinal Newman's famous hymn, "Lead, kindly light, amidst the encircling gloom." The Jesus Prayer designed especially for this particular moment of the mystic way is perhaps the best known of all. "Jesus, Son of God, have mercy on me, a sinner."

At moments when I felt touched by the presence of God who seemed absent for so long, I turned to phrases of praise and thanksgiving to express how I felt, but that was not often, at least in the early stages. The important thing is to choose something that genuinely embodies how you feel at the time and what you feel you most need from God to help you. It is no good pretending with God. He knows exactly how you feel so it is no good trying to soft-soap him. What is important to remember is that these short prayers are used to keep helping you turn back to God from the distractions that would turn you away from him, while at the same time helping you to remain open to receive his love in return, that comes in his way and in his time.

Please do not feel you have to choose what appealed to me. Choose short prayers that you feel appeal to you, but use them in the way I suggest, to help you to keep acting selflessly, keep repenting, keep turning and opening yourself to receive the only love that can lead you from Paradise lost to Paradise regained. A regrettable and unforeseen consequence of clear systematic teaching on the practicalities of how to pray in contemplative prayer is plaguing the contemporary Church. Huge numbers of good serious-minded people have been led to believe that the endless repetition of a word or a mantra can lead them into the sort of mystical prayer described by St Teresa of Ávila. This is totally false. *My Soul Thirsts*, a document issued by the Spanish Bishops in 2019 rejecting mindfulness and other eastern meditation techniques makes this abundantly clear. In the contemporary "Me-Me" society that demands instant self-satisfaction, it is easy to see why the promise of instant mystical experience seems irresistible. The very essence of all authentic Christian prayer is that we continually try to raise our hearts and minds to God in acts of selflessness, and not in seeking instant self-satisfaction in the way of inner peace or mindfulness.

When St Peter was asked how to receive the outpouring of God's love on the first Pentecost he answered, "repent," just as Our Lady keeps asking us to keep repenting in prayer. For it is here alone that our acts of love enable us to receive God's love in return. The first commandment is to love God with all our heart, with all our soul, and with all our mind. Love has to be learned and prayer is the place where this is achieved through the practice of selfless giving that opens us to the only love that can make us new.

Chapter 47

How to Pray in Mystical Contemplation III

Two months after my brother died, my sister-in-law said what she missed most was simply walking with him, hand in hand in the countryside without speaking a word. There were times when they expressed their feelings for one another in short expressions of love, but the time comes when all you need is to be together in silence to savour the love that binds you together. A similar development takes place in divine love. When we meditate and reflect on what Christ has and is doing for us now, it leads to heartfelt expressions of love, often filled with feeling and emotion and sometimes even tears. However, the time comes when words fade away leading to silence which some spiritual writers have called the Prayer of Simplicity or the Prayer of Simple Regard. At this point in our spiritual development, our desire to love God has been so clearly manifested that God leads us on into a deeper and more testing spiritual environment where our love can be more perfectly refined. We are therefore led into the Dark Night when all the feeling and fervour that sometimes accompanied our previous prayer is taken away and we are asked to go on loving without seeming to receive anything in return.

If we persevere, our love can be sufficiently purified to enable us, in years rather than months, to come to experience something of God's glory that is our final destiny. When we pray in the Night, however, we are not praying to Christ who felt so close to us before, but now we are actually praying in him, with him and through him to the Father in mystical contemplation. It takes some time to realize that far from having left us we are actually in him, praying to God himself for whom we now yearn like never before. However, because it will take time practising selfless giving before we can be sufficiently purified to experience something of his love, we feel all alone in a spiritual desert and the first form of prayer that begins to rise to God is not full of feeling as before. It is, in fact, full of expressions of our need for God's help in the sorry plight which we now feel envelops us. That is why, when I found myself in this predicament I began to pray, pleading for help, "My God, My God, why have you forsaken me?" My mother's favourite short prayer was "Jesus mercy, Mary help". What I found, and what you will find, is that in time the full sentence used to express your inner desire for God or for his help will be too long. You will feel the need to reduce it to say simply, "My God, my God", or "Out of the depths", or "Lead, kindly light", or "Have mercy on me, a sinner". Then the time will come when a single word will be all you need, like "God", or "God help me", or "mercy". The great Abbot Macarius is thought to have been the author of the Jesus Prayer before it was written down by St John Climacus in the form that we have come to know it today. Abbot Macarius used to teach his disciples simply to call out "Jesus" or "Lord to the rescue", or simply "to the rescue", or to use St Peter's prayer, "Lord, save me" (Matthew 14:30). The author of the *Cloud of Unknowing* suggested that if you are drowning and you come up for breath, you do not waste time on many words, you just cry out, "help" or, "Jesus help me". I cannot give you rules when to change down from many words to few. You will know for yourself.

It is like changing gears in a car; once you become familiar with them, you know automatically when to change down. Some people like to count the words or the phrases on their rosary beads. My mother found this helpful, as do I. It is not essential, but if it helps to keep gently fixing your gaze on God in the darkness, that is all that matters. These suggestions will help you to practise the prayer of the heart, or what many prefer to call the "prayer of faith" because there is little feeling in it. It is here that repentance is learned better than anywhere else. This repentance of heart that is practised in the darkness is worth ten times that practised in the light. It is easy to pray when the well is full and brimming over, but far more difficult to pray when the well runs dry. This is why it is of paramount importance to give exactly the same time to prayer that you gave when prayer was full of feeling and fervour. And it is in this way that you show by the very consistency of the daily time you give to prayer that you are there for God alone and not for what you receive. Then, as you pray, day in day out, year in year out, you will so demonstrate your unconditional love for God alone that your love will be purified, enabling you to come to know and experience something of the breadth and length, height and depth of God's love that St Paul said surpasses the understanding.

If you continue persevering in prayer, come what may, the subtle magnetic force of God's love becomes stronger. Then, as this process continues and you feel you are going nowhere, a welcome change takes place. When your purification has been sufficiently advanced you are able to experience the love of the Holy Spirit enveloping you ever more deeply as St Teresa of Ávila explains in her masterwork *Interior Castle*. As this experience deepens and heightens you are left with no doubt that you are experiencing the love of God. Then suddenly your prayer changes. It is no longer inspired by anguish, but joy. Short acts of love, thanksgiving, praise and adoration fan the sparks of love into a flame that wishes only to give glory to God for being God, before pausing in moments of pregnant awe-filled silence to relish the love you are receiving. All you wish now is to remain still and gaze in awe upon the One whom you feel drawing you onward into the peace that surpasses the understanding.

All these short acts of love are like the oars on a boat that you use to guide it downriver towards the sea. At first, you have to keep rowing to get the boat moving forward towards its destination, but when the momentum has been built up you can sit back and rest for a while as it moves silently forward. The moment the boat starts to slow down, drifts towards the bank or is caught in tidal currents, you have to start rowing again to keep it moving in the right direction. And so you keep journeying on, at one moment rowing to keep the boat on course, at another resting, enjoying the beauty of the surrounding countryside. As you approach the sea you need to row less and less as you experience the pull of the tide drawing you onwards. Once you have left the river you can put aside the oars and set up the sails. Now you can travel with ease and with speed, with the tide on your side and the wind in your sails. Another power takes over to do for you what you could never do for yourself.

All this takes place in that part of the Dark Night of the Soul that St John of the Cross calls the Dark Night of the Senses, where it is predominantly our senses that are purified. However, another Night is on the way which the traveller will find far more testing. It is important to note that when this second Night, called the Dark Night of the Spirit commences, the Dark Night of the Senses continues. They operate simultaneously, as I have already explained. In the Dark Night of the Spirit which involves the purification deepening to the foundations of our inner spirit, our deep pride and prejudices have all to be purified away before the new person can emerge.

Towards the end of the Dark Night of the Senses, our purification so far enables us to experience moments of joy as we encounter brief moments when something of God's glory seems to reach out to touch us. But we can be deceived into believing that we are on the threshold of the Mystical Marriage when the union that we desire more than anything else takes place. However, before this can happen a far deeper mystical purification must finish its course so that mystical union can be consummated. The analogy of the little boat that has hoisted its sail and seems to be sailing with so much ease towards its destination can be deceptive, as any seasoned sailor would warn you. At any moment the wind can drop and the sails can be useless as the boat finds itself adrift in the doldrums. Then dangerous cross-currents can threaten to set the boat off course permanently. Sadly that is not all; at any moment terrible gales, storms, and hurricanes can suddenly erupt, threatening disaster. However, for those who persevere, they will eventually pass through them all and it will be a well-seasoned and wise sailor who will steer the boat into harbour.

In the spiritual life, the traveller will arrive safely because it is the Holy Spirit himself who is at all times at the helm. These terrible storms symbolize the powerful and painful purification that will finally destroy all the evil impulses, inclinations, prejudices and perverted pride that separate us from union with the perfect man who will lead us into the mystical marriage.

Chapter 48

How to Pray in Mystical Contemplation IV

When going through a particularly testing period in my own spiritual journey some years ago, I could find no one to help or explain what was happening. How was I to continue in what I later found was called the Dark Night of the Spirit by St John of the Cross? I prayed continually to God for help and the help came from a most unlikely quarter. Tired and exhausted both mentally and spiritually, I found myself watching a "Western". The fort was surrounded by enemy forces and it only seemed a matter of time before the enemy would break in and slaughter the inhabitants. There was only one hope. A messenger was sent to pass through enemy lines at dead of night for reinforcements. Just when all seemed lost the trumpet sounded and the cavalry arrived. The messenger made it through, reinforcements came and the fort and all its inhabitants were saved.

Suddenly I saw my predicament more clearly than ever before. I saw what must be done with such simplicity. When we are in the Dark Night, when we find ourselves in a spiritual wilderness and all hell seems to have been let loose within us, there is only one thing to do. That deep primordial desire for God that is deepest within us must become the messenger to raise the siege. We are besieged by all the animal instincts, urges and drives that rule us from within. We may be rational animals, but from time immemorial history has shown that unaided human reason is incapable of reining in the powers of evil that hold us captive. Only one thing and one thing alone can save us and that is love, the love implanted deep down within us by God when he created us by his love in his own image and likeness. We cannot possibly defeat the powers of evil that hold us in its thrall. They surround us, just as they surround others, just as they surround the Church to which we belong and the world into which we have been born. History is the story of what this evil has done to the human race and will continue to do unless help is sought.

Our predicament can now be seen in its stark simplicity. We cannot possibly overcome the powers of evil in ourselves, never mind in others, let alone in the world in which we live. Only one thing can help us and that is reinforcements. A messenger has to be sent. Fortunately the messenger is deep down within us. It is the deep-down primeval desire for the fullness of love that ultimately resides in God. The sort of prayer I have been describing has one purpose and one purpose alone; to help support and guide our weak human love through the forbidding powers of evil. These powers rise from our lower selves which seem to have formed a dark threatening cloud to contain and rule us and prevent all forms of escape.

Our prayer, albeit in darkness that at first seems purposeless and futile, is our only hope, for the messenger must get through; love must pierce through the dark clouds that seem to incarcerate us. If we try any other way we will be doomed to failure and may be destroyed in the process of trying to do what only God can do with the reinforcements that only he can bring. Eventually, after many months or rather many years of practising selfless giving in prayer, our purified loving eventually gets through. It has been so purified that it reaches out and into God where our weak human loving is transformed by his. Now our love becomes like the lightning rod that directs the love of God down to raise the siege. Now and only now can the powers of evil be confronted and confounded. As Jesus said to Martha, only one thing is necessary and that one thing is love. This is the only power that we possess that if purified and refined can be united with the only love that can transform us and make us new.

It can now be seen how ultimately the spiritual life is so simple, although I do not say easy. It is so simple that the most unlettered among us can both see and live it. This is not the wishy-washy, here-today-gone-tomorrow sort of love the world thinks is the real thing. This is the love that is learned in years by endlessly giving without receiving. This is the true love that can alone change us on earth and prepare us for the fulness of love in heaven. The sadness is that all too often many scholars spend their lives in abstract theological thought and speculation and so are blinded by multiplicity from seeing with the simplicity that characterizes the teaching of Jesus. All too often, instead of seeing the simple truth they only complicate it, and far from guiding the faithful they bamboozle them and even mislead them with the latest fashionable falsehoods. The history of spirituality shows time and time again that God hides his most profound truths revealing them only to the simple and humble of heart. "I bless you, Father, Lord of heaven and earth, for hiding these things from the learned and the clever and revealing them to mere children" (Matthew 11:25).

When in the aftermath of Quietism the mystical theology that emphasized the ever-presence of God's love and how our love can be purified to receive it, fell into abeyance, a new devotion came to the rescue. It was thanks to the revelations given to St Margaret Mary that a new popular devotion began to represent not just Christ as he was, but as he is now, with a glorified body bursting with uncreated love. The Sacred Heart is the same as the Pantocrator, but now he does not appear as distant, for he rules with all the human love that filled Jesus whilst he was on earth but transformed by what became of him in heaven. When a new brand of theologians were beguiled by what came to be called the "New Biblical Theology", many quasi-intellectuals like me were guilty of throwing the baby out with the bathwater. Many ancient and proven Catholic devotions like devotion to the Sacred Heart were disdained if not discarded. This was a scandal. After all, who is the Sacred Heart but Our Risen Lord burning with love for us, presented in a way that all can be inspired and revitalized by his love? The Sacred Heart is not just incarnate love but incarnate loving, who will transform all who open their hearts to receive him.

If devotion to the Sacred Heart has at times been trivialized by bad taste in the cult surrounding it, and the art used to promote it, it should nevertheless not be forgotten as it proclaims a profound truth, the central truth of our faith. Jesus is not dead, he has risen and is alive now, bursting with uncreated life and love that pours out of his heart relentlessly and into the hearts of all who would receive him. For two centuries this devotion counteracted the damage done to a Catholic spirituality shorn of mystical theology. It also helped to counteract a form of "Catholic Calvinism" or Jansenism that grew up and spread from France with its narrow-minded "kill-joy" moralism. The Sacred Heart proclaims the love of the Risen Christ in a way that even the simplest can understand. No one should allow their artistic sensibilities to prevent them from appreciating this profound truth that was revealed in a unique way to St Margaret Mary. I am quite clear in my own mind that these revelations represented God's divine intervention to set before everyone in the clearest possible way the reality that his love is always with us, ever present to those with hearts open to receive it. If there is no statue to the Sacred Heart in the church to remind us of his loving presence, then the sanctuary lamp is there to remind us too.

When I was a young teenager I was a rosary crusader in my first fervour, not only dedicated to spreading the rosary that Our Lady of Fatima asked us to say, but something else. We wanted to lobby all parish priests to ensure that the sanctuary lamp was enclosed in a container of rich red glass to symbolize the fire of God's love bursting out of his Son present in the tabernacle. That this love is ever present to us is of no doubt. That is not in question. The question is, what are we doing to receive it? We have sadly been doing so little and that is why in the past two centuries Our Lady has appeared time and again with one and the same message. The message is to repent and pray and in particular say the rosary. It is only by praying and in the act of praying that repentance is practised. For it is only by daily turning away from self-absorption that we can become absorbed in the love of God that is continually poured out upon us by his son, Jesus Christ. God continually loves us and that is why he continually remains with us. But if we continually refuse to listen to Our Lady, that love can do nothing for us or for the Church which is in such desperate need.

Lord, that we may see. Lord, that we may hear. Lord, that we may rise again from the dead, that your kingdom of love may come in us and through us into your ailing Church.

Chapter 49

God's Holy Angel

The Jewish religion began with God-given love and divine revelations and became a religion of man-made laws and human regulations by the time of Christ's coming. The love that Christ had for his own beloved people can be measured by the forceful way he attacked those who had misled them. There were over six hundred rules and regulations determining everything that a person said and did. The extra exertion of riding a donkey astraddle was forbidden on the sabbath, but sitting side-saddle was allowed. Eating bread baked on the Sabbath, and an egg if the hen transgressed by thoughtlessly laying it on that same day, was another of the petty strictures and restrictions that plagued daily life. With what Jesus called the "one thing necessary" forgotten, love was lost to sight. The love of Jesus that would reverse and renew everything was poured out on the first Pentecost Day, onto and into all who were prepared to receive it. Although this love would endlessly be poured out to the end of time, St Peter said that only those who, after being baptised, chose to repent and repent continually, could receive it. In Aramaic, the language in which St Peter was speaking, there was no word for a person who has repented but only for a person who is *repenting*. If you are repenting you are continually open to receive the Love of the Holy Spirit. But if you are not, then you are not receiving him and are therefore only a nominal Christian.

Spiritual Theology teaches us how to receive the Holy Spirit. We learn how to repent, relentlessly turning and opening our hearts and minds to God, firstly through the way we practise selfless acts of love inside of prayer, and secondly by the way we practise selfless giving in all we say and do outside of prayer. Although we may know in a superficial sort of way that we are afflicted by pride, envy, gluttony, lust, anger, greed, sloth and other evil desires and urges, few know that the source of these powerful drives are to be found deep down in our unconscious mind. Unless they are rooted out, we will never be able to repent successfully, enabling us to raise our hearts and minds to receive the fullness of God's love, because these base drives continually drag us down to earth.

Mystical Theology is that branch of Spiritual Theology that teaches us how to continue to try to love God when we are led into the Dark Night of the Soul, our purgatory on earth. When we persevere, we enable his love to destroy the roots of evil in us at the source. When mystical theology was no longer generally taught or practised after the condemnation of Quietism, Catholic Spirituality only generally survived on a fairly superficial level. That is, in comparison with the hundred or so years after the Council of Trent when, according to Monsignor Ronald Knox, Garrigou Lagrange OP, Adolphe Tanquerey, and Henri Bremond, Mystical Theology was both taught and practised on an unprecedented scale. For without the theology that teaches how to enable God's love to destroy the seven deadly sins at source, they will continue to rule us. Precepts and laws, rules and regulations may try to contain the effects of evil but they can do nothing to destroy it.

Aristotle defined man as a rational animal, but until our reason is ruled by love it will regularly be deceived by the powers of evil from within, making truth extremely elusive. At the Reformation, everyone was told to read the Bible and use their own reason to interpret it for themselves, and anarchy inevitably ensued. Scores of different religions were founded as different interpretations prevailed and hundreds of misunderstandings of the truth caused further anarchy within each different denomination, down to the present day. As a cynic once put it, a Protestant, Bible in hand is his own Pope. Their reason was sadly at the mercy of the ingrained pride and prejudices that influenced them from within.

The same thing happened at the Enlightenment. It arose at the beginning of the eighteenth century to proclaim the primacy of reason at almost the same time that Mystical Theology, proclaiming the primacy of love, was being systematically dismantled. For the next four centuries, the most intelligent of men and women in every branch of human learning would believe they were dispassionately guided by reason. However, it was not only their intellectual findings that were adversely affected by the evil forces but also their moral lives. In his sonnet "Batter my Heart" the metaphysical poet John Donne put it this way:

Reason, your viceroy in me, me should defend,
But is captiv'd and proves weak or untrue.
Yet dearly I love you, and would be lov'd fain,
But am betroth'd unto your enemy;
Divorce me, untie or break that knot again,
Take me to you, imprison me, for I,
Except you enthrall me, never shall be free,
Nor ever chaste, except you ravish me.

It is only love, not ours but God's love, the Holy Spirit, who can free the reason from all the malignant influences that corrupt it from deep in the unconscious. The spectacle of arrogant human beings proclaiming their version of the truth can be laughable, a "Divine Comedy", but such pride and prejudice has wreaked havoc throughout human history and is anything but a joke. When I was young I looked up to the great and the good who governed us, looked after us, policed us, judged us and made all the important decisions for us with unquestioning equanimity. However, the older I become the more I am horrified that so many of my elders and betters, no matter how intellectually brilliant they may be, and with the best of intentions, are as influenced as I am by the demons that dwell in the nether regions of our personalities. Climbing the ladder of secular success without any attempt at climbing the ladder of spiritual perfection, can influence not just our moral lives but our professional decisions too. We can become so accomplished at covering our failures, with our peers quick to defend us, that we become assurance for each other when caught out, and so become invulnerable to justice.

A Nobel prize-winning geneticist recently said that although humankind has made massive intellectual and technical strides in the last three thousand years he could see no evidence of any noticeable emotional and moral progress. If you think this is pure hyperbole you have not been listening to the world news in recent years! When we look at the naked, battered and bleeding body of Jesus on the Cross, we are looking at what unrestrained evil can do that lurks deep in every unpurified human being. What was done to him will always be done by the powers of evil from within to other individuals, peoples, races and nations whenever allowed to express itself without restraint. The evil that we read about in our newspapers, hear on our radios or see on our television screens is but the outward projection on a global scale of the unconquered evil that resides within us all. That is why St Catherine of Siena said, "The trouble with the world is me." There is only one way that we can participate in the annihilation of the evil that is within us all. A messenger must be sent to take with him the offering of our selfless loving, making it possible for the fullness of love that resides in God to come and destroy the evil that resides in us.

In Aramaic and Hebrew a divine messenger is called an Angel. In the third Eucharistic prayer that I loved so much, it is God's own Holy Angel who takes the offering of our self-sacrifices to God, so that in return we may be filled with the only love that can drive out and destroy the evil that resides and rules us from within. If other Angels have been given different tasks, only God's Holy Angel, Christ himself, whose divine love can mix, mingle and merge with our weak human love, can enable our self-offerings to be received by God, because they are offered in, with and through him. No other Angel can do this. This enables God's redeeming Angel to return again and again with the only love that can vanquish the evil that rules us from within.

Sigmund Freud detailed the unholy drives, impulses, and urges within that can enthrall our reason, in what he called the unconscious. It is only Christ and his love descending into the hell that is within us who can wipe out the evil and replace it with the love that comes from heaven. Nevertheless, when the irresistible force of God's love strikes the immovable object of a human heart captivated by evil, it takes time, a long time, even for God's love to do what is only possible to divine love. What to do, how to act and how to progress is contained in the teaching of Mystical Theology and that is why it is so important.

Baptism may well call us all into Christ's Mystical Body, but we cannot be fully united with his glorified body until what St Paul called the Old Man is put to death. When this is completed, then we can be completely united with the New Man, the Risen and Glorified Christ. Then in, with and through him, we can be united for ever with the ultimate glory that radiates to eternity from the Three in One.

Chapter 50

Death to the Demons Within

In *As You like it*, Shakespeare said that all the world is a stage and the men and women merely players, each playing their part. Their parts are rather stereotypical and superficial, but in his other plays like *Hamlet* or *Macbeth* you see murkier parts that his characters play. They mirror the real world in which he lived and in which we live today. Although they pose and posture to deceive others, they are influenced by deep desires and urges that come from below stage in the unconscious. Sometimes something suddenly triggers the stage trapdoor and all hell is let loose, at least for a time, as unholy desires and urges flood the minds of the unsuspecting. What is often called a Freudian slip happens to us all, as has happened to me, flooding my conscious mind, exposing irrational prejudices and thoughts that shamed me. I have come to realize that there must be many other pernicious prejudices lurking deep within me. Whether we like it or not they all influence us although we hardly realize it and would be humiliated to admit it. I sometimes smile to hear the politically correct holding forth, blissfully unaware of what rules them from within.

There are within all of us who are not immaculately conceived, innumerable drives and urges that if allowed to rule would destroy us, like sensual and sexual desires, the yearning for power and position, and myriad other desires and urges. If these desires are gratified, they only want further satisfaction until greed and rapaciousness destroy us, or anger and jealousy eat away at us as we try to destroy others who seem to have what we want. If we are not consciously and daily engaged in the spiritual combat that calls upon us to act selflessly, then we will be unable to admit the New Man which is Christ so that he can do to death the Old Man which is ourselves. Christ was conceived by the Holy Spirit and therefore did not experience evil from within. But he did experience evil in others, pitted against him throughout his life on earth which finally succeeded in his being condemned and tortured to death. When the love that raised him from the dead was unleashed on the first Pentecost, it meant that we could be drawn up into his mystical body where our weak human love can be strengthened and fortified to rise with his. Only the ever-increasing inflow of love with which he returns from the Father can transform our hearts. We are transformed to the measure of our daily self-sacrificial living and self-giving as we persevere most particularly in the Dark Night of purification. The example of Christ should be sufficient to alert us, that in addition to the spiritual combat within there is another conflict that we will have to face from outside.

Even the most conservative of commentators are warning us, and with good reason, that we are at present facing an unprecedented upsurge of evil both inside and outside the Church. There may well have been such wicked and even devilish manifestations of evil before in the world, but now we have to face them from within the Church and even from those to whom we should look for inspiration and guidance. It is because many other orthodox writers are revealing what I can only describe as satanic evils that are arising in the Church, that I can instead concentrate on detailing how Christ wishes to destroy them and their perpetrators through those who would receive him. What Freud has called "unruly and irrational impulses" the Desert Fathers called the "monsters in the deep" or the "demons within", that can possess those who do nothing to contain them. The love that has been leaking from Catholic Spirituality for several centuries is now finding rock bottom in large groups of powerful clerics, religious, and some laity, who are demanding sacramental status for unworthy and unscriptural forms of so-called love that they practise. They are almost a religion within a religion, frighteningly militant, and as the desires and urges that rule them are irrational it is impossible to confront them with rational argument.

Because Scientology teaches so much irrational nonsense, its adherents are told never to engage in rational debate with those who oppose them. Instead, they are told to attack viciously and personally, looking for weaknesses to psychologically undermine them. You will find the same with the new quasi-sexual religion that is trying to insinuate its erroneous teachings and practices into the Church. They cannot argue against the truth for the teaching of the Church has been against them from the very beginning. Their main weapons are stealth, or when they are discovered, they shout down opponents and anyone who would oppose them. They relentlessly attack personally and do all in their power to undermine credibility. This brings me to the most heinous heresy of all that is already on the rise although it is only spoken of in whispers and behind closed doors. It is the return of Arianism. If their teachings are to prevail, they will have to denigrate their main opponents, and then Christ himself, for he is their main opponent.

If Christ's teachings are no longer relevant today and must be adapted to the norms of our times then how can his teaching be divinely inspired? If, like Arius, they argue that Christ is not actually divine, although he is the greatest man to have lived who has said and done so much as the founder of our Church, then suddenly the way is open for the Church to be undermined from the inside. With reason on their side, they could argue that Jesus was ultimately only a man, and therefore his teaching for the ancient world was only human. It may well have been right for the ancient world, but they believe that if he had been alive today, he would be pursuing exactly the same agendas that they themselves are pursuing. For they believe that they are accurately "reading the signs of our times" and discerning the needs of the "modern world". The truth of the matter is that they are, in fact, trying to introduce into the modern Church amongst other things, sexual agendas that cannot be reconciled either by the teaching of Our Divine Lord, the sacred scriptures and the perennial Catholic tradition. In the vanguard of the coming storm it should already be noticed that Christ will be mentioned less and less and Catholic Spirituality and traditional devotions hardly at all. If you think that I am writing to shock you then you are absolutely right. The barbarians are once more "at the gates" and there is no time to lose. So many of us have been sleeping; it is time for the "wild geese" to awaken us or we will fail to see the steady downward slope down which a new breed of misguided clerics and prelates have been trying to lead the unwary.

There is only one solution and that is not yet another orthodox theology we already have, it is a person. The person is Jesus Christ Our Lord to whom we must totally abandon ourselves or we will be lost. I have continually emphasized that we all have within us a profound primeval desire or yearning to love and to be loved. This yearning arises from the love of God, implanted within us from the beginning when we were made in his image and likeness. It is an infinite yearning for it can only be satisfied by God's infinite love. Christ came to tell us of this plan, which St Paul called the *Mysterion*. That this plan be realized for us all, Christ released love without measure on the first Pentecost. Those who continually try to turn and open their hearts to receive this love are called mystics because at baptism they are drawn up into Christ's Mystical Body. But that is not all. His mystical body is not some vague, inert ethereal reality, but a living breathing supernatural person who is endlessly caught up in an otherworldly act of loving contemplation of the glory of God the Father. It is into this, his sublime, transforming mystical action that we are called to join him, by learning to love as he did so that our loving begins to synchronize with his loving. It is this that enables us to make the offering of our lives as he made the offering of his life, and then to receive the fruits of contemplation in return as he received them.

All the various ways and means of prayer that I have been writing about have been to do one thing; to raise our hearts to God in unison with the heart of Christ. In order that our prayer be ultimately successful, when it has sufficiently shown its genuine desire for God and God alone, a change takes place and we are led into purgatory on earth into the Dark Night of the Soul. This is the penultimate point in our journey into God. But by penultimate, I do not mean that the end is near because it is not. However, it is the place where our hearts are gradually purified from the influence of the "demons" in our subterranean self, to be united, not just with Christ's mystical body, but with his glorified body and his Sacred Heart as it lovingly contemplates the glory to which God has called us from the beginning. The ultimate destruction of the evil propensities that have for so long ruled our lives, is the final object of our mystical purification.

With Christ's help, our hearts are able to receive love in ever greater measure. Like a radioactive laser, this love gradually purifies and refines the mind, the intellect, the understanding, the reasoning as well as the memory and the imagination, all of which have been corrupted by the evil and irrational drives and urges that ruled us before. Now, towards the end of the Night, the mind becomes clearer to see what could not be seen before, and the feelings that were dormant for so long in the darkness are once more aroused. The Spiritual Betrothals can now take place. The longer these betrothals last, the more the mind with all its operations and the feelings with all their sensible warmth and tenderness can once more open and operate, but this time without the demons that perverted them before. The Mystical Marriage is on the horizon; the most perfect union possible in this life that mirrors albeit darkly, the perfect and everlasting marriage with God in the next life, where God's kingdom of love, of justice and peace reigns supreme.

Chapter 51

The Fruits of Contemplation – The Infused Virtues

Conventional wisdom tells us that geniuses are born. However, the Catholic metaphysical poet Francis Thompson, said there is an exception to this rule. He insists that at the moment of rebirth at baptism, the genius of God is implanted in the very depth of our being. It is his genius, the Holy Spirit who supports, sustains and keeps our hearts centred on God. In this way our love, strengthened and fortified with his begins to rise, piercing through the evil that surrounds us, opening up a mystical passageway. It is through this passageway that our augmented love rises to God, enabling his infinite loving to descend into us.

In God's time, not ours, his love prepares us for the fullest possible union with him that finally satisfies the profound primeval desire for love that he planted within us from the beginning. The love that previously set our superficial selves on fire is directed to the very centre of our human heart. This is the beginning of a profound purification in which all other impure, wayward and self-serving loves that have ruled us before are defeated and destroyed at source. This purification takes place in the Dark Night where we see what ruled us before as it is being rooted out. It is painful and humiliating, but it does two necessary things before the fullness of love can be received: it creates within us a humble heart and a pure heart, both of which are necessary to receive the infusion of God's love, his Holy Spirit.

The outpouring of the Holy Spirit can only be received by continually turning to receive it, as St Peter insisted on the first Pentecost day. This process may begin on a fairly superficial level, but for those who keep selflessly turning day in day out, the act of turning away from the evil world around and within them deepens. It now involves turning to God with every fibre of our inner being when the forces of evil within us are bent on turning us to their will to seek the object of their desires and their satisfaction. Gradually the battleground moves from the surface of our lives to the depth, where carrying our daily Cross involves endlessly turning away from the evil that is within us. White martyrdom now necessitates the deep repentance of heart that involves trying to keep our heart turned to and fixed on God in mystical contemplation, when at times it feels as if all hell is trying to stop it. This does not involve months but years, trying to act selflessly before the love that we desire begins to make itself present. This is what true practical Christianity involves. G. K. Chesterton said that "Christianity has not been tried and found wanting; it has been found difficult and left untried."

As our continual repentance enables us to become ever more sensitive and docile to the love of God, then that love makes our heart ever purer, ever humbler. It is then that our heart becomes like a spiritual prism that on receiving the pure love of God's Holy Spirit, refracts and reflects it. It does this in such a way that it infiltrates every part of our human being. Then it becomes visible in human acting, as all the virtues and gifts of the Holy Spirit that are one in God become many in man, the new man recreated more fully than before in the image and likeness of the perfect man, Jesus Christ.

A Christian without the virtues is like an athlete without muscles, looking the part but achieving nothing. Human wisdom enables us to see through the mind with the intellect, but it is one-dimensional, flat and instructive and can set us on the "way" with knowledge. Infused wisdom enables us to see through the heart, with spiritual insight. It is three-dimensional, alive, inspiring and sets us on the "way" with love. The first is only open to the few with brilliant minds, the second for all with loving hearts. Human wisdom can easily be subverted with error, infused wisdom never. While those with purely intellectual knowledge remain silent when errors are smuggled into the Church by stealth, those with infused wisdom speak out and are prepared to die for the truth, because they are infused with the virtue of Fortitude. Infused virtues never come alone but always together with the whole spectrum of God-given virtues because they come through the love that is received in prayer.

A spirituality that sees the acquisition of the virtues without the mystical death to self is just humanism in modern dress. Yet sadly, since the demise of mystical theology, this modern humanism has been taught to the young as the ideal in both schools and in many seminaries, religious Orders and houses of study, as if the infused virtues can be acquired by human endeavour alone.

St Francis of Assisi is adamant that no one can attain any of the God-given or infused virtues unless we undergo the profound mystical death that I have been detailing.

> All holy virtues, God keep you, God, from whom you all proceed and come. In all the world, there is no one who can possess any one of you without first dying to self. (The Praises of the Virtues, Saint Francis of Assisi)

Daily dying to self is the very essence of the journey in the mystic way that leads to the sustained contemplation through which all the infused virtues are received. Julian of Norwich makes this point so clearly when she uses the example of Our Lady gazing upon God in profound mystical contemplation.

> The greatness and the nobility of this contemplation of God filled her full of reverent awe, and with this she saw herself so small and so humble, so simple and so poor in comparison with her Lord God, that this reverent awe filled her with humility. And so, founded on this humility she was filled

with grace and with every kind of virtue. (Revelations of Divine Love – Long text chapter 7)

What happened to Mary happens to all who through dying to self are eventually led into mystical contemplation with her, in her Son, our Divine Lord. This divine loving, which is the Holy Spirit, draws us not only into the life of the risen Christ, but also into his action, into his unending loving of his Father. We cannot see the profound mystical prayer that enables God to enter our human being, but what can be seen are the virtues that are generated as God's love enters human action. That is why Jesus said, "You will be able to tell them by their fruits" (Matthew 7:16), and most especially as Jesus insisted at the Last Supper, "By this love you have for one another, everyone will know you are my disciples" (John 13:35).

As the stoics continually failed to practise the virtues they preached to others, and as paganism seemed ever more superficial and senseless, the ancient world turned elsewhere. It turned to Christianity because it could be seen how Christians lived the love they preached, animating and inspiring everything they said and did. They saw not just an obscure teaching, but in their action, the fruits of the contemplation in which they died to self to live for God and for his Kingdom of Love, Justice and Peace. What they came to call the "prayer without ceasing" was nothing other than the continual practice of turning to God directly in prayer and indirectly outside of prayer by turning to him in the neighbour in need. "In so far as you did this to one of the least of these brothers of mine, you did it to me" (Matthew 25:40). This was the offering they made together at their weekly Mass that summed up their whole lives and made their whole lives into the Mass.

This means that at all times they were open to receive the genius of God, the Holy Spirit, who made them into the living likeness and image of the greatest loving Genius who ever lived.

Early Christianity was full of spiritual geniuses who they referred to as the "saints". These saints become so sensitive, docile and open to God, that he implants into them his own DNA, namely the Holy Spirit, who inspires and animates them with the same love that animated Jesus and embodies in them the same virtues and spiritual gifts that animated him. It is precisely because God has implanted into all of us the profound and deep desire for infinite love, that anyone can become the genius that love can make of us. Only those with hearts of stone are excluded. However, even these hearts can be melted to be remade and remoulded by the love that is open to all who are radically prepared to abandon all else for the pearl of great price, the treasure hidden in the field. The conversion of the ancient pagan world to Christianity in such a short time still baffles historians who only have reason for their guide. It was brought about by spiritual geniuses, or saints, transformed by the same love that raised their Risen Lord from the dead. What was done then can be done now through those who persevere in the profound mystical contemplation that creates pure and humble hearts to receive the love that is endlessly pouring out of the heart of Christ, remaking us into his image and likeness.

Chapter 52

Renewal and Family Love

Anyone who has known moments of intense joy will know that these experiences would be diminished if they could not be shared with another. Surely this is why God created other beings to receive and return his love, to know and experience true joy on earth and the fullness of happiness in the world to come. This is why he created both male and female, to bring to birth others who would enjoy forever the happiness of loving and being loved by God for all eternity. The very fact that in doing this would not add a single jot or iota to his own happiness makes God's plan all the more incredible, and all the more adorable.

Whenever I am invited to a wedding I wonder whether the couple are aware of the privilege that God has bestowed upon them. Their mutual loving binds them more deeply to each other, but also to God who has destined them to generate new beings. Their children will not only populate the world but heaven too, where they are destined to experience the ever-expanding ecstatic bliss of contemplating the infinite glory of God to eternity. I wonder if they are aware of their responsibility to help prepare their children for this otherworldly destiny, most of all by bestowing on them their mutual love. It is this above all else that they are called to deepen and enrich with each passing day. I find it awe-inspiring to realize that God's breathtaking plan to share his glory with others depends on the love of ordinary mortal men and women, stained by original sin yet called to this sublime Sacrament of Love. Without their cooperation, God's plan could not be brought to completion.

It was not just accidental that Christ's first miracle was performed at Cana in Galilee, nor was it accidental that the wine ran out. This was the necessary precursor for what followed. St

John did not refer to what happens next as a miracle, but rather as a sign. In fact, he calls all his miracles signs, for what they signify is far more important than the miracle itself. The miracles happened at particular moments in history, but their significance is for all time. The miracle of the feeding of the five thousand would be a sign that he would feed many myriad millions more with his own body and blood. The miracles of raising Lazarus from the dead would be a sign that he would raise all from the dead who believed in him, and the miracle of giving sight to the man born blind, that he would give spiritual sight to those in need of his wisdom.

In the same way, the miracle at Cana signified that married love would become a sign that natural human loving would in the future, become supernatural loving. The water of human love would, by virtue of the Sacrament of Marriage, be surcharged with the wine of Christ's own life and love. They would not only receive this love on their wedding day but every day, enabling their weak human love to be permeated by the divine. As the ministers of holy matrimony, the couple who are wed transmit not just their own human love to one another, but Christ's own love, the love of the Holy Spirit to fortify and strengthen their own. That is why they are each able to reach out, not just to one another's bodies but to their very souls. Those who are aware of this often call each other soul mates for that reason. It is only the mutual giving and living for one another that can induce divine love to enter into human loving, enabling it to rise to as much perfection as is possible in this life.

Now that their human love is mingled with the divine, each can penetrate the primeval desire for God that abides deep down in the other, enabling them to love God and each other simultaneously, strengthening and supporting each other. This is the quality of mutual loving that leads to the generation of new and very special children to people God's kingdom in this world and in the next. It overflows onto them, as they grow from childhood to adulthood preparing them to do for their own future families what their parents did for them. In this way, more and more of those created in God's image and likeness through marital loving will find their fulfillment and final destiny in him.

As the temptation to act selfishly would always be there, so too would the Sacrament of Reconciliation, when after confessing to one another they would seek God's forgiveness for transgressing against this holy Sacrament of Love. They are the ministers of this Sacrament, so it is in their daily dying to self that they minister God's love to one another and so participate in the mystery of Christ's death and Resurrection by being drawn ever more deeply into the mystical body of Christ. As they try to love one another and their children, their love synchronizes with the loving of their risen Lord. It is in this act of contemplative loving that they will first glimpse the glory which will one day be theirs to enjoy together for all eternity.

All that I have said and written about the quality of love that is born in the Dark Night applies in every detail to the Dark Nights that all married couples will experience, both in prayer and in their married life. It is not in spite of them but because of them that their love will grow ever deeper and ever more profound with the years. From the very beginning mystics have used the analogy of human love to explain and understand divine love, and the beautiful "Song of Songs" was used time and time again by the Fathers of the Church with which to describe the journey along the mystic way. This song would have been sung by Jesus and his disciples at the marriage that he attended at Cana, and it was sung by the wedding guests as they accompanied the bride from her old home to the new home of her husband. I only really came to understand the profound correlation between human and divine loving after my mother died. As I have related many times, my father came into my room with a cup of tea after his sleepless nights. He told me the story of his love for my mother over their long and fruitful marriage. He told me that in the last eighteen months of his life he had been closer to her and loved her more dearly and more deeply than at any other time in their married life. I have told this story in detail in my book *Wisdom from the Western Isles* because it enabled me to see the mystic way as never before, and from the lips of my own father.

I know as a matter of fact, that if it was not for my parents' holy love for one another that overflowed onto me, my life would have been quite different. If it was not for them and their love that gave me such inner confidence and security I would never have been able to push on through many dark nights. I would never have come so far in my life without them nor would I have been able to write this and many other books on mystical theology. Whatever I have accomplished by the grace of God that first came to me through their love, continues to sustain me although they have been dead for forty years. It was for this reason that I quote St Bonaventure again, who wrote that "contemplation is learned at the mother's breast". He was speaking both metaphorically and really.

When next you recite the litany of the saints you will be asking many great men and women to pray for you. You will be praying to great saints, mystics and martyrs, the founders of the great monastic, mendicant and apostolic Orders, renowned Popes, Bishops and Priests and holy teachers, writers and Doctors of the Church who all have one thing in common. They all had fathers and mothers and for most of them it was the sacramental loving that they received from their parents that was the making of them. In some of the darkest days that Catholic spirituality has undergone, when all seemed lost, it was the Sacrament of Marriage that has come to the rescue. When the ministers of the other Sacraments failed the Church, it was the ministers of the Sacrament of Marriage who came to our aid. The "love that springs eternal" continues to rise in them to become sacramental as they minister that love to each other and to their families. We have need of such leadership in the Church today perhaps, more than at any other time. The place from where they will come is from good, loving, caring Catholic marriages. Now is the time for the laity to take the lead with the help of the one whom I have called "my senior partner", the Holy Spirit.

All the sacraments have two things in common. First, they channel the love of God through the heart of Christ to human hearts. Then, through prayer those human hearts must be prepared through purification to receive that love. So, for marriage, as in all the sacraments, the importance of prayer is paramount for its success. By this I mean the prayer that precedes the marriage and the prayer that must always accompany any successful marriage. Then the old adage will come true that the "family that prays together will stay together". If, as the years go by they are physically separated, they will nevertheless always be spiritually one. Not even death will mean separation because in Christ they will all be reunited together once more, to travel as one on the final journey into the fullness of love.

Here they will experience loving and being loved in ever greater measure and will see how they and all their loved ones become transformed and transfigured like Christ before them. The joy that each experiences will be multiplied many times over to see that what is happening to them is happening to all they have loved and held dear. Then all they will want to do and say is, "Thanks be to God", *Deo Gratias* and *Gloria in Excelsis Deo.* All they ever wanted, all they ever yearned for, all they ever desired has been brought to completion beyond even their wildest dreams.

Chapter 53

To Contemplate and Share the Fruits of Contemplation

In 1215 when Magna Carta was being signed in England, the most successful reforming council for a thousand years was taking place in Italy. It was called the Fourth Lateran Council. St Dominic, St Francis of Assisi, St Bonaventure, St Thomas Aquinas and four major new religious Orders were involved in spreading the reform all over Christendom. When asked why these new mendicant orders were teaching and preaching outside their monasteries, it was St Thomas Aquinas who replied simply: their job was firstly to contemplate, and then share the fruits of their contemplation with others. These words summed up the new reform which St Francis saw as nothing other than the "Gospel of Our Lord Jesus Christ", but it also summed up the spirituality of the first Christian communities before monasticism was founded. It was the fruits of this contemplation, the infused virtues and the gifts of the Holy Spirit that dazzled the ancient pagans with a quality of pure human goodness and loving selflessness that was never seen before.

If the Second Vatican Council had produced a document detailing a modern representation of the ancient God-given spirituality that his Son handed on to his first followers, as it should have done, then its conclusion would have mystified its readers. The measure of the shock and bewilderment that would have reverberated around the Church would be the measure of just how far we have departed from our spiritual origins. Priests and prelates, as well as the laity would look at one another in disbelief, for the mystical prayer they were told "began in mist and ended in schism" would be back on the agenda. There would have to be an authoritative restoration and reinstatement of mystical theology in all seminaries, houses of religious education and Catholic universities to teach the profound prayer that enables the Holy Spirit to lead us through meditation to the mystical contemplation of God, in, with and through Christ. Mystical theology had been long since taken off the syllabuses in seminaries and houses of Catholic further education. However, deep renewal will only get underway again when it is reinstated and taught by practitioners.

When I was the managing director of Walsingham House retreat and conference centre in North London, I asked my old theology teacher to become the principle visiting theology lecturer, a post that he filled until my tenure came to an end in 1981. When after several years I asked him to take on the role of teaching mystical theology I received the biggest shock of my life. He simply said that he knew nothing whatsoever about the subject. My shock was multiplied many times over as I approached other theologians and received the same sort of response. I had to teach the subject myself, for all the theology in the world would quite literally be pointless unless it is underpinned by the Church's time-honoured teaching on how to die to self and carry a daily cross in prayer beyond first beginnings.

When I asked why I was summonsed to Rome at the end of the 1970s to teach Mystical Theology, I was told there was no one else able to do it except from a purely academic and historical point of view. Invitations then came in to speak from all over the world on a subject that since the condemnation of Quietism nobody seemed to know anything about. For many years to come my initial findings that very few priests and religious were taught how to pray was confirmed over and over again. The enthusiasm of those who, after attending my courses in Rome encouraged their superiors to invite me to speak, was not matched by the vast majority of my audiences. And yet when the terrible cases of sexual abuse by priests and religious hit the headlines everyone was flabbergasted and could not see the reasons why.

If only the meditation that leads to mystical contemplation had been taught in all houses of clerical and religious education, the selfless loving learned in contemplative prayer would have introduced them directly to the love they would otherwise have experienced in the Sacrament of Marriage. We all need to love and be loved. If those who take a vow of chastity are not simultaneously taught how to come to know and experience God's love, then they could eventually seek counterfeit love elsewhere, sometimes with the disastrous consequences that we have all seen. Unfortunately, the gap created by the demise of true authentic Christian mystical spirituality has been filled by psycho-sexual-anything-goes New Age movements that are to be deplored. However, I do not want to end on a sombre note. I have come across many good people who are cooperating with the Holy Spirit and have travelled far and deeply in the spiritual life, but sadly with little help and usually much opposition.

I was fortunate to be taught theology by a theological genius who studied Scholastic Theology in the 1950s during the revival of Thomism. He received the highest attainable distinction, a *summa cum laude* and was carried on the shoulders of his fellow students to celebrate his achievements. Although it was not a subject that could be studied formally at the time, he managed to master the "New Biblical Theology" that would be so vital for the Second Vatican Council that was about to be called. I want to make a clear distinction between what was called at that time the New Biblical Theology, and what after the council came to be called the "New Theology" with which I want to disassociate myself. It became like a hydra with many heads, each head becoming increasingly blind to authentic Catholic teaching and tradition as the years have progressed.

In 1964, I hoped to continue my studies on a higher level, first by going to Rome to study Scholastic Theology in more detail, followed by further studies in Biblical Theology in Germany,

France and at the École Biblique in Jerusalem. It was then that I met a Franciscan priest, Fr Anthony, who said I should rather go to San Giovanni Rotundo in Apulia to sit at the feet of Padre Pio. He would not be able to add to my knowledge of Thomism and had probably never heard of the New Biblical Theology, but I would find in him the fullest possible embodiment of the "Primacy of Love". Sadly, by the time I was able to arrange a visit to San Giovani Rotundo, Padre Pio had died on September 23rd, 1968.

However, I was privileged to meet a monk who had reached the pinnacle of the spiritual life at the end of one of my lecture tours in Africa. Fr Gregory was in my opinion another living saint. He was a Cistercian monk who was trained at the Trappist monastery of Mount St Bernard, near Coalville in Leicestershire, England. He and several other monks opened a daughter house at Mbengwe in the republic of Cameroon many years before. When I was privileged to meet Fr Gregory who was eighty-five at the time, only he and three others remained from the original group. The Nigerian Abbot presided over a large and spiritually thriving African community that I likened to the paradise described in James Hilton's book *The Lost Horizon* called *Shangri-La*.

Fr Gregory told me he spent thirty years in the Dark Night, in which there were moments when he thought he had lost his faith. Then one day he became ill and was confined to the monastery's infirmary. From the moment he was laid up in bed he experienced what he called a weak but ongoing ecstasy that he not only experienced in his head but in his whole being. By that he meant that he was at all times lost in God, but at no time did the experience render him unconscious nor less capable, but rather more capable of his work than ever before. Then on three separate occasions just as he was about to receive Holy Communion, he heard these words, "Only you have been keeping me out." He emphasized that he knew without a doubt that he was listening to the voice of Christ himself. Furthermore, he insisted that the words were not spoken to him in his head, but out loud and in words, "as loud as you are speaking to us in the monastery church".

He told me how he had found the most help from the book *The Cloud of Unknowing* in what was the most testing period of his whole life during those years in the Dark Night. We both agreed that the book is a mystical masterpiece brimming over with the sort of practical wisdom that can only come from a fellow practitioner. What few critics it has had, sadly reveal themselves to be out of step with the Catholic mystical tradition. I would give it particularly to those who thought themselves well advanced in the spiritual life, and able to lead and guide others. If they "clasped it to themselves with hoops of steel", I would know that they were genuine practitioners, on the right path, and able to guide others too. If, however, they dismissed it or condemned the work, then they would be condemning themselves and the role they had set for themselves as a guide for others through the darkest moments of the spiritual life.

That there be no misunderstanding let me be quite clear that the prologue to the book makes abundantly clear that, if I may paraphrase the author, it should be positively hidden away from the general reader for it would indeed mislead them and they would in their turn misguide others. A good example of this is how those who belong to the many mantra movements that are unfortunately so popular today, misuse it. They do this regularly by claiming that its use of monosyllabic words are, in fact, mantras as used by gurus from the East and the West to attain almost instant mystical states. In fact the words used by the author of the Cloud are not techniques to generate inner psychological states of mind, but short prayers, acts of love directed towards God.

They are known in the Catholic tradition as "prayers of the heart". Even then they are not recommended for beginners but only those who after meditating on God's love as embodied in

Christ, and for many months, more usually years, the Holy Spirit gives them the gift of contemplation. It is only then that the book can be recommended to those now in the mystic way. The author wrote the book for a twenty-four-year-old young man who had just been led into the Dark Night of the Soul. Anybody in the same position as the young man or the sisters for whom St John of the Cross was writing, will find this book just what they are looking for, a spiritual lifeline, and the help and consolation for which they are in dire need. The very essence of his teaching is that all we can do is to keep making simple acts of love to penetrate through the "Cloud of Unknowing". He takes this phrase from the Fathers of the Church, who in order to describe the mystic way, liken it to the ascent of Moses up Mt Sinai, passing through the clouds to receive God's laws at the summit.

Like all who would follow him to seek the new law of God, which is love, the mystic has to pass through a "Cloud of Unknowing" as Moses did. The "prayer of the heart", as the Desert Fathers called it, or short prayers of love were taught from earliest times. They were used to express the deepest desire of the mystic and to support what the author of the "Cloud" called our "naked intent upon God". What was originally called the "prayer of the heart" often came to be called the "prayer of faith" by weather-worn travellers who knew the reality of travelling through the Dark Night most especially at the beginning when the "prayer of the heart" was all but bereft of heartfelt feeling. But the time comes when God becomes the sole giver and we become the receivers. When this happens God sends out a spiritual light of incredible power that pierces down through the "Cloud" to penetrate and then possess the mystic. However, the author will not take upon himself to speak of this with his "blabbering fleshly tongue". So, dear reader, if you want details of ecstatic mystical states then you will have to look elsewhere but if you want good orthodox inspiration and advice for your journey "when the well runs dry" then look no further than to this spiritual treasure and do not listen to counterfeit mystics who malign it. I find it grossly offensive when those who cannot understand this "holy work" do not just condemn it but ridicule it.

From time immemorial human beings have tried to keep the evil that is in us all in check by issuing laws, rules and regulations, with sanctions and penalties for offenders to keep the demons within from bursting out. However, despite the laws, the evil that is within does burst out, not just to commit individual crimes, but national and international atrocities as internecine wars commit unmentionable acts of brutality and barbarism. Only an arrogant fool believes that we can oppose this evil and destroy it ourselves. Endless fascination with the evil in the world and in the Church can become like a pernicious drug addiction that can at best paralyze a person into inert apathy, or at worst can make us porous to evil, possessing us with the stuff that sinners are made of.

There is only one power that can destroy this evil at its source within us, and that is the power of infinite love. When we do all in our power to invite infinite love into our hearts, we are doing the most important thing we can so that evil may be defeated and good may prevail. There is hope then and we can do something, precisely because we have been created in the image and likeness of God and yearn to love him and be loved by him. This hope becomes more than a vague longing when we try to do all in our power to strengthen and fortify this longing with the infinite loving unleashed on the first Pentecost. It is this love that continually flows out of the Risen Christ that enables us to generate and practise acts of selflessness in prayer. When, through practice, divine and human love combine, it is to produce a new and invincible brand of contemplative loving that cannot be penetrated by evil. It can open up the passageway through which our love can finally enable God's unalloyed and infinite love to do what is quite impossible without it.

It was from Fr Gregory that I first heard a monk explain to

me how he chose short prayers from the liturgy to support his longing for God when mystical darkness enveloped him. It was in this action with his attention fixed on God, that divine and human love combined and contemplative loving was generated. He was adamant that this was the practice of countless monks before him, as far back as the Desert Fathers. I have never forgotten Fr Gregory because I believe that in meeting him I met the man I am striving to become, at least in some small way, a living embodiment of the man who rose again from the dead on the first Easter day.

Chapter 54

Traditionalism and Tradition

In an earlier chapter I told the story of how a scripture scholar who wrote a book in the 1920s, was condemned for maintaining that not all the psalms were written by King David. He was condemned for telling the truth which nobody today would deny. The best and the most moving of the Psalms are as fresh and alive today as they were hundreds of years before Christ came, and were clearly written by men who were, in the words of St Augustine, intoxicated with the love of God. How had such people come to love God with such enthusiasm and with such fervour long before Christ was born? The answer is quite simple; they had been told regularly and reminded in much detail and in such inventive ways, just how God had loved them in the past, how he was loving them in the present, and how he would love them in the future with a glorious destiny promised by him through the prophets.

Each time they celebrated the great feast days that reminded them of what God had done for them in the past, they did not just remember them in their minds but in every part of their being. Their feasts were for them sacred dramas in which everyone took part so they would never forget the daily and dynamic love of God that was always active in the past, in the present, and as it always would be in the future. The verb to "remember" meant in their language, not just to call to mind, but to make present again today. When they celebrated the Passover for instance, they celebrated the time when God's avenging Angel passed over their homes to reap vengeance on the Egyptians, as they prepared to escape from the daily humiliation of slavery by eating a hearty meal of lamb, and other nutritious foods to fortify them for the journey ahead through the desert to the promised Land. When this sacred meal was celebrated each year at what we would call Easter, the father of the family would retell the story of their deliverance and the meaning of the sacred God-given food.

When they celebrated the feast of tabernacles or tents, they would remember the time they spent in the desert and the hardships they underwent in the form of a sacred drama in which all took part. For a whole week they would relive this experience by living out of doors in tents and eating the same meagre food their forebears had to eat, remembering and reliving what they endured. They experienced for themselves the cold nights and the craving for food and water, until God finally came to their rescue, as he always would to slake their thirst and relieve their hunger and do whatever was necessary for his people who he loved. All the great feasts were sacred dramas that taught the believers who participated in them how God would continue to show his love for his chosen people for whom he had prepared a great destiny, not just in this world but in the next world too. Every day at every meal time the prayer said at table by the father would remind everyone once again that the food they were eating was the fruit of the land of "milk and honey" that God had given them. And then God would be thanked for the love that he always lavished upon them. And when they went to the synagogue three times a day, they would return God's love in kind by solemnly promising to love him with all their hearts and minds and souls and with all their strength. The Talmud details the religious teaching and practices of the Jewish people, and the external acts of worship that were the backbone to a daily life totally given over to manifesting their love of God. Myriad short prayers, and acclamations were taken from the psalms, the canticles and the prayers on which they were brought up, to precede and follow almost every action they performed in their daily life to sanctify their day and offer it to God.

The first Christians were predominantly Jewish, so these

practices would have been practised by them, and taught to new Christian converts. However, they would no longer be taught to concentrate on God's love as it was demonstrated in their distant past, but on how it was demonstrated for them in the recent past, in God's love made flesh and blood in Jesus Christ, in his death and Resurrection. Gradually they began to celebrate their own sacred dramas and to participate in a new form of prayer, the meditation that would lead them on and into their new Risen Lord. The old Jewish spirituality that taught them how to consecrate their lives to God would not be discontinued but transformed. They could now be drawn ever closer to their God, because the "light inaccessible" became accessible, because of the love that Jesus poured out on the first Pentecost day and every day. This love would draw all who would receive it into his mystical body and into his mystical contemplation of the father, to the degree in which their own love was sufficiently purified to be united with his. They would not only come to know and experience God's love through the Risen Lord through meditation, but they would consecrate their daily lives to him as their spiritual ancestors the Jews did, by daily prayer and acts of love that would saturate their daily lives. These acts would simplify into what came to be called the "prayer of the heart" by the Desert Fathers.

When, as happens in any marriage first enthusiasm begins to wane, it is not the end of love, but the beginning of a new form of love. When a person is purified from the selfishness that pollutes all love, it enables love to grow, until that love becomes stronger and more totally absorbing than ever before. The same eventually began to happen to the new people of God once the first enthusiasm that had been set afire in "meditation" petered out as it always does for the reasons that I have already detailed. If unwilling, however, to rekindle their faith, punctiliously performing all the words and actions, all the rites and ceremonies in the vain belief that this was sufficient to please the God who had said, "These people only worship me with their lips, but their hearts are far from me" (Isaiah 29:13), it gradually becomes reduced to holding on to, and tenaciously observing what were originally the expressions of their faith, or what they think were the ancient practices of their faith. That is what has come to be called "traditionalism" giving rise to the slogan, "Traditionalism is the dead voice of the living, but Tradition is the living voice of the dead". The truth of the matter is true tradition never essentially changes because it is the work of the Holy Spirit speaking and acting through those whose lives are always open, always sensitive and docile to receive Christ in deep personal prayer, at any time, in any place and in any century.

When the meditation that can become heart-warming, and spiritually uplifting, suddenly comes to an end, it is not because it has failed, but because it has succeeded. It has so succeeded that the heart reaches out and upwards within the mystical body, to be united with God, as all it wants now is to love God and to be united with him. It has to the exclusion of all else a fixation on God, just as after "lift off" the astronauts no longer have any interest in the world they have just left, because they are now intent on the new world to which they are travelling. The pull that draws them Godward is such that the heart, or the will, is so fixed on its destination that it loses its power over all the inner faculties like the memory and the imagination that were used before, making meditation impossible. This ligature, this spiritual binding of our heart to the heart of God, will grow stronger and stronger. Finally when all these inner faculties have been purified then meditation becomes, not only possible as before, but far more vivid, far more graphic, as if what was seen before in black and white is now seen in technicolour.

However, what is experienced at the beginning of the mystic way is called by St John of the Cross "obscure contemplation". It is contemplation, namely a simple gaze, but the object of its vision is disrupted by endless distractions and temptations rising from the unbridled memory and the imagination. These, as the *Cloud of Unknowing* insists should be placed under a "Cloud of Forgetfulness" enabling ones heart's desire, supported by acts of love, to reach God by piercing through the "Cloud of Unknowing". That is why now and for the far foreseeable future, the prayer of the heart becomes the daily prayer of the spiritual traveller both inside and outside of prayer. However, as these short prayers have to be made in dryness and aridity and surrounded by myriad distractions and temptations without the feelings that could once be experienced in meditation, it was called the "Prayer of Faith" or the "Prayer of Naked Faith", as it is not clothed with any feeling. This is the most important moment in the spiritual life when, as I have already said, 90% of searchers pack up and run away, not just from the mystic way, but from any serious spiritual way, and some can even lose their faith.

In any branch of human achievement a person, who wants to arrive at perfection inevitably comes to the famous brick wall. The person may be a golfer, a tennis player, an athlete or a musician, they will at some point come to a brick wall that stands between them and the perfection they are seeking. Some years ago I spoke to the concert pianist Vincent Billington about this fateful brick wall and what has to be done to overcome it. The reply he gave me applies to the search for perfection in the spiritual life, as in any other form of secular perfection. "You redouble your practice and keep on going come hell or high water," he said, "until the breakthrough finally comes for those who persevere." This is the most important moment of the spiritual life, the moment to persevere in practising the "Prayer of Naked Faith" come what may. Gradually, more likely in very many months, rather than weeks, the Holy Spirit who is guiding you enables you to become aware that Someone is drawing you to himself. Eventually when this Someone begins to make his presence felt, if only very subtly to begin with, the "Prayer of Naked Faith" comes to be called the "Prayer of the Heart". Although both are short, the former is characterised by cries for help, the second is more usually characterized by cries of thanksgiving, praise and adoration that lapse into the silent gaze upon the One who is the All in all. When an aspirant friar spied on St Francis at prayer to see if he was genuine, he heard him pray throughout the night, continually saying, "My God and my all". The Latin version of this Prayer, *Deus Meus et Omnia*, became the motto of the Franciscan Order. If a graph existed to chart the spiritual life on earth, then meditation at the beginning, would be hardly more than 5% of the journey. Contemplation, characterised by practising acts of love that leads to perfect loving would constitute most of the rest of the time, before the union after purification, makes possible the return of meditation, this time in technicolour, and in high definition.

As we have seen when a person is taken up into Contemplation, and precisely because they can no longer meditate as before, they return to the vocal prayer that was at first their staple diet, as did the first Christians. Like them they gradually discover that their spiritual needs induce them to simplify these prayers into shorter prayers, prayers of the heart. That this prayer leads into mystical prayer we know, not just from later mystical writers, but from our earliest ancestors. The only sign by which you can definitively know that someone has come to perfect prayer is not because they experience mystical phenomena, have visions, or revelations, but by their fruits, namely by the love they have for others; not just for their own families or their own fellow Christians, but for their fellow human beings, and even for their enemies. The almost incredible spread of Christianity, and on such a massive sale, can only be explained by the love generated in prayer that enabled them to receive the fruits of contemplation, namely the infused virtues and the gifts of the Holy Spirit.

Many early Christians who were inpatient to receive in full measure this water of life, freely chose to become virgins or remain virginal after their partner's death. They came to be called the *virgines et continentes*. Some remained alone in their own homes, others gradually began to come to gather in communities. Before entering into the desert it was to one of these communities that St Antony went with his sister to arrange for her to join their community. The Fathers of the Church used to write little treatises for them called *Ad Virgines*. One thing above all else that they emphasized was that if they did not so deepen their prayer life, to come to know and experience God's love, then all the miseries of the loveless would be visited upon them, as no one can live without love. Then far from becoming leaders in their communities they would soon degenerate into being no more than blind leaders of the blind.

The centre of unity for everyone was the Mass that was in those day so alive, so vital and spiritually dynamic, precisely because at that Mass Christ himself would be made present amongst his people. While he was on earth every moment of every day Christ was caught up in doing his Father's will which was that he should love his Father with all his mind and heart with all his body and soul and with his whole strength, and love others as he himself was loved. When he was dying on the Cross, a lifetime of selfless sacrificial loving was drawn together as one, in the final most testing, most agonising act of selfless sacrificial loving that he had ever made. At the ultimate moment of self-sacrificial loving, when all was given to the last drop of his blood, what the Greek Fathers called his *kenosis*, his self-emptying was brought to its completion, to be filled with what they also called the *pleroma*, the fullness of his Father's love. This is how their Lord and Saviour returned to be made sacramentally present to the early Christians every Sunday, when they came to celebrate their weekly Mass. He was not, however, present as someone who had played a part in their history in their past, but as someone who was playing a part in their history in the present, because the dynamic loving that was uniting him with his Father was simultaneously overflowing onto and into all those present who were open to receive him. As they received him, as the bread of life, he would draw them up and into his life, into his mystical body and into his mystical loving of his father. To the measure that they had learnt to carry their daily cross, as Christ had done before them, then they would enter into his selflessness, his self-emptying, his *kenosis*. Then they would receive something of the *pleroma* that he received.

What happened at Mass continued to happen in the believers' daily domestic acts of selflessness and self-sacrifice, that preceded and followed each Mass as they gradually became more and more at one with their Risen Lord. As promised he became the New Temple in whom the new offering "in spirit and truth" was to be made by his followers, whose physical offerings in the old temple would now be replaced by spiritual offerings in the new temple, which was none other than the mystical body of Christ in whom they now "lived and moved and had their being". It was because their offerings were now made in, with and through him that they had a power and an effectiveness, and therefore a success, that could not have been counted on before. This meant that the love they received, in, with and through Christ, enabled them to be ever more deeply united with him who was the supreme prophet, the one sent, as they would now be sent in his name, to both embody and teach the truth to others. And the ultimate truth is that God is love and that he wants everyone to receive this, his love, to be like him, to be one with him, not just in this life, but in the next, and to all eternity. All who are baptised into Christ's royal family are called to be viceroys of Christ the King, and to spread his kingdom that will always be characterised by love that does not reign to "lord it over others" but to serve, be they friend or foe. Christ promised that the true proclamation of God's kingdom by his viceroys on earth will always be accompanied, not just by white martyrdom, but by red martyrdom too. An unpurified world impregnated with evil recoils like a viper from goodness and truth and is ready to kill and destroy psychologically or even physically, rather than have its true nature laid bare. Even the very presence of goodness for some is enough to incite them to evil for fear it might hold up a mirror to what they cannot bear to see for themselves.

When you see the battered and bleeding body of Christ writhing in agony on the cross you are seeing the physical embodiment of human evil that could not listen to the teaching of pure unadulterated love promised since time immemorial by the prophets. Yes, we are called to become prophets, priests and kings in imitation of Christ, and his love has been sent to ordain each one of us to this end at Baptism. Further to this his Mass is there to continually remind us of his presence and support us in our calling, but something further is required. Prayer and continual prayer, as Christ himself prayed, is necessary so that we may continually be open and available to receive the only help and strength that will enable us to be faithful to the end.

True tradition then is allowing true love to be handed on. That is what the word tradition means. It is continually handed on to be received by each successive generation by the Risen Christ through his sacraments. This handing on is symbolised by the laying on of hands through which the love of Christ continues to be transmitted to his people. The person whose hands touch you when you were baptised, for instance, received power from the Bishop, who laid hands on him at his ordination and that "tradition" can be seamlessly traced back to the first apostles and to the loving touch of Christ. This is true in all the sacraments, but most particularly in the sacrament of marriage, when love is communicated by touch by the ministers of this, the sacrament of love.

But love is not magic and that is why it is only those who in ever-deepening prayer enable that touch of love to suffuse their weak human love with Christ's divine love that brings him back to life again in us, and through us in his Church. That is how true tradition is established.

Chapter 55

Contemplation Made Simple

There is an unwritten law in every religious order or congregation that no one should interfere with the person in charge of the novices. When the Bishop made me the director of his Retreat and Conference Centre, the mother superior of the Dominican convent who owned the property gave me their Novice Mistress as my personal assistant and secretary. It was then that I made a "private vow". I would do nothing to influence either her or her novices who looked after the domestic arrangements in Walsingham House. This I think was the reason why our relationship ran so smoothly, and my relationship with her novices never strayed beyond a certain superficial friendliness. That is until the revolution suddenly rocked the Dominican community at Chingford whose convent was next to the retreat centre. My first book on prayer had been published, the courses that I had introduced on prayer were now in full swing, and the Novice Mistress was away for eight months following the new Dominican renewal course in Rome, when it happened. I was beginning to wonder whether or not my courses on prayer, more particularly mystical prayer, were having any effect at all, when one morning I was besieged by seven novices and junior sisters. They all wanted to leave together to form a new congregation with my guidance and leadership. I found myself in an unenviable position that was not of my choosing. What I preached, it seemed, could not be lived in their congregation. Unaware of my "private vow" and the punctilious way that I had observed it, a new superior from South Africa totally blamed me for seducing them. I had done nothing but write a book and give talks on prayer to which the Novice Mistress freely chose to send them.

311

Eventually a compromise was reached. They would await the return of the Novice Mistress before leaving, in deference to her, and to avoid the centre being closed down for lack of their help, in deference to me. When she returned further compromises were made and we carried on as before, but in the next few years they all left one by one. In fact, in twelve years that I worked at the centre, not one of her novices finally remained. I do not know whether or not the Novice Mistress secretly blamed me, as our personal relationship never wavered, but she herself never showed any interest in my teaching on mystical theology, nor did she listen to any of my courses on the subject. It was only the year after she had attended the Dominican renewal course in Rome that I was incorporated into the team, to teach the mystical theology that was part of their heritage. When, with my help therefore, she was the main mover in the revolt against psycho-sociological renewal that was everywhere apparent in the late 1970s, the renewal that she asked me to help her bring about was back to the status quo rather than forwards to something new.

Leaving what had been my home and my family of the last twelve years, I was headhunted for another job that also enabled me to return to the road as a travelling speaker. On my travels individuals did respond to my teaching, but in the prevailing state of religious life that was daily deteriorating and diminishing, it meant that even those who wanted contemplative prayer, were so busy keeping the show on the road that there was no time to do that for which they yearned with all their hearts. Inevitably then many more joined the massive exodus that never seemed to stop on both sides of the Atlantic. Even before the Second Vatican Council was called some did realize that some form of new spiritual renewal was necessary, but they were the few and did not seem to know where it should come from. The biblical scholars, liturgists, and moral theologians who I had seen as my mentors, and whose works I still have to hand, and whose influence can be seen in all that I write, never developed spiritualities in which mystical prayer played any practical part. Some have tried and lamentably failed, because they too had all been affected by the spiritual dearth that had prevailed in the aftermath of the condemnation of Quietism. Compared to the rather dry intellectual scholasticism which first formed me, what came to be called the "New Biblical Theology", even before the Council, was to me and many others new and exciting. It opened up the biblical theology to me that touched my heart as well as my mind, but the prevailing apathy to true mystical theology prevented its adherents developing a spirituality deep enough to lead people back to the great mystical tradition of our faith from its first foundation in the mystical body of Christ. It was here, in, with and through him that believers were drawn up and are still being drawn up into his mystical contemplation of the Father, to receive the fruits of this contemplation.

For instance, in the late 1950s the great man whom I have already referred to as my mentor, Louis Bouyer, was commissioned to produce a new book on spirituality by the French publishing house *Editions du Cerf.* It was to replace the old-fashioned spiritual manual written by Père Adolphe Tanquerey. Although Louis Bouyer's work has many commendable qualities there is nothing in it that he has not said elsewhere in his writings and nothing to show he has any sympathy for, or knowledge of, personal prayer beyond first beginnings and therefore to help serious searchers along the "mystic way". When I first read his *Introduction to the Spiritual Life* I could have wept to find that a man whom I so admired and who had so influenced me with his exciting brand of biblical theology had been so exposed by being enticed to write on a subject upon which he had no practical experience, as anyone can see for themselves who has read his memoirs. Of course, it is full of good things; how could it not be, but on the subject of the "one thing necessary" it is sadly and lamentably deficient. On the surface Tanquerey's master work on the spiritual life may seem a bit old-fashioned in its language and in its presentation to a modern reader, and it is after all a manual, but its content is extraordinarily accurate, orthodox and safe, most particularly on mystical theology.

A more serious attempt to write on prayer was made by, possibly the greatest theologian of the twentieth century Hans Ur Von Balthasar. However, although I would recommend his book to anyone for the brilliant and beautifully written summary of Catholic theology, its teaching on mystical prayer is non-existent. An uninformed reader might protest that he uses the word "contemplation" more than any other, but he does not use the word in the way that it has been used in the Catholic mystical tradition from the beginning. As a trained Jesuit he uses it to denote a certain form of meditation introduced by St Ignatius that I once found very helpful as a novice. This method of meditation or contemplation as he uniquely calls it, helps a person gather together and galvanise all the sensual faculties to help them enter into the different episodes in the life of Our Lord. As I was in the middle of this form of meditation when the call to true mystical contemplation led me on, I became a lost soul for almost two years, because nowhere in the teaching of the Spiritual Exercises could I find the help to journey on; that is until I found the teachings of St John of the Cross and St Teresa of Ávila. Their writings of course post-dated the writings of the Spiritual Exercises, so unfortunately St Ignatius could not have been influenced by the two great mystical doctors of the Church. Harness the practical teaching on how to meditate on the person of Christ for beginners, as taught by St Ignatius in his "Exercises", with the teaching of the great Carmelite Mystics, and put it into modern accessible language and you would have a perfect blueprint for spiritual advancement and for the constitution on the spiritual life that we are still awaiting.

None of the great biblical theologians who were called as experts to participate in the Second Vatican Council had any but a superficial understanding of deep traditional Catholic mystical theology, and some had none at all. How therefore could they have complemented an excellent constitution on the liturgy with one on traditional Catholic Spirituality in which the mystical theology, once banished without trace, was reintroduced to enrich the Church. This is the only teaching that can support a person through the purification that must precede union with God. In short, true renewal could never prevail no matter how perfect a liturgy might be that may galvanise the faithful. As Lewis Carol pointed out in *Alice in Wonderland*, you cannot have a cat with a smile but no substance. The liturgy is the expression of the collective personal relationship of the profound and substantial encounter of the faithful with God. Without this deep personal relationship, the liturgy will soon degenerate into no more than the smile on the face of the Cheshire cat. Of course, the liturgy can inspire, but it is predominantly the expression of love, of the love that is primarily learnt in prayer. The greater the love, the more the liturgy is transformed with the light that only love can give. Cut off the source of this light and what was once pulsating with life can gradually become spiritually lifeless, even though onlookers may be impressed by its aesthetic beauty.

If you, or someone you love wishes to join a religious order, do not be deceived by externals, whether they be of liturgical grandeur or of liturgical simplicity; make sure that time for freely chosen personal prayer is sacrosanct. That there will be time in the day for what is usually called "meditation", at least in the apostolic orders is to be expected, but something further is required. Something further must be built into the timetable if meditation is going to lead on, or more precisely, if the Holy Spirit is going to lead a person on and into mystical contemplation. Those young religious, who finally left the Dominican Convent at Chingford left because they came to search for and to love God, but the opportunity for the personal prayer that they needed had been denied them. Let me explain how this was provided for in the Franciscan order where I went to try my vocation. When

Compline ended at about 7.30pm, everyone was free. You could go to the library, to your room, for a walk around the garden or spend the time for further prayer in the Church or elsewhere. The same was true for both novices and students. Because the very essence of love is that it is freely given, choosing to give one's time to God, from a variety of other options, is worth far more than the regimented time for prayer that is part of the official daily time-table and therefore monitored.

It was during this time that a dramatic change took place in my own prayer life. It was because I had already been taught how to meditate at school and taught how to meditate by using the method encouraged by St Ignatius in his Exercises, that the sudden change seemed so dramatic. Using what he called "contemplation" I loved going back two thousand years in my mind, with the help of my memory and imagination to visualize the great mysteries of Christ's life and to participate in them, be inspired by them, and allow my natural human reactions to express themselves in heartfelt prayer. I used to look forward all day to this, the most exciting part of my day for which I would prepare by reading the scriptural passages that represented the mystery into which I was going to enter. Then one day when I was ready and prepared to go back into salvation history, I felt as flat as a pancake and so did all the inner faculties of my heart and mind that had made meditation so enthralling before. Nor did things return to what I had come to think was normal, no matter how I tried nor how long I waited. Only one thing remained and that was my desire for God but even this desire seemed to be going nowhere as dryness and aridity prevailed where sweetness and light had prevailed before and temptations and distractions drew the attention of my heart's desire, that I wanted to focus on God, elsewhere.

This is the most important moment in the whole of the spiritual life. It is now that a person is presented with a question. Do you go to prayer for what you get out of God or for what you want to give him, with and through Christ who died for us on the Cross? For now you will be asked to carry the cross, and within prayer itself. Every Catholic will nod their head in agreement when asked if they realize that the spiritual life involves carrying the cross, but when they encounter the cross in prayer, the vast majority simply drift away from prayer, or seek to move on by embracing the counterfeit forms of mystical prayer to which I have already referred. Sadly, if they only knew it, they are saying no to participating in the very act with which Christ wrought our redemption. The reason for this is according to St John of the Cross ignorance of the mystical theology that still prevails even more in our day than in his day. Even such a great theologian as the Jesuit Hans Ur Von Balthasar lost his way at this point, but this is a matter to which I must return later.

Chapter 56

Obedient Men

When most of our school friends were dreaming about becoming astronauts, high-flying multi-millionaires or rock-stars, my best friend, John Duffy, and I were dreaming about becoming Jesuits. By the time we were eighteen I had enjoyed nine Jesuit retreats, he seven. We loved their no-nonsense, down to earth, straight from the shoulder spirituality that took the stoical spirituality that was inculcated by the secular priests who taught us to a higher level. We were not just committed Catholics, but we wanted to dedicate our lives as active members of the Church Militant. If you want to sign up to fight for Christ then you want to join the spiritual equivalent of the Grenadier guards, the Commandos or the SAS. That is how we saw the Jesuits. While John's brilliant mind meant that he was always top of the class, my dyslexia meant that I was at the bottom, so when he went to the Jesuit noviciate I went to the Franciscan noviciate, because my older brother who preceded me, had so dazzled his superiors with his academic credentials that they did not bother to ask for mine. When we compared notes at the end of our respective noviciates it turned out to be something of an eye opener for me. It was not so much that our experiences differed, but the Catholic stoicism that we were taught at school was far more intense and far more exacting in the spirituality inculcated in the Jesuit noviciate.

There are some strange anomalies about the Jesuits that took me some time to understand. Ask a dozen of them if their founder was a mystic and they will say yes. But ask them a week later if you should join their congregation because you want to become a mystic, and they will tell you to join some other order, for mystical theology is no part either of their training or their way of life. If I were to name twenty priests who impressed me most then the majority of them would be Jesuits. Priests like Fr Bernard Bassett SJ who helped me at a key moment in my life, Fr Clifford Howell with whom I ran a Parish retreat, Fr James Walsh the editor of the spirituality magazine *The Way* who told me that it took twenty years before he was ordained a priest. Then there was Fr Lachy Hughes SJ, the canon lawyer with whom I worked for years helping to found a new Dominican congregation gain acceptance with Rome. He rang me to tell me that he had a conversion experience in Medjugorje when he saw the sun "dance in the sky". He died a few weeks later. Then another great Jesuit was my good friend Kevin Donovan SJ, who used to give lectures on the liturgy for me at Walsingham House the Conference and Retreat centre that I ran in London. He seemed amused that he was an accepted expert on the liturgy, as Jesuits are not normally known for their liturgical finesse. He said, if you want to confuse a Jesuit put him in charge of the Easter Liturgy!

Kevin was simply the most pleasant, the most decent, the most affable, the friendliest and the most perfect human being I have ever met. I could go on and on naming more great Jesuits whom it has been my privilege to meet. It led me on to study the Ignatian Spirituality that had formed them in the hope that something of what formed them might help to form me too, but I was to be disappointed. I finally concluded that it was not the Ignatian Spirituality that made them great men, but that great men were attracted to the Jesuits, as John and I had been. Then you had to have something great about you to survive the punishing formation that many of my good friends had called a terrible treadmill. They were great, not because of the spirituality that formed them but in spite of it. They were great men in the making when they joined. When I did manage to read the Ignatian Exercises and the interpretations given by modern Jesuits, I was in for a shock.

The congregation was founded at the height of the Renaissance when the spiritual forces that thrived in the old pagan Empire once more reared their ugly heads and began to seep into the Catholic spirituality that had kept them at bay in the early Church. I am referring in particular to Stoicism, Manichaeism and Neoplatonism, all of which have deeply influenced the Spiritual Exercises. I was saved by my dyslexia, because if I had joined the Jesuits and survived I would have been destined to follow a spirituality developed at the height of the Renaissance which was devised for beginners, recently described as the place where pagan moralism meets Catholic fundamentalism, and where mysticism is replaced by emotionalism. However, with the Jesuits it was always a restrained emotionalism that is often more powerful than when it is overt. Although I always loved the spartan spirituality that inspired me in their retreats I was always a little ill at ease when the retreat master became emotional when speaking about devotions particularly those associated with Ignatian Spirituality.

If, as his followers maintain, St Ignatius was a mystic, then believe me, as a mystical theologian who has studied the subject for over sixty years, this is simply not true. Or to be more precise there is no evidence for this in the Spiritual Exercises that he composed. In fact, all the evidence shows that he was not, at least, when he composed them. It is a spirituality in which human endeavour is paramount, with no knowledge of, or teaching of the mystic way, where love is purified for the Union with God, which no amount of human endeavour can achieve. It is no good saying that there is always the grace of God, when in practice, human endeavour receives all the emphasis. And furthermore, the mystical purification of the heart in the dark night that enables a person to have ever-deeper access to the grace of God in the sacraments, plays no part in their spirituality. Once you have been inspired by the positive sort of "contemplation" that St Ignatius teaches, then it is off into the world to practise "contemplation in action". This is long before you have been purified for this purpose in true mystical contemplation. Then, rather like all religious revivalists, when the fire begins to simmer down it is back to the Exercises to be reinvigorated once more by practising the art of conquering oneself and to be re-invigorated by the semi-self-generated love that flickers into flame in "active or acquired contemplation".

At the very beginning of the Spiritual exercises, St Ignatius writes that they have been written to enable a person "to conquer oneself". The way this is done is by embracing the stoicism kept at bay in the early Church but introduced into Christianity at the Renaissance by such people as John Colet. As we have already seen, stoicism was put in pride of place in the English education system where it has survived to the present day, most particularly in the public schools. However, in the Spiritual Exercises stoical practices to make oneself holy are far more evident. Let me quote from the words of St Ignatius himself to make my point. If the first two ways of mortifying the body are not enough to frighten you then the third way certainly will. "The third way is to chastise the flesh by giving it sensible pain which is given by wearing haircloth and cords, or iron chains next to the flesh, by scourging or wounding oneself and by other kinds of austerity" (Fr David Fleming's presentation of the Spiritual Exercises page 56). That is not to mention his strictures on fasting and deprivation of food and other means of mortifying the body that are more exacting than any others that I have ever come across. The Jesuit in the making has to carry beads with him to count how many times each day he has attempted to root out sin, primarily by his own endeavour, helped by twice daily examinations of conscience. Their efforts to uproot evil habits and implant good habits must be written down to ensure that he is always attentive to the task of making himself holy. There is therefore always much food for thought at the twice daily examinations of conscience, in which past failures have to be faced up to, and future successes planned.

That this stoical anthropocentric spirituality is still being used was confirmed by my best friend, John Duffy. He insisted that the way Ignatian Spirituality was taught and practised was exactly the same as it had been fifty years before, as detailed by Dennis Meadows in his Book *Obedient Men* and presumably, as it was taught and practised by Jesuits from the outset. If in the intervening years it has been changed by introducing modern socio-psychological techniques and depth psychology to enable man to do what is predominantly the work of the Holy Spirit in an authentic Christian spirituality, then it is cause for even greater concern. All would-be Catholic stoics should heed the words of Epictetus the founder of Stoicism. "Show me a stoic if you know one. You will show me thousands who speak like stoics, but let my old age gaze upon one, for so far I have never seen one."

One thing should be clear to any objective student of Ignatian Spirituality, most particularly as exemplified in the Exercises, and that is that their Spirituality is aeons away from the God-given spirituality practised by the first Christians. Ironically this spirituality, that was the life blood of the early Christians, has been perhaps described better than anyone else by great Jesuit scholars such as Joseph Jungmann SJ, Jean Daniélou SJ, Henry de Lubac SJ, and Hans Ur Von Balthasar SJ, amongst many others who were inspired to return to the early Christian sources by St John Henry Newman. They all helped me and enabled this book to be written. They have enabled me to give the theological dimensions to the study of mystical theology that was in the past almost exclusively described in terms of the psychological experiences of those trying to follow the mystic way. However, because of their inbred antipathy for mystical theology, these great scholars, thanks to their Jesuit training, never understood or taught the theology that teaches how human love is purified by the Holy Spirit in the true God-given contemplation that prevailed in the early Church. When one of my favourite books was published, *The Bible and the Liturgy*, by Jean Daniélou SJ, it was described, as Louis Bouyer tells in his memoirs, as brilliant but lacking in depth. This review sums up all those great scholars, who taught me so much about early Christianity.

Chapter 57

Humanism Rides Again

Please do not think that I am only singling out the Jesuits for criticism, because all the other religious orders and congregations and secular priests have also been affected by ignorance of mystical theology since the condemnation of Quietism. However, the Jesuits have to be singled out because they are different. Why? Because since the Council of Trent they have been numerically bigger than all the other religious orders and their influence has been correspondingly greater too, particularly after the condemnation of Quietism at the end of the seventeenth century. The anti-mystical lobby in the Church that was busy seeking out and destroying every vestige of mystical theology in all the other religious orders left the Jesuits untouched, because they did not have any mystical theology or mystical tradition to destroy. Further to this their particular brand of, what the spiritual theologian Louis Cognet called "Devout Humanism" was seen as the ideal from which other religious could learn and incorporate into their own spiritualities to fill the gap left by the absence of mystical theology. The spirituality therefore that you can find writ large in capital letters in Ignatian spirituality is to be found in lower case in other orders. So virtually all religious orders today, even those who have a mystical tradition, have been stripped of mystical theology.

In doing this they have been deprived of the unique prayer that has from earliest times been the place where selfless loving is learnt, enabling the purification to take place that enables them to be united with Christ and with his mystical contemplation of the Father. This is the only way that we can participate in Christ's redeeming action and it is therefore the only way that we can attain our destiny, the destiny that God has conceived for us from the beginning. Sadly the "Devout Humanism" that has been all but universally accepted since the condemnation of Quietism, without the majority even realizing it, has been transmitted to the faithful instead of the profound mystical theology that Christ first gave to them in the early Church. It prevents them from doing for a modern pagan world what they did for the ancient pagan world. Jesuit spirituality is still the most influential spirituality in the Church today. The terrible irony is that religious orders who were originally fountains of authentic Catholic spirituality have become the purveyors of the Devout Humanism in which human endeavour attempts to do what only the love of God, his Holy Spirit can do through those who abandon themselves to receive him.

This is the modern malaise from which contemporary Catholic spirituality is suffering. However, what is particularly worrying and that is why I have highlighted the Jesuits, is that while the older orders like the Benedictines, the Dominicans, the Franciscans and the Carmelites do have a long and rich mystical tradition to which they can return, the Jesuits do not, and, in their ignorance, they continue to oppose others, both lay and religious who seek to return to the mystical origins first introduced into Christianity by Christ himself.

For other religious orders, training on how to cooperate with the Holy Spirit to enable him to purify their weak human love for union with God, was of paramount importance before the rise of Quietism. From the time of St Bernard to the condemnation of Quietism the greatest mystical works ever written were produced by the greatest number of mystical writers the Church has ever known. But there have been virtually no Jesuit mystics or mystical writers, and the very way their spirituality is insulated from all others, ensures that no other spirituality is allowed to influence them. The Exercises that are used continually during their training are returned to year after year. For years they insisted that no religious from another order was allowed to give them retreats, for fear that the purity of their own tradition be sullied. So they have insulated themselves from any possibility of being influenced by authentic Catholic Mystical theology. Their retreats are always based on the Ignatian Exercises that clearly only deal with the very beginning of what has been called the purgative way.

It was my admiration for the Jesuits that happily introduced me to the way St Ignatius had perfected the meditation that is always taught to spiritual adolescents. However, I am only referring to the meditations, or what he calls the contemplations, that concentrate on the person of Jesus Christ and on his love, not those calculated to fill us with fear. As I have already described, it was in practising what he calls "contemplation" in the middle of my noviciate that I was so filled with the love of God, made flesh and blood, in the person of Jesus Christ. It was this love that made me yearn for some deeper and more lasting union, that induced the Holy Spirit to lead me on and into the mystical prayer where I was to be purified. It was as if, at this point in my spiritual journey I had so consistently shown my desire for the real thing that it was as if the Holy Spirit said to me, "If that is what you really want, come, I will lead you forward." Without the knowledge that I could not find in Jesuit spirituality I would have been destined to languish without help and succumb, as so many do, to what the Desert Fathers called *Accidie* before giving up what appeared to be a senseless and pointless journey. Fortunately, I came across or was led to the great Carmelite mystical masters.

The teaching of the two great saints raised up by the Church as Mystical Doctors, namely St John of the Cross and St Teresa of Ávila are, at least practically, unknown to Ignatian Spirituality. Yet it is the Church who calls upon us to listen to and implement their teaching for the good of our spiritual lives. These two spiritual giants sum up better than any others the teaching of their predecessors, in particular those myriad mystics who adorned the Church since St Bernard. In the Catholic Mystical tradition, any spirituality that excludes them will not only be impoverished, but condemned to leaving their adherents to remain, at best, as spiritual adolescents, ignorant of the mystical teaching that can alone enable them to grow to full spiritual maturity. This spiritual maturity is attained in years of selfless giving in mystical prayer where human love is so purified that, through union with Christ it can enable them to be led on, in, with and through him into union with God. Until self-centred human beings, and that is how we all begin, are purified they cannot be united with Christ, nor through him with the Father. Nor can this union be attained in months, or even years, more likely in decades of dedicated dying to self, at least for most of us. Surely this is not some sort of esoteric knowledge reserved for a chosen few. Ordinary common sense should make this truth evident to any objective reader. The imperfect cannot be united with the perfect until all the imperfections that prevent this union are purified away.

The daily practice of the "prayer of the heart", under the tutelage of the Holy Spirit, will be the main support that will help believers to keep raising their hearts and minds to God come hell or high water. A spirituality for beginners, no matter how great these beginners might be in human terms, will not be sufficient to remake and remould them into the person of their Risen Lord. Nor will continually returning to them to recharge their batteries throughout the rest of their lives do it either, as if they were continually returning to their prep-schools to be re-invigorated to change the world with a spirituality that is no more than a beginning for beginners. Sadly, without the deep and penetrating purification that their spirituality knows nothing about, they will never be more than pilgrims trapped in a spiritual no-man's-land. This spiritual no-man's-land is located between the first fervour that once set them on fire, and the "mystic way" that has not yet begun, because no one has taught them how to journey onwards, into and through it. In fact, they have been knowingly insulated against it, although to the world they may appear as intellectual giants.

The deep mystical purification about which the great mystics write, not only enables us to observe the first of the new commandments that Christ gave us, but the second too, which is to love others as he loves us (John 13:34–35) and (John 15:12–13). The very idea that a person who has not yet been sufficiently purified to receive the same love that animated Jesus Christ can love others as he did, is to believe that pigs can fly. In his book *Ignatian Spirituality* David Fleming SJ says that Jesuits show their love for God "not in words, but in actions". But a person who has not been purified of the selfishness that always perverts the best of human actions, performs them, without realizing it, not predominantly for the honour and glory of God, but for the honour and glory of themselves. That is why perhaps the only Jesuit mystic that I know of, Louis Lallemant SJ (1578–1635), said that "you can do more for God in a month with contemplation than in a life-time without it."

And the same is true for those who believe that the semi-self-generated love that develops in meditation, or as St Ignatius would call it "contemplation", can permanently change anyone. For the truth is that it is nothing more than the love of a spiritual adolescent. Spiritual adolescence is not, however, unimportant, any more than is the honeymoon period in any good marriage. The love generated and experienced there will fill the heart and mind with feelings and with beliefs that will be stored up in the memory to sustain them "when the well runs dry". Furthermore, it strengthens the will and sharpens its desire so that it wants nothing more than to leave all else behind to reach out to the One whom they now desire above all else. However, only prolonged purification in the Night can transform a person permanently for the better. For only purification can transform our inadequate human love into the love with which Christ loved his Father, and the love with which he loved others. St John of the Cross' masterwork, *The Dark Night of the Soul*, is written precisely for those for whom the first fervour that reaches its heights in the emotionally-filled feelings of adolescent love suddenly comes to an end. The end comes when our heart's desire for God is re-sited by the Holy Spirit to attention on God, not as we imagine him or have tried to depict him, but as he is in himself, or in his Son through whom we reach God, when the purification that is about to begin is sufficiently completed.

This purification constituting 90%, if not more, of a believer's spiritual journey here on earth, cannot be completed by endlessly going back to a spirituality devised for beginners to revive the love that can only be brought to perfection in the Dark Night of purification. Long before the sort of experiences of God's love are felt in this journey, as described in St Teresa's *Interior Castle* and without realizing it, the humility that is learnt in perseverance enables the Holy Spirit to give wisdom to those who believe they are receiving nothing. And this wisdom is given ever more fully as they soldier on through the Night. Only perseverance in the purification of the dark night will generate the true purity of heart, and the true humility that will enable them to become true apostles filled with the God-given love, and the wisdom that it is their privilege to communicate to others.

Chapter 58

Not by Suffering but by Love

At the first Jesuit retreat that I ever attended, Fr Gittings SJ, the retreat master said that the first Jesuits were the Apostles. They were the first to be admitted to the "Society of Jesus" for almost three years before Christ's death and Resurrection. The invitation was left open and I wanted to accept it. Who would not want to be admitted into the "Society of Jesus" like the first Apostles? I was only about twelve at the time, but my mind was made up. When the time came for me to take the step that I had been planning for years and my dyslexia ruled it out, it did not stop me wanting to know more about Ignatian Spirituality although I had become a Franciscan. The more I came to know about it, as you have already gathered, then the more disappointed I became. It became evident to me that although Fr Gittings had every right to suggest that the Apostles were the first to enter into the society of Jesus, at least metaphorically, their spiritual journey did not end there, nor did they immediately start out "to set the world on fire". After the Resurrection they did not immediately rush out to convert the world. They had to wait for the sending of the Holy Spirit, and then wait for that Holy Spirit to remake and remould them into the image and likeness of the One whom they were going to represent.

The first, the sending of the Holy Spirit was instant, but enabling the Holy Spirit to remake them into the image and likeness of their Lord took much longer. It took them many years living in retreat, in Jerusalem, while another apostle, St Paul took almost ten years doing the same in the Arabian desert, and then near his own home, Tarsus. Before the sending of the Holy Spirit they had indeed been members of the "Society of Jesus", if you want to put it that way, but after the sending of the

Holy Spirit the apostles were invited, not just into the society of Jesus, that they had so enjoyed before, but into an even greater deeper and more profound relationship with him. They were invited into, what would later come to be called Christ's Mystical Body, where, as Jesus had promised at the Last Supper, they would become closer to him than they had ever believed possible. However, love is not magic, nor is the love of God, his Holy Spirit. It has to be freely received, and in years rather than months to bring about an inner purification, so that the fruits of God's love could animate them, as it had animated Christ. This love would fill them with all the infused or God-given virtues, that they needed, to do what Christ had done in the Holy Land, in the rest of the world.

That is why the Apostles sought out the time and place for this mystical purification, to prepare them for a union with Christ that could not have taken place before his glorification. The Apostles did not just teach the truths that Jesus had told them to hand on, but the most sublime truth of all, that all were called to a mystical marriage with their Risen Lord for which they would have to be purified, not just for a few years because their purification would, for the vast majority, last for the best part of a lifetime. This purification took place inside the mystical body of Christ, and as it developed, the Apostles were further united with their Risen Lord. It was a mystical union with his mind and heart, with his body and soul, and with his human emotions and feelings too, so that through his human but glorified body, they would be united with his loving of his Father. Remember once again that the word mystical only means invisible, unseen and therefore secret, because onlookers could not see this mystical journey progressing though they could see its fruits in the extraordinary behaviour of those who had been taken up into this Mystic Way. Those who chose to take up their daily cross in prayer to follow this mystical journey came to be called mystics, and their teaching, that grew into a body of specialized knowledge, came to be called mystical theology.

As the most important part of our spiritual journey involves the mystical purification that makes possible our mystical marriage with Christ, for which we were created, it seems incredible that those who choose to join the "Society of Jesus" know nothing about this mystical purification, or the mystical theology that explains it. To deny this teaching, belittle it or even pour cold water on it, and then positively take steps to insulate themselves against it is unforgiveable. It is indeed unforgivable not just to fail, but to refuse to teach young men how to love God by entering into a mystical union with Jesus Christ, by denying them the ancient, age-old teaching of mystical theology, that will alone enable them to do this. Furthermore, it is outrageous to put in its place a programme of self-help, self-awareness, and methods of self-perfection so that they are asked to do for themselves what is primarily the work of the Holy Spirit. In the mainline Catholic tradition, renewal always means going back to prayer, most particularly the mystical prayer where alone a person can be prepared for the mystical marriage to which they are called. In Ignatian Spirituality it means endlessly going back to a programme for beginners that is predominantly anthropocentric, which they not only see as the best possible way to perfection for themselves, but which they endeavour to impose on all others whether they belong to the older orders which are theocentric, or not. The meditation that is detailed in the Exercises is clearly God-centred but when it leads a person to true mystical contemplation there is no further teaching that can lead them onward in the mystic Way, as I, like many others found out for myself. Rather than realizing that the fervour that is lost is one of the signs that may indicate that mystical contemplation has begun, it is more often than not seen as a sign of personal sinfulness or some psychological problem that needs to be resolved before ongoing fervour can be resumed. Always putting the blame on some sort of personal blockage that comes from a person's spiritual or psychological life is one of the reasons that prevents a director seeing that the Holy Spirit has led a person on and into mystical contemplation. It also absolves them of giving the sort of spiritual help for which they have not been trained and have no knowledge. In this way what is called gaslighting takes place in which the person who is being called to mystical contemplation and purification is made to feel that they are the problem when the problem lies within the ignorant spiritual director who is only competent to help spiritual adolescents. He is only able to help with minor problems, not to assist the Holy Spirit in the major problem of preparing an unpurified human being for union with God. Sadly, this form of spiritual gaslighting is not confined to the narrow boundaries of spiritual direction. When the Jesuit Superior General, Fr Everard Mercurian, heard that one of his priests was supporting St Teresa of Ávila on her mystic way, he immediately sent word that under obedience he had to lead her back to the Exercises devised by his founder. If she had listened to a beginner from another tradition, instead of to her own tradition, the Church would have been deprived of one of the greatest mystical Doctors of the Church. If Jesuits are capable of doing this to St Teresa of Ávila, then they are capable of trying to do it for all, and anyone, as they have been doing for over four hundred years, and to the great impoverishment of the Church.

They must be told forthwith that they must stop spiritually abusing the "great men" that they attract, by omission. By omission I mean by failing to teach them the fulness of the Catholic Church's Spiritual tradition, and that of course includes its mystical tradition. They must start teaching it from the very beginning of their training in the noviciate, including the teaching of the two great Mystical Doctors of the Church, St Teresa of Ávila and St John of the Cross. If they will not comply then they must be denied the privilege of receiving new novices until they do. If they continue to defy the authority to whom they are bound like no other congregation, then they should be supressed as should other orders and congregations who follow their bad example. For if this is not done, they will continue to pervert those who come to them, and the faithful at large, not just by omission but by positively propagating pernicious teachings that always prevail amongst all who do not live out the fulness of the Catholic Spiritual tradition. It is not enough merely to live in the "Society of Jesus" as did the first apostles before Christ's death, they must choose to go onward to die with him, and to die to what St Paul called the "old man" so that they can be reborn by the action of the Holy Spirit to become the "new man" which is Christ.

Their own endeavours may well be able to make them into the image and likeness of Marcus Aurelius, but never into the image and likeness of Jesus Christ. Only love, not our love, but God's love transforming our love from within can do this. No amount of self-imposed ascetism or suffering can do this, as so many had come to believe in the "Dark Ages", until God chose to reveal again what he had revealed before, to a lowly draper's son who abandoned his life to him in such a radical way. This revelation is so important that I would like to tell the story of how it happened, and its implications for a Church desperately trying to renew itself at the beginning of the thirteenth century. We need to hear this revelation again, at the beginning of the twenty-first century, or we will continue to think, behave, and act, as if we can do what only God can do, working through those, who are prepared to radically abandon themselves to him, as St Francis did.

On the morning of the fourteenth of September, the feast of the Holy Cross in 1224, St Francis was praying with his arms outstretched in the form of a cross immediately after Mass and before sunrise. He began to pray for the two things that he believed would enable him to attain perfect identity, with the one he called Brother Jesus before he died. Firstly, he prayed that he would be given the privilege to experience the suffering that Christ endured on the Cross. Secondly, that he would be given the privilege of experiencing the love that drove him to give his all for others. As he was praying he felt a flame of love burning within him with ever increasing intensity. Then he looked up to see an angel that he was given to understand was a "Seraph". Although it had six wings, two above its head, two to cover its body, and two with which to fly, it had a human body, the body of a crucified man, which he saw was Christ. As he gazed upon the vision with fear and trembling, he was simultaneously filled with joy.

When the vision finally disappeared Francis experienced Christ's love as never before, while at the same time his body was transformed into the likeness of the crucified man before him who was enfolded by the wings of the "Seraph". The sources are all in agreement that he was left not just with wounds, but with nails in those wounds. The heads of the nails were in his palms and on the top of his feet while the sharp ends curled round underneath in such a way that it was possible to put a finger through the ring that they made. He was unable to walk until St Clare made a special pair of shoes for him. There have been other Saints who have received the stigmata after St Francis, some invisibly like St Catherine of Siena, some visibly like St Padre Pio, but none of them experienced the pain of the nails in the wounds. This was no psychosomatic phenomenon. It was the real thing never experienced before or after St Francis in quite the same way. Although he tried to hide his wounds from his brothers, the blood was such that it soaked his clothing, particularly the blood from the wound in his side. Despite this Francis was in a continual state of joy which he expressed in a hymn that he composed praising the God who had granted him all for which he had prayed, followed by his beautiful poem to Brother Sun, when he returned to Assisi. In order that we do not misunderstand or misinterpret the meaning of the sufferings for which he prayed, and which he eventually experienced, it is important to understand the secret revelation that Francis received from Christ moments before he received the stigmata.

It was at this moment that Francis received a revelation that would determine the very essence of Franciscan Spirituality and the profound theology that it would inspire. The revelation was simply this. He was given to understand that although he had prayed to experience something of the sufferings that Jesus had experienced on the cross, believing this to be the way to union with him, it was in fact not by suffering, but by the inner flame of God's love that he would be transformed into Brother Jesus. The very moment that the vision faded he began to feel that flame within him, whilst at the same time he began to notice the marks of the crucifixion looming large on his body. The sublime union that was now taking place, however, was not caused by the wounds that he could see as they became ever more visible, but by the invisible flame of love within that consumed him. For those who could see, this revelation represented a shaft of light that pierced the thick pall of gloom that hung over mediaeval spirituality, giving hope where all seemed hopeless before. A new spirituality was born with a new theology to explain its profound implications. It was Francis who inspired this new spirituality that proclaimed the *Primacy of Love*, and it was Blessed John Duns Scotus who made it the starting point for the most profound and spiritual theology of love ever written.

From the beginning, authentic Catholic spirituality has been besieged and even overrun at times with alien pagan philosophical "spiritualities" that insisted that the body is evil, or the prison of the soul that must therefore be subjugated by harsh and harmful forms of asceticism that you find nowhere in the Gospels. This is the suffering they chose to bear through self-imposed asceticism, that they believed would lead them to union with God. The Gospel says otherwise. God is love and it is only by love that we can be united with him. It is not our love, but the love of God, sent on the first Pentecost day and on every day to those who are open to receive it. The first Christians were taught how to come to know and love God, by loving his love-made-flesh-and-blood in the person of Jesus Christ through daily meditation. As they learnt to love him and continued to love him when contemplation followed meditation, the deep inner transformation began. In the very act of loving him, these acts of love became a habit of loving that raised a sort of spiritual superhighway that enabled their love, as it can still enable our love today, to rise to him and his love to descend into us. In this way divine and human love meets, mixes, and then merges into one another, enabling us to be united with the God for whom we have yearned for as long as we can remember.

This is the way to God, the way to true happiness and the way, to experience even in this life something of the eternal happiness that God has prepared for us in the next. That is why the revelation to St Francis about the primacy of love was of such absolute importance to people emerging from the "Dark Ages". It was not revealing a new doctrine of the Church but an old one that had been forgotten; they had forgotten the God-given "spirituality of the heart" that prevailed in the early Church, and how to generate a new form of love in which human love was so suffused and surcharged with divine love that the intimate union with God that had been inconceivable before became, not only conceivable, but possible for all. It was not even the suffering of martyrdom, whether it was "blood martyrdom" or "white martyrdom" that united you with God, but love; the love of God that penetrated pervaded and propelled human loving, that was developed in deep personal prayer, and purified and perfected in mystical contemplation.

If there were some acts of heroism, and even eye-catching feats of asceticism in those early days, they were not the acts of Catholic stoics trying to make themselves perfect. They were outward expressions of men, women and children animated by and inspired with the love of God. Later admirers who were inspired by them and wished to emulate them, made the mistake of thinking they had to copy their acts of superhuman asceticism if they wanted to follow them. What was in fact needed, as the revelation to St Francis underlined, was that they should rather generate the quality of personal prayer that could alone enable them to generate the love that could unite them with the One who makes all things possible, even the impossible. It was for this reason that, as you can still see today all over Franciscan Italy, hermitages were built to enable the friars to generate this love, and the mystical contemplation in which their loving would synchronize with the loving of Christ directed toward God in prayer, and indirectly in loving God in the neighbour in need.

Salvation, sanctification, and sanctity then does not involve the arduous task of trying to free oneself from a world in which all things are evil or infected by evil and imposing on oneself a form of inhuman ascetism that you find nowhere in the teaching of Christ, but everywhere, where the influence of Manichaeism still abounds. Nor does it consist in submitting oneself to a code of Spiritual Exercises that promise to make you perfect by methods, techniques and practices that have more in common with Socrates, Seneca, and Marcus Aurelius than with Jesus, Mary, and the first apostles. That is why the ideal for personal and communal renewal is not to return endlessly to man-made programmes to make oneself into a perfect human being, but to God-made love to make us into the perfect man which is Christ. In his diary, St Ignatius wrote that above all other saints he wanted to emulate St Francis of Assisi. What a pity that he never really understood him and the revelation of love that enabled him to re-introduce the God-given spirituality of love that prevailed in the early Church.

I have never been privileged to receive any revelations except one that I was so unpurified that it took years for me to understand it, so it took years for it to get through to me. However, I did finally get the message that I now hand on to you. Give all the time and energy that you have been giving as a Catholic stoic to making yourself perfect, to God. More specifically give it to him in daily prayer as the first Christians did, and he will do what you can never do for yourself, through his Holy Spirit. Then I promise you that the perfection that you desire will be brought about by being transformed, not just into a perfect human being, but into the most perfect human being who God created for that very purpose. What happens next is, "as they say", history, the Salvation history that we experience being brought about within us, as it is brought about in all who, like that young draper's son, abandoned himself totally to the Lord of History.

Chapter 59

Marcus Aurelius Rides Again

The Renaissance (circa 1350–1620) was not caused by the Black
Death (1348–1350), otherwise known as the Plague, that began in
the middle of the fourteenth century, but the spread of its moral
teaching was certainly deeply influenced by it. The Plague was
so horrific, so widespread and so destructive that people began
to ask how God could allow such a thing to happen. Where was
he when the collective prayers of Christendom rose up to plead
with him to stop it. Where was he in those apocalyptical times,
and why was his Church on earth so impotent to prevent almost
half the population of Europe dying terrible gruesome deaths.
Instead of looking to God and his Church then, many started to
look elsewhere for spiritual guidance, for principles on which to
base their lives. When the Renaissance conveniently unearthed
the ancient philosophical religions that the early Church had
condemned, they began to turn to them. This was most especially
true of what came to be called humanism that did not depend
so much on, as they thought, passively waiting on God, but on
man actively taking charge of his own destiny and the moral
principles that promised to secure it. Soon, statues or busts of
Socrates, the father of these ancient philosophical religions were
to be found in major European towns and cities alongside statues
depicting Christ and the saints.

From this time forward two spiritualities began to travel side
by side, one emphasizing human endeavour the other divine
endeavour. In the fifteenth century these two trends could
actually be seen depicted in architecture. In Italy, for instance, the
cradle of the Renaissance, magnificent buildings proclaimed the
glory of what man's action can achieve while humble hermitages
were being built by the great Franciscan reformers amongst

others, to proclaim what the glory of God's action can achieve in the poor and humble of heart who seek him in prayer. In the sixteenth century the trend that over-emphasizes the importance of human action in personal spiritual renewal, could be seen in the Exercises of St Ignatius, while simultaneously, the emphasis on what God's action can achieve could be seen in the works of great mystical writers like St Teresa of Ávila and St John of the Cross. These two trends or pathways continued to journey on side by side in the seventeenth century until at the end of that century the condemnation of Quietism unleashed a powerful anti-mystical lobby that permanently undermined the classical teaching on mystical theology. Henceforth, the two different pathways would disappear as the spirituality that maximised the action of man's endeavour became a single major highway along which man's endeavour became paramount. In other words, the emphasis already seen in the Exercises of St Ignatius seeped into every other order or congregation to a greater or lesser degree, drawing them together on the same man-made highway to God.

Generalizations inevitably lack the finesse of more detailed and more nuanced explanations, but they do have the advantage of giving a bird's eye view, that a serious student can develop for themselves in more detail at ground level. I insist that the bird's eye view is not wrong, and if you are tempted to doubt it, it can be seen today mushrooming at ground level in the Church and to the highest level. Here, human endeavour and fallible human processes of seeking the truth, like "discernment" are preferred to the God-given truth received through the infused virtues and the gifts of the Holy Spirit given to all in the profound mystical prayer which has been lost to sight. What I saw breaking up a Dominican congregation over forty years ago, has been doing the same to many other religious institutions in the intervening years. It is alive and well, and actively doing the same today, not just in, but to the whole Church, and at the highest level. It does not just seek to discern what it has already decided to do, without any meaningful dialogue, but it subtly condemns the God-given spirituality that Jesus Christ introduced to the early Church with catch-all-phrases such as "clerical rigidity". But let me take a look in a little more detail to see how man's endeavour to seek the truth and renew himself can be undermined by the original sin that has undermined us all.

The Credo of the humanism that was born at the Renaissance was, "I believe in man, what man can do, what man can achieve with his unaided human endeavour." The Credo of Christianity that was born on the first Pentecost is, "I believe in God, in what he can do, in what he can achieve with his divine endeavour, working in those who open themselves to receive him." The new religious congregations founded after the rise of humanism then, like the Jesuits, were deeply influenced by what man can achieve, working alone by his own endeavour. Those founded before the rise of humanism are more influenced by what God can achieve working through those who firstly turn to him, and continually turn to him in prayer, so that he can work through them to do what is impossible without him. The discernment process that you find in the Exercises of St Ignatius are a good example of these two different approaches. For the older orders it is in mystical contemplation that the Holy Spirit, gives the wisdom and the other infused virtues that enable a person to see the truth about oneself, about God, and what he wants of you. As the Jesuits have no mystical tradition, they have devised the process of what is called "discernment" to do for them what the Holy Spirit does in mystical contemplation. The only effective way that a person can discern God's will for themselves, or for others is in the light of the Holy Spirit, not in the light of man-made rules or instructions. Even if they were divinely inspired, they will be misunderstood and misapplied by those who have not been sufficiently purified in the mystic way to receive the "infused gift of Wisdom".

In order to understand the discernment process in the

Exercises, I must remind you of what I have said earlier. That the devil exists is the teaching of the Church. That he is seen to have attacked Christ is clear from scripture, but from the outside. It must be quite clear that the Evil One could not get inside Christ either when he was on earth or in heaven, which is good news for us. For although the Devil is the ultimate personification of Evil, he cannot enter into the glorified body of Christ, so those who enter into his mystical body are safe from direct confrontation with him. Therefore, although we may be assailed by powerful temptations, we are safe from direct confrontation with the Evil One, or the "Enemy", as he is described in the Exercises.

When I have spoken in the past about the "demons within" I made it clear that I am using the phrase metaphorically. I am therefore referring to the unruly passions and urges, the consequences of original sin that keep threatening to destroy us. I am not referring to demonic creatures, agents of the devil, that dwell within us like pernicious gremlins gleefully plotting to destroy us. This is an important distinction that must be made as, beginning with the Desert Fathers this distinction can become blurred so that you cannot always tell when a person is speaking literally or metaphorically. In the Exercises, however, it seems that the active presence of the "Enemy", who is, as St Ignatius puts it is "known by his serpent's tail and the bad end to which he leads us", is to be taken literarily, as are the good and bad Angels, or good or evil spirits to which he repeatedly refers (see Fr David Flemings presentation of the Spiritual Exercises page 216). It gives rise to the simplistic imagery of the good angel standing on one shoulder whispering into your right ear trying to get you to do good things while a bad angel stands on the other shoulder trying to seduce you into doing bad things.

If such a presentation of the spiritual combat was helpful over four hundred years ago, I cannot help feeling that modern readers would find it far more helpful to be told the truth that coincides with their experience. That is, that the evil that we do comes from our fallen nature as St Paul experienced for himself without any reference to good or bad angels, to say nothing of the "Enemy" as a serpent with a perceivable tail. He writes, "I fail to carry out the things I want to do, and I find myself doing the very things I hate.... and so the thing behaving in that way is not myself, but sin living in me. When I act against my own will, then, it is not my true self doing it, but sin which lives in me" (Romans 7:14–20). In recent years this discernment process has been taken out of the Exercises and presented as a programme for spiritual advancement in its own right. Anyone who has been dazzled by the expertise of a sincere and competent presenter would be advised to read the rules for discernment in the Exercises for themselves. Then see them in the context of the other teachings in the Exercises. They would then see that even the greatest of presenters is doing no more than trying to modernise practices that would be better left to be studied by spiritual antiquarians to understand a specific expression of the faith at a particular time in Church history.

The rampant humanism that inspires them, guarantees that they are riddled with the semi-Pelagianism that always prevails when a spirituality places all the emphasis on personal endeavour to make themselves perfect despite a perfunctory reference to grace. The relentless concentration on oneself and on trying to discern one's motives, inevitably leads to the scrupulosity that the Exercises are forced to address, for they are the inevitable consequences of self-centred spiritual monomania. All the great Jesuits, with whom I have raised the question of their spiritual training, take the whole matter with a "pinch of salt", that they try to laugh off. If pressed, the only good point to which they draw your attention is that it is such a "terrible treadmill" that it ensures that only those with deeply embedded psychological security will survive. Many other survivors of the "spiritual" training programmes of other orders would, in my experience agree with them, and point out that at least they would be far less harmful than psychological programmes with which some religious orders tried to replace them. I have noticed over the years that despite the emphasis that the Jesuits put on the Exercises, most of the high-flying Jesuits whom I have known over the years, are a little embarrassed by the rather crude and simplistic language in which their founder wrote them. This is not to mention the undisguised stoicism and the biblical fundamentalism that makes them rather defensive. I have also noticed that few, if any, of the well-known Jesuits run the retreat centres where retreatants are guided through the Exercises. It is usually a job left to lesser-known Jesuits, or to religious men or women of other orders and sometimes even to lay-devotees.

If all the time given to trying to understand this questionable programme for perfection, with the endless examinations of conscience that all concentrate on self, were used to concentrate on God instead then spiritual advancement would be far safer, far quicker, and far less dangerous. Notice that the solution to the predicament that St Paul found himself in did not induce him to turn within to try and discern the source of his dilemmas and seek the wisdom of current pagan religious philosophies but, in his own words, he could only be rescued, "Thanks be to God through Jesus Christ, Our Lord" (Romans 7:25). In the very next chapter, he goes on to expand on precisely what he means when he writes, "For I am certain of this: neither death nor life, no angel, no prince, nothing that exists, nothing still to come, not any power, or height or depth, nor any created thing, can ever come between us and the love of God made visible in Christ Jesus our Lord" (Romans 8:38–39). In short, and as I keep emphasizing, the devil cannot exist in, never mind operate within the glorified body of Christ and in those who have been led there after baptism as their new home where they "live and move and have their very existence".

Quite apart from the predominance of concentration on self

rather than on God, those who do take the Exercises seriously, and try to update them for the faithful at large can, and have done, serious damage both to individuals and to communities. In my own personal experience that I have described, it broke into two a large Dominican Congregation by using methods of discernment taught at the Jesuit renewal centre in Denver, Colorado, USA. The Dominicans sent to be trained there discerned that those other Dominicans who wanted to follow the Classical Dominican Tradition instead of the latest pop socio-psychological techniques to change themselves, with a lot of "help" from Professor Rulla's depth psychology, were being led astray by the "Enemy". I have to own up to a certain vested interest in this affair, as it was discerned that I was possessed by the "Enemy" and only exorcism could free me. Forty years later, those who did the discerning have completely disappeared off the religious map. Those who returned to their own Dominican tradition are now thriving as a new Dominican Congregation, and the one who led them astray is just finishing his tenth book on prayer, so you can judge for yourself whether or not he is still in need of exorcism!

Sadly and more seriously, many of those abused by the Jesuit academic, Professor Rulla and his devotees schooled in his evil psychological machinations, are still suffering from post-traumatic stress. This I know from experience, helping those harmed by the misuse of depth psychological techniques in the spiritual life. Their arrogance implicit in believing that they can do and do far more quickly what only the Holy Spirit can do in the spiritual life, has the sulphurous stench of evil about it. Even now after forty years I am still helping one of them. The instigators of this particular form of psychological abuse and their perpetrators are in my opinion devilish, and I am not speaking metaphorically. Of course I believe that possession is possible for those who are outside the mystical body of Christ, and I believe there will be devilish rewards awaiting them. I do not know precisely where Dante would place them in his

Inferno, but I have a few ideas of my own!

At the end of my first year of Philosophy I had to write a dissertation on Stoicism. In the oral examination Fr Germaine Heron, the professor of Philosophy had only one complaint about my work. "It seems that you are a fan," he said. "I expected you to provide me with a criticism, but all you have done is to produce a eulogy!" He was of course quite right. I was a fan of the stoical ideals that had sunk into my spiritual DNA that had been presented to us at school by the secular priests who taught us, and by the Jesuit priests who gave our annual retreats. Nor had the training in the noviciate done anything but encourage my stoical endeavour to make myself into a saint. I clearly remember deciding to master a different virtue each month to make myself into a saint, so that when my parents came for my first profession at the end of the year their erstwhile and errant offspring would be no more. The familiar shape and form would still be there but it would be no more than the outer shell that enclosed the new-made man within. If I achieved my objective, which I did not, he would have been far more like Marcus Aurelius of Rome than Jesus Christ of Nazareth. However, unknown to me at the time a change was beginning to take place deep down within me. Inside the dark chrysalis into which my prayer life had plunged me in the noviciate, a transformation was gradually taking place from which in God's time a new creature would emerge. If this creature would not be like a butterfly, then at least it would be like a man who would know that without a shadow of a doubt, that only God and his love could do what the stoicism to which I had once aspired could never do.

Professor Heron was adamant that the stoics were the most arrogant of men, because they believed that they could make themselves into perfect human beings by their own unaided endeavour, and those others too, whom they tried to change into their own image and likeness. This was the arrogance that I saw in those at whose hands I suffered, with so many others, when the new evangelists from Denver, Colorado, came to force a new modern form of stoicism on others and tried to destroy those who stood in their way. Classical stoicism was bad enough, but when the new stoics had their own pop-psychological techniques, that they believed were infallible, to add to, if not replace the man-made, anthropocentric spirituality of the Exercises, then the Pelagians, with whom St Augustine had fought so long and so hard, were back in town. In the God-centred spiritualities that puts all the emphasis on God and what he can achieve through those who are ever open, ever docile, and ever submissive to receive his Holy Spirit, the faithful are always characterised by humility. It is the humility of those who know without a shadow of a doubt that they are doing nothing and he is doing everything.

It is the Holy Spirit who leads a person to perfection with the loving kindness that gradually shows them all that separates them from the union that they desire and supports and sustains them through the purification that is his work, not man's. That is why St John of the Cross says the "Dark Night" is safe for it is the place where God's love is ever shining. It continually shines through the darkness to be received by those who it makes ever humbler. This is where true humility is learnt, not by being humiliated, by their stoical task masters, but by experiencing he who is mighty doing great things within them. As their humility deepens it magnifies the light of love that is purifying them accelerating their spiritual growth that Christ may be born again, this time in those who are made humble enough to receive him.

I have been spending so much time writing about Ignatian Spirituality because since Quietism and the demise of traditional Catholic Mystical Spirituality it is Jesuit spirituality that to a greater or lesser degree has seeped into most other religious orders most especially orders of women. The Jesuits have in the past and continue to produce great intellectual and theological scholars that can match and even excel in the world of secular scholarship. However, when the infused gift of wisdom is required that only comes through mystical contemplation, then they are found, not only wanting, but often in serious error. From the outset it has been their proclaimed objective as Catholic humanists to understand and harness the ever-progressing wisdom of the world for the good of the Church. But pure secular knowledge and learning, no matter how great, without the infused virtues given by God, most particularly wisdom, will prevent them from doing what is part of their very *raison d'être*.

I have already shown how the serious misuse of psychology by Jesuits, and others, has had on my life and on that of many others. However, what is happening today by Jesuits in the very highest positions of influence in the Church, without the gift of Wisdom that comes from God through contemplation, is turning out to be little less than catastrophic. They are expressly using and encouraging others to use the discernment that they learnt in their training to come to frightening conclusions that even, or especially the humblest of the laity, can see are light years away from the teachings of Christ. It is so easy to use discernment to arrive at the conclusions that you have already come to before you even begin the process. This man-made process, that purports to include the Holy Spirit, is seriously wanting. However, it continues to deceive the innocent that their conclusions are not just infallible but inspired by the Holy Spirit.

The many thousands of different denominations, that grew out of the Protestant reformation, should be proof enough that those who deceive themselves into believing that they are able to discern what the Holy Spirit wants of them or wants of others are deceiving themselves. This is especially true of those who have rejected the mystical prayer and the mystical purification that alone enables the Holy Spirit to give the infused virtues, and in this case the infused virtue of wisdom, to those who need his guidance. Self-centred, sinful human beings who have rejected the purification that comes from carrying the cross in prayer, believe in magic if they believe that their man-made methods and techniques can give them a direct line to the wisdom of God. I am reminded of the members of a Catholic Youth club, who were totally convinced that the Holy Spirit was guiding them through the Ouija board that had taken over their lives. They were amazed at how they were being guided to some incredible conclusions by the Holy Spirit who never failed to answer their questions. Once I put blindfolds over their eyes the answers that they received from the "Holy Spirit" were reduced to gibberish! If it were possible to put spiritual blindfolds on to those who believed they were being led by the Holy Spirit, then the answer that they received would be gibberish too. That they come to the answers they want, more usually the answers they had decided upon before the process of discernment begins, is a clear indication that, like the children in the youth club, they are deceiving themselves and for that matter others too.

In the last forty years or so since I first experienced the misuse of the discernment process, I have no idea how many other priests, religious, and laity have had their lives or their way of life ruined by unprepared, misinformed and unpurified crusaders trying to renew others with what would later ruin their own lives too. What I do know is that their methods are still with us and being implemented on a wider and an even higher level than ever before. That synods have been used by the Church in the past and used successfully for the good of the Church is undeniable, but the very ingredients that once made them so effective do not seem to be verified in what is coming to be called "synodality". For synods to be successful then dialogue is essential. Dialogue with God, with the people of God, and with oneself – with one's own conscience, in which listening is paramount. For dialogue with God to be effective and enable the participants to participate without personal sinfulness, self-interest, pride or prejudice or the other moral imposters destroying this process, then prayer and the purification that makes deep prayer possible must be sufficiently advanced in all taking part. Only this safeguard can guarantee that the participants are listening to God and not to themselves. For genuine dialogue with the people of God to take place, and not just with the like-minded, a certain basic degree of personal holiness learnt in prayer beyond first beginnings is essential. Finally, dialogue with oneself through one's own conscience can only be guaranteed when the reason has been sufficiently purified to enable it to apply the traditional teaching of the Church to the matters in hand.

In AD 537 the greatest church in Christendom was built in what was then called Constantinople, in honour of the Holy Spirit in thanksgiving for his part in implementing Gods plan in the first Christian centuries. Understandably then it was called *Hagia Sophia* or Holy Wisdom. At the Last Supper Jesus promised that the Holy Spirit would come to fill the apostles and his future followers with his Wisdom so that they could continue the work of our redemption. He put it this way at the Last Supper. "I still have many things to say to you, but they would be too much for you now. But when the Spirit of Truth comes he will lead you to the complete truth" (John 16:12–13).

When in about AD 48 fifteen or more years after the Crucifixion, several serious questions that were dividing the early Christians had to be resolved, a gathering of the faithful was called together to settle the matters. St Peter presided but other apostles were there too, including St Paul. This conclave that came to be called the Council of Jerusalem was seen as the prototype and forerunner of the later ecumenical councils. Please notice that those involved had come, not to take part in some sort of discernment process devised by human beings, but in serious debate and discussion that was successful because deep and prolonged prayer had sufficiently purified their minds and hearts, making then porous to the wisdom of the Holy Spirit. We have seen how this had taken place over many years in the lives of the apostles in "retreat" at Jerusalem and in St Paul's "noviciate" in the Arabian desert and in Tarsus, where they had been radically purified in such a way that they were open and docile to the inspiration of the Holy Spirit. Furthermore, their experience had led them to insist on at least two years of prayerful preparation for all those who were preparing for baptism, after which this preparation would become part of their daily lives, as described by the fathers of the Church.

The fruitfulness and effectiveness of all later Councils, Conclaves and Synods depended on prolonged and serious arguments and debates of the participants who for many years had their minds, their reasons and their hearts purified in profound contemplative prayer. It was the quality of the collective prayerfulness of the participants that preceded these conclaves that determined the quality of the presence and the power, the influence and the inspiration of the Holy Spirit. Their conclusions therefore would always be attributed to the Holy Spirit working through those who, through their prayerfulness were at all times open to receive his wisdom. That is why when announcing the results of their deliberations at the Council of Jerusalem, St Peter uttered those famous words. "It has been decided by the Holy Spirit and ourselves" (Acts 15:28).

In Catholic Councils, Conclaves and Synods it is primarily the Spirt who is at work, but his work depends on the collective quality of the holiness of those who are sufficiently open to receive him. This is how God's will is sought in the Catholic Church. The same means of seeking his will was copied by the monks in their monasteries and the mendicants in their priories and friaries through their chapters. It was only when later congregations like the Jesuits had rejected contemplative prayer and the purification that would make the working of their minds and heart both sensitive and open to the Holy Spirit, that they had to devise man-made methods and techniques to discover or in their words "discern the truth" to which only the Holy Spirit can lead people. That other priests and religious have all but forgotten the profound purifying prayer that can open them the more readily to the Holy Spirit has prevented them from seeing clearly and so opposing a semi-Pelagian means and methods of seeking true Wisdom. True God-given Wisdom is only fully open to those who have become poor in spirit and humble and pure of heart, in the purification that only comes through encountering He who is mighty, in profound contemplative prayer.

Thanks to the reasons that I have given to show why this prayer has been all but abandoned in the Church in general, the so called discernment process that once thrived at a lower level has been adopted at the highest level in the Catholic Church. Then, to add insult to injury, religious communities dedicated to contemplative prayer are being attacked and dismantled while inviting all and sundry to take part in discernment processes in which, often enough the conclusions have already been decided before the "discernment" begins. Although, as I have insisted that other religious orders have forgotten the contemplative prayer that was once their spiritual bedrock, they have not, like the Jesuits, invented their own man-made methods of trying to discern God's will and become actively involved in spreading it to others. That is why I have singled the Jesuits out.

If they would only read the first few chapters of St John of the Cross's masterwork *The Dark Night of the Soul* they would see enumerated all the sins and selfishness, all the faults and failings and all the wickedness and the wrongdoings that necessitate the Holy Spirt leading a person into contemplative purification. Just as all these human evils that are present within everyone at the beginning, prevent a person from entering into the pure God-given contemplation as detailed by St Teresa of Ávila, they also prevent the process of "discernment". They prevent this process from achieving, not just what it claims to achieve, discerning God's will but often leads them to do the very opposite. For the truth of the matter is the one they call the "Enemy" can rule through the unpurified and unbridled evil instincts, drives and impulses that are still very much alive and active within them. In short, they deceive themselves and they deceive others and with disastrous consequences.

Such universal Synods as the Councils of Nicaea, Chalcedon and Ephesus are examples of how the Holy Spirit can work through those who are open to receive him, in an age when the dominant spirituality was theocentric not anthropocentric. Synods are not just for saints, but for sinners too who persevere in the prayer that opens them to Wisdom, not to man's wisdom but to God's Wisdom. When anthropocentric spiritualities predominate, any sort of discernment process, and at any level is fraught, because it can so easily be taken over by the self-serving Ego within, as I have seen often enough for myself. This is one more reason why I have written this book, so that we can learn to return to the theocentric spirituality that Christ himself gave us. It is in this spirituality that what St Paul calls the "old man" can be destroyed in us, so that the "new man" which is Christ, can guide us by his wisdom.

One of the frightening features of a discernment process in the anthropocentric spirituality that predominates today, is that when a person comes to the conclusions that they have usually come to before the process begins, then they believe that their conclusions are, "of God". When this happens, woe betide anyone who tries to argue with, or stand against, anyone who believes that they are being led or inspired by God. This time it will not be Marcus Aurelius, but Oliver Cromwell who rides again! In anthropocentric spiritualities it is predominantly human action that promises to bring about their version of heaven on earth. In theocentric spiritualities it is predominantly divine action that promises to bring about God's version of heaven on earth.

Whenever their anthropocentric spirituality is questioned then the questioner is put in their place by reminding them that of course the Mass, the sacraments and the grace of God are necessary. But as always, they are in fact assumed rather than emphasized and not given the emphasis that they are in the theocentric spirituality given to us by Christ himself. The sacraments and the love of God that pours out of them are not magic, they can only be fully received by the pure in heart who have been purified in the profound mystical purification that takes place in the contemplative prayer that has played no part in their spirituality for over five hundred years. Yet for centuries they have gaslighted all who oppose them by making them feel that they are some form of inferior spiritual species for not seeing and accepting without question a spirituality that is long since dead, but sadly far from buried, to the continual jeopardy of renewal in the Church.

If their discernment processes were predominantly "of God" then they would have long since discerned how to discern when and how the Holy Spirit leads a person from meditation into contemplation. It seems hardly believable, but they have not only been unable to do this, but they have continually rejected or undermined those who could, including such great Doctors of the Church as St John of the Cross, St Teresa of Ávila and St Catherine of Siena. This failure alone should make any objective observer question a discernment process that they seem to think should be accepted without question. It seems hardly credible that a religious congregation that insists on a far longer period of preparation than any other should exclude the deep purification of the heart at the expense of the education of the mind. That they do this with the best of intentions, is unfortunately not enough to redeem them from being blind leaders of the blind who, unless they radically return to authentic Catholic spirituality should be stopped.

Just as we know that this spirituality was originally in balance by its acceptance by the Church, the imbalance into which it has fallen is proven by the evidence of subsequent history, most particularly modern history, some of which I have been able to draw to your attention. Its imbalance is now so evident and therefore so dangerous that it must be called to book. Its adherents, however, are well adapted to defend themselves. When, despite their renowned intellectual prowess in other matters, they find themselves disadvantaged by rational debate in this matter, they tend to reduce the argument to the personal. Like the scientologists they attack and undermine the credibility of their opponents rather than engage in objective discussions of what has clearly deviated from the theocentric spirituality that Christ introduced into the early Church. A false sense of charity, that is more akin to political correctness, has prevented other clergy from outwardly expressing their misgivings even though we are in the last minute of extra time, and if we do not return to the Spirituality of the Gospels without delay then the consequences that are already in motion could quickly escalate into complete pandemonium.

It is important to remember that St Thomas Aquinas said the vocation of God's apostles in every age is to contemplate and then share the fruits of contemplation with others. When we all start to do this then we will be back on the road to do what God had created us for in the beginning. When at the end of his life St Thomas experienced the love of God like never before he stopped writing. That is why his great *Summa* was never finished. Compared to the love of God that he then began to experience, all he had written before was he said, no more than straw. This love of God and all the infused virtues that are communicated through it are for all, high or low, educated or uneducated, lay or religious, enabling them to do what God has created them for in this life and to enjoy eternal life in the next. They cannot be obtained through discernment, but only by dying to self as St Francis taught, that can alone induce the Holy Spirit to possess us and bring Christ to birth again in us. Then we will be guided by his love and the infused virtues contained within it, for our salvation and for that of the whole world. Seek first above all else, God and his Kingdom of love, and everything else, including the wisdom that you seek, will be given to you.

Chapter 60

The Last Minute of Extra Time

The Greco-Roman Stoics were all inspired by the words of the Delphic Oracle to "Know Thyself". This was for them the beginning of wisdom. They believed that until self-knowledge was in place then you could not even begin to change yourself, never mind others. Fr Bernard Bassett SJ used to say in his retreats that if your friend would not tell you the truth, pay an enemy to do it for you. It was a lesson that he would have learnt the hard way in his Jesuit training where the famous "Ring" was used to do what you might otherwise have to pay an enemy to do for you. Each had to take their turn, and regularly, in this degrading charade. The famous Jesuit obedience would ensure that nobody would hold back from denouncing the faults and failings of others, who one by one had to stand at the centre of a ring composed of one's peers whose accusations would regularly reduce even the toughest to tears. This usually happened when the presiding priest would then compare the moral mess that you were, to the moral perfection of the man you aspired to become. Nor would this telling the truth be confined to the "Ring" as it was part of the training to inform superiors of any misdemeanour of others and check up on whether or not another was "at prayer" or examining their conscience at the prescribed times to further their own personal endeavour to achieve their objective of stoical perfection.

In the years after the war when God was in his heaven and everything seemed well with the Church it would never have been considered "cricket" to criticise the spirituality of other religious orders, at least openly. After all, "dog does not eat dog" in the Catholic Church. But seventy years on when the religious orders and the religious congregations of both men and women have in many places all but disappeared and the laity are in a spiritual topsy-turvy land, with the leadership all at sea, it is time for the truth to be stated openly and clearly. If the truth cannot be told at the eleventh hour, in the last minute of extra time, then when can it be told?

If I have singled out the Jesuits to stand in the "Ring", it is because in the last four hundred years or so, since the Empire has been striking back under cover of the Renaissance with the teachings of its Pagan Philosophies, they have been the most influential congregation. Furthermore, they have been the most emulated even by those who do not realize it. They are such a good example of what goes wrong when love is lost in religious life, that I am using them as an example, but by no means the only example of what can be seen in almost every other current religious order or congregation. Here I would like to include a more modern congregation or institute in the Church known as Opus Dei that has some characteristics in common with the Jesuits, but sadly far more in common with contemporary cults. They are just as anti-mystical as the Jesuits.

I cannot speak in detail for others but in the Franciscan order that I joined to try my vocation in 1957 there were almost three hundred friars with missions in India and South Africa. Now, however, I would be surprised if there are more than ten left with an average age of over seventy. I have no doubt that similar statistics could be gleaned from other religious orders, including the Jesuits. For years the blind have been crying out that this modern generation do not have the idealism that inspired us, being too lost in materialism to seek the spiritual. In my experience this is not true. The problem is that even if it were not for the sexual scandals perpetrated on an industrial scale by men and women vowed to chastity, they see nothing in the vast majority of modern religious to inspire them. That the perennial desire that always rises in the young to seek what is good, what is just, what is right, and what or who is spiritually loveable, is there today as it always has been, is not in question.

Religious life has to be radically reformed and without any further delay. It may well be true, as I have argued that it was lay leadership that was paramount in early Christianity, before religious life existed, and when the majority of religious orders or congregations that we know today were more than a millennium away. But since they came they have exerted a leadership role amongst the laity in matters spiritual that must be replaced, not necessarily by new religious orders, but by old religious orders returning to what they once were. We are indeed in the last minute of extra time so let me suggest a way that the Jesuits might like to take the lead and how others might like to follow their example. I would call a dozen of the greatest Jesuit minds to Rome and ask them to form a ring around their "Spiritual Exercises". Then under obedience casting off any familial affection for the "treadmill that formed them" criticise what may well be an interesting historical document, once used to train trainees in a bygone age when humanism was rife, but which is today no longer fit for purpose. When the strictures of holy Obedience has freed them to say what must have been lurking in their minds before, introduce specially selected members of other orders, older religious orders who have access to a tradition that they have long since rejected, to learn how they can both profit from what has long since been forgotten, or at least in practice, no longer lived.

The Exercises begin by teaching us that it is by coming to know ourselves that we can be changed. The Gospels begin by teaching us that it is in coming to know God that, his love alone can change us. The Exercises teach us how it is primarily by mastering stoical methods and techniques of asceticism that we can change ourselves from the sinners that we are, into the saints we want to become. The Gospels teach us how it is by coming to love God, as he is embodied in Our Lord Jesus Christ, that his love can change us from the sinners that we are to the saints that we want to become. The first draft of the Exercises was written by St Ignatius at Manresa in 1522, at the height of the Renaissance, when he was only a novice himself, so he could not help being influenced by the principles of humanism that was in full swing.

If they are to be re-calibrated so that they can be made fit for purpose they must be redesigned to become theocentric not anthropocentric. The whole attention from the outset must be focused on coming to know and love Jesus Christ, and away from morbid concentration on self. In order to do this we need look no further than the Exercises themselves in which St Ignatius holds up three great saints, not just to inspire his followers, but for them to be emulated. They are St Augustine, St Bernard, and St Francis of Assisi. St Augustine teaches us to follow our heart's deepest desire that will never be satisfied until it rests in God. St Bernard teaches us that it is only by entering into a profound mystical marriage with Christ in which our love and his love can mingle, mix and merge, that it can rest in God, beginning now in this life. Moments before he received the stigmata St Francis, as we have already seen, received the revelation of the primacy of love. Christ said to him that it was not by suffering, most particularly by self-inflicted suffering that you can be united with God, but only by love, his love. The spiritual life then begins in earnest, not by trying to take upon ourselves the punishing forms of asceticism with which we think that we can change ourselves, but by receiving his love to do what no earthly power can ever enable us to do. It does, however, begin with asceticism but with the "asceticism of the heart" that seeks out the quality space and time in which to open our hearts to the love that only God can give us through his Son Jesus Christ.

That is why, first and foremost, and above all else, the unique and meticulous teaching of St Ignatius on how to meditate should be introduced to novices on day one. Not those calculated to fill us with fear, but those with which to fill us with God's love as we find it embodied in Jesus Christ Our Lord. And this should be done for every novice both male and female of every other order or congregation. And the same should be done for secular priests too for whom noviciates should be introduced for this very purpose. If the first apostles and St Paul needed a noviciate then so also do those who have never seen Christ, else they will never really come to know and love the person whose life and love they are called to introduce to others. That this has not been done, as it should have been done for centuries, is the scandal of what the aftermath of Quietism has done to religious and clerical education. That it has not been done was what I had to find out for myself, in many years of auditing the priests and religious, who came to my retreat and conference centre and to whom I gave retreats for over twenty years. The lay reader will be shocked to be told that very few of them had experiences much different from my own, who in seven years of training in the Franciscan Order never had a single instruction or talk on personal pray or on how to pray. The only congregation that did were the Jesuits. But why, despite the unique opportunity that St Ignatius gave to his followers, this meditation never led on to mystical contemplation is still a mystery to me. That it was wrongly believed that what St Ignatius called "contemplation" was what the great spiritual writers called "mystical contemplation", is a mystery to me too. It led those who generated this prayer to believe that they had experienced the mystical union that is the culmination of the mystical journey here on earth. It was this that made them, and likeminded evangelists, to go out to share the fruits of their predominantly "man-made and emotional contemplation" with others, and to return to it when their "well ran dry". This is not what St Thomas Aquinas meant by and defined as contemplation in concert with the whole Catholic mystical tradition.

There is a general consensus amongst spiritual theologians that in seventeen-century Europe the teaching and the study of mystical theology reached its height, and this practical teaching began in noviciates. Many novice masters and novice mistresses, not only believed, but showed how in practice, meditation could be taught from the outset, and their novices could be led into what St John of the Cross had only recently called the Dark Night before the end of their noviciate. The advantage of this was enormous, because before they began their future studies, they would have, not only been told that they had entered the "Dark Night", but that what St John of the Cross called "contemplation", and they could therefore be taught how to adjust their prayer life accordingly.

All that I have said in this book to sum up the Catholic mystical tradition should be taught to novices including the new simpler form of Prayer based on different forms of the "prayer of the heart", the practice of which would eventually lead to the purity of heart that would enable them, as the beatitudes put it to see God. One thing must be said and underlined. The whole point and purpose of this purification is that at the end of it, the mind and the heart, the feelings and the memory and the imagination, together with the whole human personality, will be so purified both physically and spiritually that they can be united with Jesus Christ Our Lord like never before. This means our whole body, blood soul and humanity with his body, blood soul and humanity, so that through the hypostatic union where his humanity and his divinity form one person, we can go on, in with and through him to the Father, in whom is our ultimate destiny in the next life and our joy in this life. To begin with we showed our belief in this profound union into which we are invited in words, in prayer, in liturgy, but now once purified it takes place in reality. In short, we begin as Catholic nominalists, but if we persevere through purification we end up as Catholic realists.

All the great mystical saints knew this, but so many others, who claim to be practising Catholics, despite Christ's incarnation, despite his life and his ignominious death on the Cross, remain in practice "spiritual hybrids", semi-Gnostics, semi-Manichaeans, semi-Neoplatonist or simply materialists, who only believe that Union with God can take place through some sort of direct pseudo-mystical knowledge, in this life or in the next, that is and can only be, purely spiritual? The whole point of God's plan, his *mysterion*, as St Paul called it, is that union between the infinite and the finite can take place, because of our real personal and human union with the glorified humanity of Jesus Christ. But without the purification that prepares a human being to be united with his human being, then such a union is, and can be, no more than a pipe dream. Hence the mystical renewal that must begin now, not just for priests and religious but hopefully with their support and leadership, for everyone, so that from being no more than nominal Catholics they can become real Catholics, because they are in every way united to the real living and glorified body of Jesus Christ, Our Lord and Our Saviour.

For the last four hundred years or more we have become blind, living like the prisoners chained up in Plato's famous cave, only gazing at shadows on the back wall of our prison. The shadows of the real world are so indistinct that each manages to see in them what they want to see, and they create their own little worlds and their own self-made spiritualities. When someone like Socrates came to awaken them with the truth, they killed him as they killed Christ and most of the prophets who insist on trying to tell them what needs changing, what they fail to see in their blindness, and what they think they see in their ignorance.

In recent years we have had a Jubilee Year, a Year of Mercy, a year in honour of St Joseph. What we now need is a year of repentance, reparation and prayer. Repentance to turn back to Jesus Christ and make him once more, what he was in the early Church, the heart and the soul of our daily personal prayer. This must be made clear by the way we do first and foremost what was done by the early Christians beginning the very moment when they chose to become one of God's people. Namely, they went to Christ whom they were taught to come to know and love through the new form of prayer called meditation. Then, how to journey on by carrying the cross with him both inside and outside of prayer to be purified so that their bodies can be prepared for Union with the Body of Christ who converted a Pagan Roman Empire into a Christian Empire through them, as he can still do again today through us. It must be a year of reparation too, reparation for countless thousands of abused children, and even more abused women, and for the scandalised laity too, both inside and outside of the Church by loveless priests and religious, who sought and continue to seek counterfeit love for the love they never learnt or received in their training. In addition to the physical, psychological, spiritual as well as the financial reparation that must take place, that this may never happen again, all priests and religious must be taught as their first ancestors were taught, not just to give their lives over to Christ in words, but in a deep and ongoing prayer life from the moment that they enter a house of religious training. To this end those who receive Novices must be trained, not just to teach their charges to meditate from the outset but how to contemplate when the Holy Spirit leads them on.

If, as in very many instances, novice masters and novice mistresses, who are able to do this are not available, then noviciates must be closed down until they are, else more loveless priests and religious will be deformed to give scandal to the faithful. If it is seriously sinful to perform sexual crimes then it is also seriously sinful to put a person in a position where such sins are all but inevitable, because they have not been taught how to come to know and love God. If superiors demand that young men and women take vows of chastity then they must also teach them the profound mystical love that can make possible and fruitful what cannot be achieved without it. All religious orders or congregations, who fail to return to this Christ-centred mystical spirituality that once flourished in the Catholic Church must be suppressed until they do and supressed permanently if they permanently fail to do what is demanded of them.

I leave it to others to detail the scandalous moral malaises that prevail even in the highest positions in the Church. This is not the place to detail them; others have done and are still doing this for me, but simply to say that without the contemplation that St Thomas Aquinas once said should prevail at all levels in the Church then spiritual anarchy will continue to ensue. For the fruits of contemplation – God's indwelling love, and all the other infused virtues given by the Holy Spirit, especially wisdom, will be lacking and the spiritual chaos that inevitably follows when human wisdom alone is used to solve spiritual problems, will continue to be evident everywhere.

If what I am demanding seems outrageous then it is only because those who are outraged, have come to accept as normal what is slowly destroying the Church. Surely we all know and accept the two new commandments that Christ gave us. The first from which the second flows states quite clearly that we are to love God with our whole minds and hearts, with our whole bodies and souls and with our whole strength. This universal commandment for the whole Church can only be realized to the degree in which each member of the Church is taught how this love is first learnt and then grows and develops in the years ahead in personal prayer. For there to be spiritual directors and leaders who are at the disposal of the laity for this purpose, every priest and every religious must, from the outset, and above all else, be taught how to practise this the greatest of all the commandments that begins in deep personal daily prayer. Furthermore, and from the very beginning of their training they must be taught how to read and understand, at least in theory, the great mystical Doctors of the Church. Then, when the time comes when they are led into the mystic way, they will know where to go to look for the help if they cannot find it elsewhere.

That is until the great spiritual revival that is already underway provides wise and prudent practitioners who are once more as commonplace as they were in the past.

Chapter 61

The Father of Counterfeit Mysticism

Before moving on to end this book with some simple practical examples, and what I call the "ascetism of the heart", I would like to pause for a moment to warn my readers of a fraudulent mystic, who has been called the father of counterfeit mystical theology.

There were two very important thinkers born within a hundred years of each other who were later called saints and mystics. One was the real thing, the other was the counterfeit. St Augustine was born in the fourth century after Christ, the counterfeit mystic a hundred years later. They were both converts to Christianity from Neoplatonism. The old Platonists followed the teaching of the Greek philosopher, Plato who believed that you could find all life, all truth, all beauty and all goodness in God. This meant that it was possible to glimpse something of God's transcendent glory in the glory of his creation.

Like St Augustine many of us have had such experiences. They are so well known that they have come to be called "natural mystical experiences", or experiences of the "numinous", as the Romantic poets called them. St Augustine writes about such an experience when converting from Neoplatonism to Christianity.

> I tasted you, and now hunger and thirst for you. You touched me, and I have burned for your peace. So, I set about finding a way to gain the strength that was necessary for enjoying you. And I could not find it until I embraced the mediator between God and man, the man Christ Jesus, who is over all things, who was calling unto me and saying, I am the way, the truth, and the life.

Many people have experienced God in this way, most especially in their youth. While some spend their lives trying to transpose these experiences into words or capture them in sublime poetry like the Romantic poets, Augustine rushes on to seek the source from which they came. His search led him to Jesus Christ for he finds in him the Masterpiece of God's creation. The fragments of God's beauty and goodness and truth that are scattered in the rest of creation are to be found fully in the Masterwork. Finally, in, with and through Christ he was led on to a Union with God that drew him into a profound contemplative stillness. When Augustine was led on to experience ever more deeply the presence of God in mystical contemplation, the light of love that reached out to him all but blinded him. It made him realize like so many before and after him that he would have to undergo a deep and penetrating purification before he could come closer to the God with whom he yearned and wished to be united. This is how he put it:

"I knew that I was far from you in the region of unlikeness, as if I heard your voice from on high. I am the food of grown men; grow and you shall eat me."

After many years of journeying on in what St John of the Cross later called the Dark Night of the Soul, what Augustine was able to experience more fully and understand more deeply, was the profound contemplation about which he was able to write like none before him. Sadly, for him and for us, the counterfeit mystic either had not heard of St Augustine's mystical journey, or he ignored it and remained so locked up in his Neoplatonic philosophy that he simply did not progress like Augustine in the authentic mystic way. For, while the original Platonists were purely philosophers, reasoning about the God of beauty, truth, and goodness, the Neoplatonists wished to come to experience him, as far as this would be possible. St Augustine found the way, in with and through Christ. The counterfeit mystic, otherwise known as Dionysius the Pseudo-Areopagite, did not, as Christ played no part in his mystical journey. If this is not made eminently clear by a quick reading of his Mystical Theology then let me quote from *A History of Philosophy* by the famous Jesuit historian, Frederick Copleston.

The Neoplatonists objected to the Incarnation and although we cannot be justified in asserting that the Pseudo-Dionysius denied the Incarnation, his acceptance of it does not well adapt itself to his philosophical system nor does it play much part in his writings. One may well doubt whether his writings would have exercised the influence that they did on Christian mediaeval thinkers, had the latter not taken the author's pseudonym at its face value. (Vol 2 Chapter 9)

Fr Copleston is referring to the fact that in order to pass off his clearly Platonic method of contemplation as Christian, he deceives his readers into believing that he was writing, not in the middle of the first millennium about AD 500, but more than five hundred years earlier in Apostolic times. He claimed to be St Dionysius the first Bishop of Athens, friend of St Paul and the other Apostles.

Dionysius was in fact a pagan convert from Neoplatonism who wrote somewhere between AD 490–530, four hundred years after his supposed friendship with St Paul. These works are heavily dependent on the writings of the Neoplatonism of his previous pagan teachers. He was writing long after the Church's reaction to Arianism had created a completely different spiritual landscape from that which prevailed in the aftermath of Christ's Resurrection. He was as far away from Apostolic times as we are from Tudor times, but in order to give a false credence to his pagan philosophical ideas he pretends to have lived in apostolic times himself, and to have been on familiar terms with many great Christian personalities whom we rightly revere. To do this, Dionysius assumed the name and the persona of a well-known personality and saint – the first bishop of Athens, who was acquainted with St Paul.

It is one thing to write in another person's name; this is not an uncommon convention for a writer and is usually quite harmless. But to do it in such an emphatic way, in order to deceive readers into believing in the quality and in the orthodoxy of all that is said, is taking the matter too far. This deceit has had the most pernicious consequences for the Christian mystical tradition. The veneration that was given to this man and his writings in the Christian West where his works were translated into Latin, cannot be exaggerated. For many hundreds of years almost all Western mystical writers looked to him as to one of the Apostolic Fathers, whose works therefore were even more authoritative than the Fathers of the Church and hardly less sacred than the scriptures themselves. He was even referred to as St Denis.

He did not just claim to be the Bishop of Athens and friend of St Paul, but a friend too, of St John, Timothy, Titus, Justin, Carpus and Polycarp. He claimed to have known Mary the mother of Jesus and although he did not profess to have been at the Crucifixion, he did claim to have witnessed the solar eclipse mentioned by Matthew (27:45) and Mark (15:33) that took place when Jesus was dying on the cross. There are many more deceits in his writings, and all with one aim, to fool others into accepting his own Neoplatonic presentation of Christian theology that is aeons away from that of St Augustine and the mainline Christian tradition. The great sadness is that in the aftermath of the heresy of Arianism, the Christ who was so obviously the Way, the Truth and the Life for St Augustine, whom he called the "mediator between God and man", had all but disappeared from sight, compared with the way in which he had been at the heart and centre of early Christianity.

In his History of the Catholic Church, Monsignor Philip Hughes simply describes Dionysius, not as a convert to Catholicism but to Monotheism (History of the Catholic Church Vol 2 pages 164–5). In other words, Dionysius, does not believe in the Hypostatic

Union, namely the divine and the human natures, indissolubly united in the person of Christ. Naturally therefore, Christ and his love can play no part in his mystical theology which is in fact no more than the Neoplatonic philosophy of the cult from which he partially converted. The only way to union with God therefore is by some strange form of mystical knowledge that first consists of emptying one's mind of all images, thoughts, and desires that normally reside in the mind, so that what he calls "unknowing" resides there instead, enabling some sort of esoteric intellectual intuition to rise to God. No later Catholic mystical writers would deny the need to empty the mind when the Holy Spirit leads them into contemplation, but not to fill it with "unknowing", but rather with acts of love to pierce through the unknowing caused by our human sinfulness.

The authentic Catholic Tradition righty insists that it is only love that can unite two different persons together. Knowledge may inspire a person to desire union, but it can never bring it about. What is true of human relationships is equally true of divine relationships. Human loving may unite human beings with each other, but only divine loving can unite human beings with God. Divine loving comes to us through Christ, and Christ alone. As Christ plays no part in Dionysius' mystical theology it is condemned to do no more than lead searchers into a dead end. Nevertheless, his impeccably assumed credentials fooled many later Catholic thinkers to believe that the intellect could do for them what only the heart can do. That is what the two new commandments of Christ are all about, not knowledge, but love – the love of God and the love of others (Matthew 22:36–40). As Christ himself said, everything else depends on the practice of these two commandments (Matthew 22:36–40).

The great canonized Catholic saints and their followers who refer to the Pseudo Areopagite and even use some of his language in later years, replaced his obscure esoteric intellectual intuition with "love". The great French Philosopher Étienne Henri Gilson put it this way. "It was one of the major problems of the later scholastics to give Denis an orthodox interpretation without baldly declaring him to be in the wrong (cf. p 85, and p. 588). The authority of the pseudo convert of St Paul was too great for it to be possible to ignore him. It was all the more necessary to find a way around him which is why we find so many commentaries on his works from Hugh of St Victor to St Thomas Aquinas himself whose aim (not admitted in deed and perhaps even unconsciously), was to extract the poison from him" (Gilson op. cit. 80 cf. pp. 80–9).

The first great Saint to do this was St Maximus (died AD 662), Abbot of the monastery of Chrysopolis near Constantinople who is usually quoted by those eager to substantiate the Areopagite's orthodoxy, because he appears to endorse all his teaching. In fact, Maximus does not do this, but the acceptance of his false credentials induced him to commend his philosophical ideas about God, and the asceticism needed to contemplate him. However, he was emphatically not a Monophysite like the Areopagite. For St Maximus the journey, not only takes place in, with and through the Christ who plays no part in the Areopagite's "mysticism" but with our love and Christ's love as one, making possible what is otherwise impossible.

The great spiritual historian Père Pourrat makes this abundantly clear in the first volume of his *History of Christian Spirituality* by quoting the words of Maximus directly.

The end of contemplation is union with God by rendering us like him and in a manner deifying us. This deification is brought about by love. Through love the will of man and the will of God become one and the same thing. But this assimilation of the human will and the divine will is realised first in Christ. In him the two distinct wills exist, contrary to the teaching of the Monophysite heresy. Christ is thus the model of our own deification. The word 'incarnate' is therefore the one centre of the theology and the spirituality of St Maximus.

While the Pseudo-Areopagite was busily employed in deceiving Christians into believing in his Neoplatonic mysticism without Christ, St Maximus was suffering terribly for his orthodoxy at the hands of the Areopagites' fellow Monophysites. They brutally scourged him, cut off his hand and pulled out his tongue to make sure that he could do nothing more to oppose their heresy. While St Maximus slowly died a martyr's death, because he refused to abandon orthodoxy, the Pseudo-Areopagite used orthodoxy to hide his heresy and spread it down subsequent centuries to the present day.

Chapter 62

Followers of the Counterfeit Mystic

Those who failed to see the essence of authentic Catholic mystical theology in subsequent centuries, and persisted in their allegiance to the Areopagite, like Eckhart and his disciples for instance, stepped outside the authentic Catholic tradition. Eckhart was originally condemned by the Church in the person of Pope John XXII. Nor is it true, as his modern disciples claim, that contemporary theologians have seen the light and totally exonerated him from the Church's false accusations. His abstruse form of mental contemplation and his teaching of how to obtain it sadly leads to, amongst many other errors, some sort of pantheism in which the individual identity of the mystic is merged into his maker. However, orthodox Catholic mystical theology teaches otherwise. Love differentiates.

This means that the love that is the only way to true union, even in purely human love, does not mean that a person loses their individual identity but rather finds it ever more fully. For the love that unites them ever more deeply to each other simultaneously enables them to become more themselves than they ever were before, as they mature into their true selves from what sin and selfishness made of them before. What is true of human loving is even truer of divine loving for the ecstatic bliss of endlessly going beyond oneself to all eternity means that we never stop growing physically, psychologically and spiritually in the journey in with and through Christ our Lord as we gradually attain our ultimate destiny. Ignorant of the nature of their final destiny, pseudo-mystics still follow their pseudo saint, and are still drawn, not to the mystical theology of love, but to the mystical theology in which the mind searches in vain for what only love can attain. It is a mysticism that is particularly attractive to intellectuals, who tend to live in the mind and have already found a sort of psychological satisfaction in intellectual pursuits, that can all too easily be wrongly identified with the mystical contemplation that is a pure gift of God.

It was almost a thousand years before anyone even questioned the identity of Dionysius, and then for four hundred years more, many eminent scholars still defended him, and for that matter still defend him, as Hans Ur Von Balthasar SJ has done for instance. Let me use the example of Balthasar for what happened to him has happened to so many others, particularly intellectuals, but also to many educated and intelligent Catholic laity too. When after the initial emotional experience of practising meditation, or what his mentor St Ignatius calls "contemplation" he found himself in an intellectual and emotional limbo land, at least in his prayer life, he was at a loss to know what to do in order to go forward in his personal search for union with God.

His prevailing experience seemed to coincide with that of the Neoplatonic mystics who concluded that you cannot possibly attain union with God through human reasoning, through the emotions or through the feelings because God is infinitely above them all. He had tried through the sort of contemplation taught by his mentor St Ignatius, but in the end it had failed to lead him to God, but only into a spiritual limbo land. That is why he turned to the Neoplatonists who taught that the only way to achieve what you desired was to strip your consciousness of the content of all these inner faculties and remain in a state of utter emptiness or "naughtism". Here you had to wait for some sort of "intellectual intuition" to lead you into an ecstasy in which you encountered God. It is interesting to note that in order to help him to do this Plotinus, the greatest of all Neoplatonists set out for the East to learn from Indian mystics how to facilitate and support this "intellectual intuition", as his spiritual descendants still do today in the many worldwide members of various types of mantra movements. For many years confreres of Balthasar have, like Plotinus, been looking to the East to help them in the spiritual wasteland that St John of the Cross calls the dark Night, or even before they get that far in their spiritual search. They call their counterfeit mysticism "Ignatian Yoga" and like children with a new toy they are trying to share it with anyone who will listen to them, and sadly there are all too many who will.

Accepting their philosophical proposition, that you cannot come to union with God through human intellect and human emotion, Balthasar was delighted to align himself with the "Catholic" Neoplatonist – the Areopagite. If he, and those who followed his example, had been educated by the Fathers of the Church, the Desert Fathers and the Catholic mystical tradition they would have followed the example of the great Christian mystics from the beginning. They would have turned to the simple "prayers of the heart" or the "prayers of naked faith" as they are called at the beginning, to help keep their deepest heart's desire fixed upon God. In short they are God-centred prayers. They are therefore in direct contradistinction to mantras, which keep a person's attention fixed on self, and on seeking self-satisfaction through seeking out inner psychological palliatives. Those who choose to use the prayers of the heart, will have to pass through dryness and aridity, endlessly plagued by a thousand and one distractions, as I have described. But if they persevere, not just in months, but in years showing their love for God in this way they will pass through the purification in which, not just their desire for God is purified, but their minds and hearts too, their memories and their imaginations with their emotions and their inner feelings.

Those who have no understanding of the full Catholic tradition that comes to us from Christ, through the Fathers of the Church, and the great mystical writers cannot see the fullness of our Catholic faith. Nor can they therefore see its implication for the spiritual life. The meditation on Christ that suddenly comes to a stop in first fervour does so, because the union with him for which they yearn cannot be furthered. It cannot be furthered never mind attained, until the mind and heart, the feelings and emotions, are purified. The memory and the imagination are so infected with the sin and selfishness that is the salary of original sin, that they cannot be united with the perfect human being Jesus Christ until a sufficient likeness is created through purification. If a plug is old and encrusted with rust it cannot be inserted into the socket until that rust is removed by purification, nor therefore can it become the means through which electricity passes to give the necessary power to all who need it. At the end of purification then believers are, not only able to come closer to Christ than before, but they are able to do what all lovers desire, namely to enter into the one whom they love, and then to receive for themselves and for others the spiritual power, which is love, that is needed.

As we enter into Christ we enter into the hypostatic union, in which the divine and the human are one in a single person, the single person of Jesus Christ. This union is not just spiritual then, as the Gnostics would have us believe, but physical too, body into body, soul into soul, flesh into flesh, blood into blood. In this way through the hypostatic union our humanity enters into Christ's divinized humanity through which we are united with God. The scriptures are quite clear about this profound and intimate union even if our imaginations cannot conceive it. This union then takes us up not just into Christ's life but into his action – into his love of the Father. Now Paradise has been regained. We are not just back in the Paradise from which we were ejected, but back into union with God, but now far more profoundly and far more completely. We can, not just walk and talk with God in the garden as Adam did, but enter into God, because now we have been united with the New Adam, who does not just walk and talk with his Father but enters into him and remains in him to eternity. This is how we come to know and experience "eternal life" beginning in this life, as St John insists, but also coming to know it in the next life where God has prepared for us our final destiny.

This is the way of, and the teaching of the Fathers of the Church and the great Christian mystics, as summed up in the works of St John of the Cross and St Teresa of Ávila. Eventually then in what St Teresa of Ávila calls the Spiritual Betrothals those inner faculties of the heart and mind come back to life and are able to meditate as they could meditate before in first fervour before the commencement of purification in the "Dark Night of the Soul". Only this time their meditation of God's love, as embodied in Jesus Christ, both before and after the resurrection is far more real, far more vital, and more enthralling than before. They, not only enable them to relate to him, more powerfully and more lovingly than ever before, but to be united with him in his loving contemplation of the Father. This sudden new development is at first intermittent, as the phrase "Spiritual Betrothals" implies. However, when this purification is completed and what St Teresa calls the "Mystical Marriage" takes place then a new spiritual, personal, and physical relationship with Christ becomes permanent, both inside and outside of prayer, as can be seen in the lives of the great saints. And so does the union with God in, with and through him, that the rationalism of the Neoplatonic Mystics had insisted was impossible. It is possible precisely because of the Incarnation, and what Christ came to achieved through the Incarnation, for those who are prepared to take up their daily Cross with him, inside prayer itself rather than seeking the self-satisfying palliatives that will never lead a person to God but only into a spiritual cul-de-sac. Now it will, I hope be appreciated, why I have found it necessary to criticise Ignatian Spirituality, and the Jesuits and their allies who actively promote it. They have, not only knowingly insulated themselves from the fulness of Catholic Spirituality, but continue to do so, and so continue to lead so many of their ardent followers astray, and into a predominantly superficial anthropocentric spirituality that was unknown to the God-centred spirituality that Christ bequeathed to our first ancestors.

Dionysius was finally exposed by Hugo Koch and Joseph Stiglmayr SJ at the end of the nineteenth century. These two scholars worked independently, and in 1895 came to the same conclusion. They discovered that whole extracts from his works had been lifted from the last of the great Neoplatonic writers, Proclus, his teacher. Further to this they found an astonishing agreement in the sequence of thought, examples and expressions that had also been taken from Proclus. So henceforth, he genuinely earned the title of the Pseudo-Areopagite. But it took well into the twentieth century before the fraud was generally accepted, although many still look to him with reverence and revere his teaching. Many still continue to allow this teaching to distort the true meaning of authentic Christian prayer, leading myriad well-meaning Christians into various forms of bogus mystical practices that will lead them nowhere.

There have been and there still are many would-be mystics both inside and outside of the Church, who look to the philosophical mystical treatise of the Pseudo Dionysius as their Bible. These include modern followers of some of the Rhineland mystics, and even of Molinos and some who belong to the various branches of the mantra movements. At the end of the nineteenth century and the beginning of the twentieth century what had come to be called "Mysticism" became fashionable again, thanks to books like *The Varieties of Religious Experience* by Harvard Professor William James, brother of the novelist Henry James. When Counterfeit mystical experiences from the East or the West became hardly distinguishable, problems arose when they led to the idea of a new religion based on a common mystical experience. It was then that the Pseudo-Dionysius came back into favour. This was because they rightly saw that his way to mystical experience did not depend on any theological teaching, so dogma could be dispensable. Everyone would be united in a new religion based on a common mystical experience which many believed could be attained by man-made techniques.

Sad to say, in this country a famous Catholic academic, to whom so many look for authoritative guidance, uses the Pseudo-Dionysius as his basis for explaining the teaching of St John of the Cross and St Teresa of Ávila, both in his books, lectures, and retreats that he leads to Carmelite Spain. I have personally read some of his books and listened to him lecture, preceded by him praying in the lotus position at the headquarters of the World Community for Christian Meditation in London. The very position that he takes up for prayer seems to visibly embody his all-embracing acceptance of the new man-made mysticism that can unite both East and West in a religion in which dogma takes second place to pseudo mystical experiences. Like other speakers who I have listened to at the World Community for Christian Meditation, they cherry-pick from the teaching of authentic Catholic mystics like John Cassian and the author of *The Cloud of Unknowing* whose teaching they wrongly believe endorses their own erroneous mysticism. It is easy to see how they feel that their mysticism is all but identical with the teachings of Indian and other Eastern Mystics. The reason why this new mysticism has such widespread support is because the methods and the techniques that they offer are so easy to adopt and promise all but instant mysticism, bypassing meditation where the love of Christ is learned as well as the purification in prayer that leads to contemplation.

The World Community for Christian Meditation was founded by Father John Main. His method of "meditation" which he had learnt as a layman in the Far East before he became a monk at Ealing Abbey London, can be summed up simply. In his own words the essence of his teaching is this. "When we begin to meditate we must say the mantra for the whole twenty or thirty minutes of our 'meditation'... I repeat this to re-emphasise what is essential and perhaps the only advice worth giving about meditation which is simply: to say your mantra" (*Word into Silence* Page 56). His successors, follow exactly the same approach that has clearly be repudiated by the Vatican.

The Vatican document, Jesus Christ the Bearer of the Water of Life (3rd Feb 2003), insists that, "Meditation techniques now used are not prayer, even if they lead to a more pleasant state of mind or bodily comfort... their meditations are self-centred, directed towards attaining feelings of inner relaxation, peace and mindfulness, and are totally opposite to authentic Christian prayer. It insists that 'Christian prayer' is not an exercise in self-contemplation, stillness and self-emptying, but a dialogue of love, one which implies an attitude of conversion, a flight from 'self' to the 'You' of God" (see also Catechism of the Catholic Church, 2705–2719).

I will end by emphasizing yet again and for the last time that the very essence of the teaching of Jesus Christ is that God is love, and his love was so embodied in his own mystical body on the first Pentecost that it could draw up into itself all who are open to receive it. Here, with the help and strength of this divine love, their human love could be united in Christ's mystical body with his mystical action – his loving contemplation of the Father, so that, as he conceived from all eternity, we could find our final destination in him and in the love that unites him to his Son.

You do not find any trace of this profound mystical teaching in the philosophical mysticism of the Pseudo-Dionysius, precisely because it totally depends not on revelation but on reason alone. It is simply impossible to generate love for Someone who is utterly unknowable. If some of his terminology and imagery has been used by later Christian mystics it does not mean that his philosophic mysticism is in harmony with all the great Christian mystics because it patently is not. As I have developed the teaching of the genuine Christian mystics in this book, from St Bernard of Clairvaux to St Teresa of Ávila and St John of the Cross, you will have seen that they were all engaged in doing the same thing. They are all teaching how our love can be so detached from all other loves that would prevent it rising to God, while being purified and refined in such a way that it can ultimately be the means of uniting us with Christ in with and through whom we can be united to God here and now and to all eternity.

Chapter 63

Contemplation Is for Children Too

After a parish priest asked me to speak to his parishioners about meditation, I approached him for the feedback that I did not expect. What I said was very interesting, it seemed, moving, inspiring even, but not actually very practical, at least not for most of them. It was for the birds, as one busy housewife put it. Or rather for religious who have noviciates, quiet chapels and cells into which they could retire to do what busy working men and women with families simply cannot find the time to do. Their understandable response enables me to highlight what is seriously wrong with Catholic Education in modern times. We have forgotten its true meaning, which is first and foremost, and above all else to introduce new converts or young children to come to know and love God's infinite loving goodness, as embodied in Jesus Christ.

This was precisely what happened in the early Church, above all else. This is what took place when newcomers were prepared for Baptism in what came to be called the catechumenate. Two years were set aside to prepare them to be taken up and into the Risen Christ on Easter night. The very essence of this preparation was to introduce them personally and deeply to Jesus Christ, so that in knowing him through the teaching, the testimonies, and the writings of those who had known him personally, and then meditating on all they heard or read, they would be prepared. This would enable them to generate the love that would prepare them spiritually, psychologically as well as sacramentally to "put on Christ" permanently through the rites of Christian initiation on Easter Night. At the end of the rites of initiation they would be clothed in a shining white garment because it was believed this was how Christ was attired when he rose from the tomb on the first Easter Day. They would continue to wear this garment for a week, until the next Sunday, to remind them, and to demonstrate to others and especially those who might ask what happened to them when they were re-born on Easter night.

A similar sort of Catechetical preparation should be given to all new converts and children today, who were naturally too young to undergo the sort of preparation for baptism that newcomers, or neophytes as they were called underwent in the early Church. As in the early Church this preparation should first and foremost involve teaching them to meditate on God's infinite goodness made flesh and blood in the most loveable human being who ever lived on this earth. As we have seen, this meditation leads those who are taught to love him as he once was, to love him as he is now in his Risen Glory. This does not take place far away in some distant heaven, but within us now where he resides, in love, as the very ground of our being. It is here that he makes his home in all who love him, as Jesus promised at the Last Supper.

That babies can be baptised, and introduced into the family of God, without doing anything to deserve it, is one of the most striking examples of God's totally gratuitous gift of love. But this inestimable privilege must not mean that they therefore forgo another privilege that was bestowed on all who sought baptism in the early Church. I am of course speaking of the privilege of being personally and intimately introduced to and taught how to love the Lord into whose family they are adopted. Because this introduction is so personal and can only be perfectly performed by those who already know and love him, the poor children often miss out and, like sex education, parents leave it to teachers and teachers leave it to parents.

I was fortunate; my mother taught me to meditate on the mysteries of the Rosary, and Fr Francis Handley, the school spiritual director, taught me to meditate in his Monday evening meditation seminars. I was so indebted to him that I dedicated my second book *Inner Life* to him with these words: "To Fr Francis Handley, who first taught me to meditate". That I should have been sent to the only school that I have ever known with a weekly meditation course was a complete chance when it should be the norm, as part of the education given in every Catholic School. Nothing was left to chance in the early Church. They even provided backup if, for whatever reason parents were unable to do what my parents did for me. They invented a new role for specially chosen people to act as godparents, a role that goes back at least to the second century. This role was given to those best suited to take the parents' place in fostering their faith if something happened to them. In Rome at the time, the average age of mortality was twenty-nine, and this must have been lower for Catholics as martyrdom was a distinct possibility, so therefore was the importance of the role of godparents.

Ideally what did happen in the early Church and what should happen now, is that a true Catholic education should teach a young person how to come to know and love Christ in the sort of meditation that I have detailed earlier in this book, that was practised by all in the early Church. This will lead them on to the contemplation which, surprising though this may seem, involves using a pure simple prayer that is therefore most appropriate and most easily adapted for those intensively involved in the world that they are called to transform through love. But instead of first teaching the heart to love, Catholic education has degenerated into first teaching the intellect how to know, and to know in detail the teaching of the Church, the catechism, the creeds and how to defend them against all comers. All too often this education never seems to get round to teaching the "one thing necessary". Once a person is taught how to love Christ then they will be eager and diligent in learning more and more about him, through the study of those who were preparing for his coming in the Old Testament and through those who knew him personally in the New Testament. Then they will want to know more and more about his Church, its teaching, its history, the philosophy that underpins it, and the apologetics that will help them to defend it. But this study must be preceded by the loving that will shine through everything else that is subsequently learnt, giving a quality of wisdom and understanding without which it can so easily become purely dry intellectual knowledge. They will become vulnerable to attack from what might be presented to them as more rational, more modern, and more sophisticated philosophies of life that just happen to be fashionable today, but which will be forgotten tomorrow.

If you want to look for scapegoats for this almost exclusive intellectual religious education then look to the Renaissance, that demanded highly intellectual minds to rediscover and savour its "treasures", rediscovered from the past – the pagan past. Then Greco-Roman education was introduced into our education system, in the form of stoicism, thanks to people like John Colet, as we have seen. Look to the counter-reformation that had to concentrate on teaching Catholic truths to counteract protestant errors, in books through the written word, from the pulpit through the spoken word and in the classroom through the catechism. In my youth this was no more than a concentrated summary of the teaching of St Thomas Aquinas that had to be learned off by heart, though the heart gained little from it. When the anti-mystical witch-hunts succeeded in taking away the means that had traditionally led to the purification of the heart through contemplation, it was to intellectual renewals to which the Church primarily turned in future to do what had traditionally been done by the "Spirituality of the Heart". This emphasis on the intellect at the expense of the heart was compounded in the Age of Enlightenment, that even influenced the Church, where the reason was the sole arbiter of everything, and love was left to the romantics. That all these movements have much to teach us is undeniable, but so too is the truth that the overemphasis on the head at the expense of the feelings has deprived us of the

Spirituality of the Heart that Christ introduced and left for us as his inheritance. The truth is that it is only love, in, with, and through Christ, that can lead us to the destiny for which our whole being craves more than anything else, and it is only love that can support, sustain, and succour us on our way.

Sadly, the intellectual emphasis that has dominated Catholic education, which will of course always be an essential part of that education, never seems to end, and the real education of learning how to love never seems to begin. There is always a sort of embarrassment, the embarrassment of non-practitioners, thanks to the legacy of the history that I have outlined that prevents Catholic teachers teaching their students how to love Jesus Christ. Inevitably they take refuge in teaching the mind how to know rather than teaching the heart how to love the source of all truth. Just over a year ago in talking about these matters to a religious priest, I said rather uncharacteristically that we must begin by teaching them how to love Jesus. If I had said by coming to love Jesus Christ, then there may not have been any reaction, but there was. It was a hardly perceptible reaction, but it was there in a slight change in the demeanor of the Priest. "You are thinking that I am beginning to sound like a Protestant," I said. His smile confirmed that I had read his mind. It is Protestants, usually evangelical protestants, who tend to talk about Jesus as their personal friend and Saviour. He is for many of them what imaginary childhood friends used to be for many of us. The sort of friend who represents what we would wish to be at our best, the sort of friend who would help us to be better people.

His presence would enable us to ask ourselves what Jesus would do in the various predicaments, the different moral dilemmas in which we continually find ourselves. Then, when our fallen nature makes us fail to live up to what he would have done, his goodness would shine so brightly that God would not see, or at any rate not count our sinfulness against us. But for Catholics, at least those first Catholics from whom we must learn, Jesus was even more than a personal friend. The profound teaching that he taught at the Last Supper makes this clear. He wants to enter into us to make his home in us, so that we can be found together in a spiritual marriage that is even deeper and more lasting than a secular marriage. But sadly, that is not possible for the first protestants, because for them human beings are intrinsically evil and so intrinsically incapable of enjoying the divine indwelling and the mystical prayer to which this leads. That is why in her book on Mysticism, the Anglican Evelyn Underhill admitted that the vast majority of mystics are Catholics. But this is all pie in the sky for us, if we do not begin to love Christ ourselves through the meditation that leads to mystical contemplation. It is in this profound prayer that we not only see Christ as the perfect human being who can teach us how to behave in every human circumstance in which we find ourselves, but much more. He is rather a mystical mentor who not only teaches us what ought to be done from within but gives us the power to do it from the place where he has now made his home within us.

Although I have spent my whole life studying and writing to teach others the essential spiritual teaching of the God-given spirituality that Christ introduced into the early Church, my emphasis on love has opened me to the criticism of being anti-intellectual. Was Jesus Christ anti-intellectual because he did not choose university professors or world class intellectuals to become his first apostles? He chose those with pure and humble hearts to confound the "wise" with the simple message that God is love and that he is the embodiment of his Father's love, and that through love we have been drawn up into his mystical contemplation to receive the fruits of contemplation. This is not just for us, but for others too, for whom we are called, that God's Kingdom of love be brought about on earth.

It was St John Henry Newman who inspired me to go back to rediscover this pure simple spirituality that is the heart and soul of his own personal spirituality, that must be rediscovered and lived again today as it was in the beginning. For this to happen he knew in the first place, that in our modern sophisticated world, this would need a highly educated laity to rediscover and understand what had been lost and then disseminate it amongst others. That is why he specifically encouraged an intelligent and educated laity, because in these difficult times their leadership was, and still is, essential. However, they too must practise the God-given "Spirituality of the Heart" that Jesus introduced into early Christianity. Those who in early times were called "saints", many of whom became martyrs, were not so called because of the quality of their intellectual expertise but because of the quality of their love. That is why although for Newman an intelligent and well-educated Catholic laity is essential to usher in renewal, it is a renewal in which love reigns supreme as it does in his writings. That is why when he was made a Cardinal in 1879, he chose the words *Heart speaks unto Heart* for his motto. It was taken from his favourite spiritual writer, who wrote that wonderous book on the love of God namely St Francis de Sales. John Henry Newman made his prayer to the Sacred Heart his prayer, for it summed up his whole spirituality of love, that intellectuals only too keen to immerse themselves in his inestimable scholarship, can so easily forget.

"May thy heart dwell always in our hearts!
May thy blood ever flow in the veins of our souls!
O sun of our hearts, thou gives life to all things by the rays of thy goodness!
I will not go until thy heart has strengthened me, O Lord Jesus!
May the heart of Jesus be the king of my heart!
Blessed be God.
Amen"
(St Francis de Sales)

Catholic faith is not firstly a body of dogmatic truths, but a body full of love that rose from the dead on the first Easter Day. It should begin then by teaching the young how to come to know and love Jesus Christ, as soon as possible, by introducing them to true Catholic meditation, by Catholic teachers who know how to do this from their own experience, and who also know where it leads. It is in the love that is generated here, as human loving and divine loving merge together as one, that enables the Holy Spirit to lead the young to Contemplation as soon as possible, even before they are teenagers. Contemplation should be the prayer of every adult Catholic. It is the prayer most easily adaptable to a person who lives their lives in a busy world that is absorbed with self-interest and take. Many lay people have had to discover this for themselves, as without due help and assistance they have had to muddle through the spiritual life alone. In the next chapter I want to give you an example of how we can reform our own spiritual lives, in such a way that they can be rebuilt on the foundations laid down for us by our early Catholic forebears.

Chapter 64

Practising the Prayer of the Heart

I never spoke to my father about his spiritual life, or my own for that matter, but I know that after reading a book on the Desert Fathers he became very interested in their spiritual teaching, and what they came to call the "Prayer of the Heart". All those early monks, like St Antony, left home where through meditation they had come to know and love Christ. It was this love that inspired and set them afire while they were in the "world" that led them into the desert. It was here that their love would be prepared and purified sufficiently for the union that they desired with every spiritual and physical fibre of their being. What was then called the "Desert" and what later came to be called the "Dark Night of the Soul" was the place where this purification took place, as they now prayed using a new form of prayer, because the meditation that had initially set them afire with the love of Christ was no longer possible for the reasons that we have seen. This new form of prayer came to be called the "Prayer of the Heart" or the "Prayer of Faith". It would help prepare them for what the Eastern Church called *Divinization*.

It must have been the way that they used this prayer, or these prayers to sanctify their day and offer everything to God that they did in that day, which affected my father most. After his death I found a quotation from John Cassian on the final page of his missal which helped him to keep his Morning Offering on course throughout the day. It helped him to live out the new worship "in spirit and in truth" that Christ had introduced to the early Church through his apostles. It helped him to offer himself up to God in myriad acts of self-sacrificial loving, as Christ had done. Thanks to the Ignatian form of meditation to which he was introduced long before he was married to my mother, he had passed through meditation and into mystical contemplation that, unknown to him, had led him into the "Dark Night". Here he learned a new form of simple prayer that he could easily integrate with his life as a business man and father of a family, precisely because it was so simple. In with and through Christ he learnt to make acts of love wherever possible even on the busiest of days.

These acts of love are like waves contained in a channel that reaches upwards to God allowing his love to reach downwards to us. Gradually the waves of love subside into a stiller, smoother, more silent sea of contemplative loving, enabling our loving to rise into God and God's loving to descend into us. In this way God imparts something of the Ocean of his infinite love to us even in this life, which will be our ultimate destiny in the next. Christ is that channel of love, the Holy Spirit the waves, whose loving gradually merges with our own leading us on and into the still and silent contemplative loving that enables us to glimpse something of the loving that has always passed to and fro between the Father and the Son from all eternity.

My Father learnt from John Cassian how to use these acts of love throughout his day, not just when all was going well but when all seemed to be going wrong too. The prayer he used most was simply, "O God come to my aid, O Lord make haste to help me". As I have already mentioned John Cassian said that this prayer was taught to his disciples by Abbot Isaac and later used by St Benedict with which to begin the divine office throughout the day, as it is still used today. Under this little prayer, my father copied out the following words from Abbot Isaac, written for the benefit of his followers.

You must continually use this prayer in your heart, whatever you are doing or whatever office you are holding, or journey you are undertaking; in adversity that you may be delivered, and in prosperity that you may be preserved. You should be so moulded by the constant use of it that when sleep comes you are still considering it so that you become accustomed to repeating it even when you sleep. When you awake let it become the first thing that comes into your mind, let it anticipate all your waking thoughts. When you rise from your bed let it send you down on your knees, and thence send you forth to your work, and let it follow you all through the day.

Abbot Macarius used to tell his disciples to say simply, "Lord to the rescue", or call upon him by name by using the holy name "Jesus" whenever they were in danger of losing their way or forgetting what they were about. Abbot Macarius was believed to be the originator of the Jesus Prayer. Later it developed into the prayer as we know it today, which was originally composed by Saint John Climacus, "Jesus son of God have mercy on me a sinner". These short prayers were not only used by the Desert Fathers but have been used continually throughout subsequent centuries. They have always been used to help Christians keep their attention fixed on their calling throughout the day and help them when distractions or temptations threaten to overwhelm them. One of my mother's favourite little prayers that helped her throughout her day was, "Jesus mercy, Mary help". My primary school teacher, Miss Holt, taught us all to say, "Sacred Heart of Jesus I put my trust in you". During the First World War, Fr Willie Doyle SJ used to give his troops his "pink pills" to use in the battle ahead. They were short pithy prayers easy to remember that they could repeat over and over to support, inspire and sustain them. We might not have to face such terrible physical battles each day, but we do have to fight very many spiritual battles, so we too have need of his "pink pills". He encouraged his men to choose their own so they could be personalised to their own individual needs. I have made my own "pink pills" – why not make some for yourself?

Morning prayer was not the beginning and end of daily prayer, for it was the custom of the early Christians to pray five times a day, as Jesus did. It is still possible for us to do this, as I believe my father did. I remember asking him why he put little stickers on his wristwatch. One was pointing to nine o'clock another to twelve o'clock, and the third to three o'clock. He merely said it was a little device to help him remember something. In earlier times when Christian Europe was predominantly rural, the Angelus bell that pealed three times a day called everyone to prayer wherever they were and whatever they were doing. This was a world that neither my father nor his forebears had known, for unlike my mother, whose forbears were recusants, they were all Protestant. His parents were converts and like them, he was always reticent to speak about his faith. When it came to the spiritual life, he was an intensely private man who found it difficult to speak about it, let alone his own. However, one thing I know for certain was that he always tried to find some time each day, in addition to all else, to enter into what my mother called his inner garden shed for his daily prayer.

As far as I have been able to gather, the prayer of the heart that he used there when he had more time did not differ from the prayer of the heart that he used during his day. He used it in exactly the same way that was suggested in Chapters 45–48, but in longer and more concentrated periods of time. Please remember something that I said earlier – time for meditation that I believe should be part of our earliest Catholic education would only take up a fraction of our life-long journey in prayer. For the vast majority of the time this journey is predominantly composed of acts of love, or prayers of the heart, made in and outside of prayer, but always within the mystical body of Christ. Then, when God chooses, he will "touch" us and moments of contemplative stillness will envelop us that will sometimes rise to shattering degrees of intensity. When you persevere come what may, in darkness or in light, in sickness or in health, in desolation or in consolation, then you will be carrying your cross and practising the white martyrdom that leads onwards and into the greatest Martyr of all, the greatest mystic the world has ever known. In his "darkest hour" Winston Churchill wrote

"Success is not final, failure is not fatal: it is the courage to continue that counts." He might not have been a saint or a mystic, but he was a wise man, at least when he said that, for it certainly encourages me in my darkest hours.

If you only journey on because you want to experience the consolations of God, rather than the God of consolation, then you are going nowhere. At least you will go nowhere until in purification your motives are purified by the God of consolation, to enable you to receive the consolations that only he can give. Next time a parish priest asks me to speak to his parishioners about meditation I will be sure to speak about contemplation too, the contemplation where the love is truly learnt, in a lifetime of loving that leads to an eternity of loving, together will all those we love and hold dear.

Let me end with one further suggestion that you might find helpful. It is taken from an ancient tradition traced back to the Desert Fathers, that I am sure my father must have used, because I know my mother did, for she taught it to me. When you are in bed say a short prayer and repeat it slowly and prayerfully. It may simply be the word, "Jesus", or the full Jesus prayer, "Jesus Son of God, have mercy on me, a sinner". This prayer and others like it came to be used most particularly in the Eastern Christian Church, with slow rhythmical breathing. It was not a device for relaxation, but for reminding the believer of the all-pervading action of the Holy Spirit. The ancient Jews believed that their breath was their life-principle, their spirit, so naturally they believed that God's breath was his life-principle, his Spirit. As a mark of respect, God's breath or his Spirit came to be called the Holy Spirit. So, deep rhythmical breathing that often accompanied short prayers of the heart, helped remind Eastern Christians of the incoming Spirit who dwelt within them with ever-increasing power the more they prayed. It can be a reminder to us too, particularly when preparing for sleep.

The prayer "Come, Holy Spirit" can accompany the slow intake of breath followed by the prayer, "Conceive Christ in me", as we breathe out. With the next breath pray again, "Come, Holy Spirit", followed by, "fill every part of me", and again with the next breath, "Come, Holy Spirit", followed by, "bring Christ to birth in me". Then the three prayers can be repeated again and again. Other short prayers can be used like "Come, Lord", or "Come, Lord Jesus", or whatever short prayer you feel helps you best. When this practice becomes a habit, it can be far more effective than sleeping pills, and there are no side effects either. This sort of prayer need not be restricted to preparation for sleep, for once you have become used to using it at night, you can use it at other times of the day too. It can be used when you are waiting for a bus, the train or the plane, when you are sitting in a waiting room, waiting for the doctor, the dentist or the consultant, or when you are waiting for a phone call, for the plumber or for the electrician to come. Instead of letting frustration take possession of you, use the time to let the Holy Spirit take possession of you instead. Then, instead of anger and impatience, you will be filled with peace.

At the end of his book *The Count of Monte Cristo* by Alexandre Dumas, the author says that all the wisdom in the world is contained in just two words – waiting and hoping. If we learn how to wait while doing all we can to invite the Holy Spirit to take possession of us, then before too long all our hopes, all our deepest desires and yearnings will be realized. For, as the Holy Spirit suffuses our love with his love, then that love can take us up into Christ where we are able to contemplate the Father, in, with, and through him. Then, we will be able to experience brief moments of heavenly peace in this world, as we are beginning the journey to experience the fullness of heavenly peace in the next, and for all eternity. When at the end of the day you have finished trying to pray as best you can, be at peace. You have done your best, now leave the rest to God, remembering the words of St Padre Pio: "Pray, trust and don't worry."

Chapter 65

The Ascetism of the Heart

I was born, and brought up, like us all, in the aftermath of the Renaissance, influenced by a spirituality that owed as much to the rise of humanism as to the Gospel of Jesus Christ. As I have already said the Credo of humanism is "I believe in Man" the Credo of Christianity is "I believe in God". Naturally, I thought that if I were to attain the sanctity to which I aspired it would be primarily the result of my own efforts. I was in effect a Christian stoic, a Pelagian who had failed so comprehensively to make myself into the saint of my dreams that I was about to give up the spiritual life for good. It was then that I came across *Pax Animae*, written by a Spanish Franciscan in 1588. It was a spiritual gem untouched by the spirit of humanism. Reading it was the nearest I came to a Damascus Road experience. It immediately enabled me to see that I had been misled into believing that I could be the architect of my own perfection. Its very first paragraph showed me why I had failed and what I ought to do to succeed.

With love you may bring your heart to do whatsoever you may please. The hardest things become easy and pleasant, but without love you will find anything not only difficult but also impossible.

In short, with love all things are possible but without love nothing is possible. The rigorous asceticism that I adopted to make myself perfect did nothing but exhaust me. Now I could see that I would achieve nothing without coming to know and experience the same love that animated the man I wanted to emulate more than any other. We make the same mistake with Christ as we do with the saints. We read their lives backwards. We read about their rigorous lives, their superhuman sacrifices, and their heroic virtue, and we believe that the only way we can be like them is to do likewise. If we would only read their lives forward instead of backwards, then we would see that they were only capable of doing the seemingly impossible because they first received the power to do it in prayer. If we try to be and do what they did without first receiving what they received, then our brave attempts will inevitably end in disaster. True imitation of Christ or any of his saints means firstly copying the way they did all in their power to receive the Holy Spirit who inspired and animated them. That is essentially all we have to do. That is why the spiritual life is so simple, if only we had the simplicity of a little child to see it.

I needed a new type of asceticism that would not dissipate my energies trying to do the impossible, but which would enable me to do the "one thing necessary". I needed to gather what little resources I had to create quality space and time in my daily life for the profound prayer that would give me access to the same love that filled Jesus Christ and inspired everything that he said and did. I knew that this love would have to be experienced if it was going to give me the inner security that would alone do for me in some small measure what it did in full measure for Christ. I had a new asceticism with which to substitute for the old, and I called it the "asceticism of the heart". Asceticism for the beginner, then, is quite simple. Do not give up anything you like or enjoy except when it prevents you from giving quality space and time to God in prayer each day. If you think it is too easy, then try it and stick to it, and you will soon find it is not quite as easy as you thought. So do not let first enthusiasm fool you into heroics that you will never sustain. Now, when you have persevered for long enough, you will gradually begin to receive and then experience the love that will enable you to do what is quite impossible without it. But first things first, if you are going to have, not just time, but quality time for prayer then you must learn how to prepare yourself for it.

Whenever you watch any sport at the highest level, you cannot but be impressed with the dedication of the participants. It is the quality of their single-mindedness that draws the attention. The moment they begin their preparation, it is as if they enter into a time-free zone where they are able to put everything out of their minds in such a way that they can live and act fully in the present. If they allow anything from the past to disrupt their concentration, then it is instantly dismissed. Nor must anything from the future disturb them either. Just a few moments' indulgence imagining themselves receiving their trophy or celebrating with their friends could mean losing their prize. It should be exactly the same with preparation for prayer. We need some sort of countdown to help us drop out from the hectic life that is so often forced upon us, to prepare to turn on and tune in to God. Just as different athletes find their own rituals, we need to find our own. It may simply be lying down for a rest, reading some spiritual or inspiring book, exercising, going for a swim, listening to music, or whatever helps to relax us. This is all part and parcel of the asceticism of the heart that is going to help us enter into that time-free zone when we begin to pray. It is here that we can first begin to enter, as fully as we can, into the present moment, by ridding ourselves of anything from the past or the future that can draw the attention away from fixing our gaze fully upon God. This is the only place on earth where time can touch eternity.

In order to sanctify this place and consecrate it to God, the early monks first practised private confession so that no past guilt would disturb them. They even confessed the temptations that might induce them to desecrate holy ground by inducing them to live in the future. God cannot be encountered in the past or in the future but only, as de Cassaude saw so clearly, in what he called the "sacrament of the present moment". That is why he said that "The present moment is always full of infinite treasures. It contains far more than you have the capacity to hold." This is the only moment when time touches eternity, and prayer is the offering that makes it a holy place, where the human and the divine first meet, mix, and mingle before being united.

The trouble is that the spiritual life seems to have become so complicated over the years that you almost feel you need a couple of degrees in theology just to understand it before you can even attempt to live it! Yet it is essentially simple, so simple that you need the simplicity of a little child to see it. You see, there is only one thing that is necessary, and that is love. Not our love of God, but his love of us. In other words, Christianity is firstly a mysticism not a moralism. It is not primarily concerned with detailing the perfect moral behaviour that we see embodied in Christ's life and then trying to copy it virtue by virtue. That is stoicism, not Christianity, and it is doomed to failure. Christianity is primarily concerned with teaching us how to turn and open ourselves to receive the same Holy Spirit who filled Jesus Christ. The more we are filled with his love, the easier it is to return it in kind, as the divine suffuses and then surcharges human love so that it can reach up to God and out to others. Then and only then are we able to "love God with our whole hearts and minds and with our whole beings and to love our neighbour as Christ loves us". Then, when we begin to practise the first of the new commandments in, with and through Christ, everything else in the spiritual life falls into place.

When a person falls in love and begins to experience being loved, then there is nothing they would not do, nor any sacrifice they would not make for their lover. In fact they positively look for things to do, the harder and the more exacting the better, to enable them to show the real quality of their love. What was impossible to self-centred egotists only a short time before becomes not only easier but also their greatest pleasure. It is exactly the same in the spiritual life. The exemplary behaviour, the extraordinary self-discipline and the heroic sacrifices made by a person who begins to experience the love of God are not the results of an arrogant stoic trying to make themselves perfect.

They are the actions of someone desperate to express their love in behaviour that could not be maintained for long without the love that sustains it. All the little pleasures and pastimes that were thought indispensable before suddenly become dispensable, and with the greatest of ease, virtues that were noticeable by their absence before, are born of the love that envelops them. When the love of God strikes a human heart, it strikes it as a simple ray of light strikes a prism. Just as that light is then diffused and transformed into all the colours of the spectrum, so the love of God is diffused and transformed into all the virtues and gifts that are needed as the believer seeks to acquire them. In short, first seek God and his Kingdom which is love, and everything else you want or desire will be given to you.

Chapter 66

From Stumbling Blocks to Stepping Stones

When I was fifteen, I fell in love for the first time. When I heard those magic words "I love you", I simply wanted to spend the rest of my life returning her love. It is the same when we first begin to realize that God loves us, and will continue to love us, not just here on earth but to eternity in heaven. Christ experienced this love enveloping him at every moment of his life on earth, so he alone has the answer to what we must do to receive and return this love.

Although God's love is infinite and infallible we can nevertheless receive it as Christ is God's go-between and our High Priest. He remained open at all times to the love that poured into him from the Father, and then he returned it in kind. The Morning Offering is the most important prayer that we can make because it commits us to making every action in the forthcoming day into an act of love. Whether we say our Morning Offering in bed, while kneeling at the bedside, while dressing or even on the way to work, it is actually being said in the New Temple which is Christ's Mystical Body. Because it is offered in, with and through him, it has a power and potency that is infinitely beyond what we can offer alone.

Nevertheless, there is a clear difference between the way Christ loves his Father and the way we do. Because there is no sin or selfishness in Christ, there is nothing within him that can prevent him from contemplating and enjoying his Father's love at all times. Because original sin has perverted our God-given impulses and drives, they are in a state of perpetual anarchy. While we try to raise our heart's deepest desire to love and to be loved by God, they relentlessly endeavour to prevent the pure and unalloyed contemplative love that was Christ's greatest joy. Before our hearts can beat in union with his, we need to be purified through the repentance we practise each day, as we try to take up our daily cross to follow Christ, both inside and outside of prayer. It is therefore of utmost importance that we understand the meaning of the word repentance, which was as totally unnecessary for Christ as it is necessary for us.

Christ did not come primarily for everyone to meet him face-to-face like a supernatural celebrity, but for everyone to enter into him through "light inaccessible" transformed into love, making it possible for all to come to know and love him in every time and in every century. Before, God was seen as the all-holy and unutterable Other who dwelt in light inaccessible, but Jesus taught that we have a Father who is accessible through love to those with hearts open to receive it. He used the word Abba, or Dad, with which to address God in the first prayer he gave his followers and the prayer that we still use today. Opening our hearts to receive this love makes it possible for every man and woman in every age to the end of time, not just to be introduced to him but to enter into him, making him, as St Augustine put it, closer to us than we are to ourselves. This is not the end but the beginning of a mystical journey, in and with him. It will take us to the home where love without measure will fill us in an ever-greater measure, as the capacity of the heart to receive it expands to receive it to eternity. Ultimate happiness then is not a state, but an ongoing and ever-more joyous journey into the light inaccessible that we now know is accessible because it is love, the love of the One who wants to be known as our Divine Dad. This is the strong vibrant faith that we have all but forgotten, but which was given to the early Church by Christ. Yet, we can return to it now and without delay simply by doing daily what St Peter told us to do on the first Pentecost, when light inaccessible was unleashed as love, making it accessible to all.

Begin at once, and I promise you that as long as you persist in turning, opening and offering your heart to God you will receive his love no matter how many times you fall, so long as you have the humility to rise and start again immediately. Christ's love, his Holy Spirit will bond you ever more deeply into him and will prepare and purify you ever more thoroughly to become perfect. You will be fitted into him, not for the journey of a lifetime, but to the end of time and beyond. The unending and ecstatic bliss of entering into love without measure to all eternity will therefore never end. If you have the humility to keep trying to practise the repentance that involves repeatedly turning, opening and offering your heart to God, he cannot fail you because he is God. His infinite loving will always triumph, even over our endless finite failures. It is only the pride and the pomposity of those who do not have the humility to keep getting up after falling, and getting up immediately, that can keep God out and prevent him leading them through the darkness of purification into the light of his love.

Although the Devil is the ultimate personification of Evil he cannot enter into the glorified body of Christ so those who enter into his mystical body are safe from direct confrontation with him. St John of the Cross is quite clear about this. Therefore, although we might be assailed by powerful temptations in the Dark Night we are safe from direct confrontation with the Evil One. When I speak of the "demons within" I am using the phrase metaphorically, as I have made clear before. I am therefore referring to the unruly passions and urges, the consequences of original sin that keep threatening to destroy us. I am not referring to demonic creatures, agents of the devil, that dwell within plotting to destroy us.

This process of endlessly repenting is firstly learned by practising it in prayer. No matter what form of prayer we may find helpful, you can be sure there will always be distractions and temptations preventing us from turning, opening and offering our hearts to God. Remember St Teresa of Ávila said that you cannot really pray without distractions. Far from preventing us from practising repentance, these temptations and distractions are where repentance is learnt. If God gives you experiences of his pure love that so lift you out of yourself so that you no longer experience any temptations or distractions, then that is his gift of pure unalloyed mystical contemplation that you cannot attain by yourself. However, you can keep trying to prepare yourself to receive the love that leads to union, by continually trying to turn away from distractions and temptations. The more you do this, most especially when you are in the darkest moments of the Dark Night, then the love is learned that does not merit, but enables you to receive the gift of contemplation.

I want to let you into a secret about the spiritual life that for some reason many people fail to see. They think they would progress in leaps and bounds if only they did not have so many distractions in prayer. The truth of the matter is you could not possibly progress in prayer without distractions. My brothers and I used to laugh at an old Victorian painting that our aunt used to hang on her kitchen wall. It depicted a brook flowing down from the mountains. The left-hand side of the brook was in all but darkness, the right-hand side was bathed in light. In the foreground there were stepping stones and under the picture written in bold Gothic script was, "Make all your stumbling blocks into stepping stones". I do not know why we found it so funny. I suppose the combination of the Victorian picture and the Gothic script made it all seem a little too twee, at least to us. But the truth of the matter is that the little epigram was true, and it still is true, especially in prayer where our stumbling blocks are in fact the stepping stones to sanctity.

It is interesting that St Teresa of Ávila said that you cannot pray without distractions. As I think I have said before but it is worth saying again – if you go to pray and fall asleep you are not praying, nor are you praying if you are swept up into an ecstasy. When you are asleep you are doing nothing and when you are in an ecstasy then God is doing everything. Prayer takes place in between the sleep and the ecstasy. In that place there are always distractions, so you are forever engaged in turning away from them in order to turn back to God, by continually raising your heart and mind to him, by making acts of love. So if you have a hundred and one distractions in half an hour, you have chosen to turn back to God a hundred and one times. In other words, you have been doing what St Peter asked his listeners to do on the first Pentecost day to receive the Holy Spirit. You have been repenting, repeatedly trying to turn back to God, continually raising your heart and mind to him, to give your love to him, so that he can give his love to you. Prayer is the place where in concentrated periods of time you practise what God wants you to do all the time, as you turn to him in all you say and do each day, and as you turn to him in the neighbour in need. That is why all the saints and all the great Christians who are held up to us as examples of how to live the Christian life, are men and women of prayer. They all knew and practised the art of what I have called spiritual weight-lifting in prayer. It was this daily spiritual exercise that, not only taught them the art of how to keep turning to God outside of prayer through all they said and did each day, but gave them the power to do it too, as their weak human powers were surcharged by the divine. As they gave, so they received, and in ever greater measure.

The more you keep trying to turn and open yourself to God in the darkness, then the more your love is being purified and perfected. The more your love is purified and perfected then the more it becomes like a spiritual pathway that enables the Holy Spirit to enter into you with ever greater energy and power. You may not feel his presence in these darkest moments but this dark and dry contemplation which is experienced is the consequence of the inner emptying that finally enables us to surrender our true self, freed from the "demons" within. It is this utter and complete surrendering of ourselves that finally enables the Holy Spirit, who has been guiding us throughout, to draw us up ever more fully into the Mystical Body of Christ. The more we are purified, the more deeply we are fitted into Christ's Mystical Body, and into his mystical action with which he at all times contemplates the Glory of God. This is the contemplation to which we are all called, our final destiny. It is here, and only here, in, with and through Christ our Risen Lord, that we first begin to glimpse something of the infinite glory of God.

Chapter 67

In the Trying Is the Dying

It should now be clear that the *Primacy of Loving* means that love is the prime objective of every moment of every day of our lives, by performing acts of love that gradually lead to a habit of loving, then to an inner disposition of loving that begins to permeate our whole lives. Begin each day therefore with the Morning Offering. Sometimes in a quarter of an hour of personal mental prayer you can make more acts of love, turning away from what your wayward self would prefer to indulge in, turning back to God, than in many weeks when you forget this important spiritual exercise. Practising acts of selflessness in formal prayer enables you to develop the habit of selflessness that not only enables you to love God inside of prayer but everyone else outside of prayer too. Prayer is for a Christian what a gymnasium is for an athlete where the muscles of your heart and not the muscles of your body are exercised, as they practise what is called "weight training" or "pumping iron". The principle behind it is very simple. By repeatedly raising weights above your head in the gymnasium you are not just developing the muscles in your arms and legs, but virtually every other muscle in your body as well simultaneously, in one simple action. The whole person is not only made stronger and more powerful but is given powers of endurance beyond those who do not use this method. It is the same in the spiritual gymnasium which is prayer. What is prayer but the raising of the heart and mind to God? It is just like weight-training. Whatever form of prayer you are engaged in, whether it is saying your morning prayers, trying to meditate or even contemplating you will always experience distractions, so you will always have to keep raising your heart and mind to God time and time again. As a person is doing this then the muscles of the heart and mind are continually being exercised, gradually transforming the whole spiritual metabolism. Athletes know that this concentrated period of physical exercise will give greater ease and facility to whatever they do in the rest of their day. The same is true for the spiritual athlete. It is not only they, but others too, who will benefit from the love generated in prayer where the muscles of the heart are developed more quickly and more fully than anywhere else.

There is no time like the present. This journey can begin now in the "sacrament of the present moment" where alone time can touch eternity. Never be deceived into believing that our continual failures will disqualify us from this journey. God judges us by how best we try no matter how many times we fall, for only he knows the power of our personal "demons" and how best we have tried to overcome them. Everyone begins life with a different hand of cards. Everyone begins with different parents or only one or even none. Even the best of parents are themselves psychologically handicapped by what nature and nurture has failed to give them, and what we therefore have failed to receive from them. But remember, God ultimately judges us by how best we have tried despite the odds that seem to have been against us from the beginning. And he judges those who have received so much and yet have given so little too. Only God knows the quality of our endeavour in comparison with what we were given at the beginning of our life, so only he can judge us at the end of it, by how best we have tried. He does not judge us by what the world may think that we have achieved, but what he knows we have achieved. There is an old Spanish proverb that says, "You see what I drink but you do not see my thirst." God does!

Only Our Lady was conceived without sin, and that means that the rest of us were not. That is why we are continually falling, both inside and outside of prayer, whether we like it or not, and that includes the saints too. The difference between us and the saints is not that they did not sin and we do. They sinned just as we do. What distinguishes the saint from the sinner is the speed with which they get up after having fallen. The saints do not waste precious time pretending they do not sin, or making endless excuses, or blaming others for what they know only too well was their own fault. When passing through Purgatory Dante noticed that now at last people saw the truth, so they did not spend their time blaming others but only themselves, for the sins that separated them from God. The saints saw this even in this life. The moment they fell, they did not waste time blaming others but only themselves and so they sought forgiveness and began again, knowing they had sinned, but trusting in the mercy of God.

St Francis of Assisi said that the very moment a person sins must be the moment when he or she turns back to God, begging his forgiveness, immediately and without delay. He put it this way in his writings,

"A man is faithful and prudent when he is quick to atone for all his offences, interiorly by contrition, exteriorly by confessing them and then by making reparation" (Admonition XXIV).

Herein lies one of the main differences between the saints and sinners like us. Only too often people simply cannot face their guilt so they run away from God and hide, as Adam did in the Garden of Eden. When God called out, "Adam, Adam, where are you?" (Genesis 3:9), God knew exactly where Adam was: it was Adam who did not know where he was. He had lost his way trying to hide his sin and the guilt that shamed him. Sometimes we can spend years on the run because pride will not allow us to admit what we have done. Our inability to eat humble pie means that we can spend half a lifetime suffering from spiritual starvation. What is even worse than the pride that comes before a fall, is the pride that follows the fall, because it stops us from getting up, sometimes permanently.

So the difference between the saints and us is not that they did not fall and we do, but that they learned how to use their inevitable failures to their advantage. Saint Paul was the first to pen what is in fact the great secret of the spiritual life. It is simply this, that God's power works most perfectly in human weakness, gradually transforming it. That is why no one can progress in the spiritual life without the humility to know their weakness and their need of the only One who can help them.

Whether in or out of prayer, the measure of spiritual advancement can always be determined by the speed with which we turn back to God from the distractions, the temptations, or the sins that try to turn us away from him. However, what all the saints discovered was that this speed can only be maintained with the help and strength from God. That is why, although they may have differed from one another in everything else, they were one in their daily commitment to prayer. They knew without a shadow of a doubt that without it they had no power to do anything of any real value or worth, let alone advance in the spiritual life. That is why each of them in different ways echoed the words of Saint Teresa of Ávila, whom I do not hesitate to quote yet again, when she said, "There is only one way to perfection and that is to pray. If anyone points in another direction they are deceiving you."

The very essence of our spiritual journey then, is in endlessly getting up no matter how many times we fall. It is in this, more than anything else, that the real quality of our love is measured.

Even if we do not have a pure and humble heart to begin with, a pure and humble heart will be God's gift for those who persevere in following their heart's desire, come what may. The most pernicious stumbling block to our spiritual advancement is the pride that follows our fall, which induces us to pack up and run away from God rather than face the truth of our sinfulness. Yet again then I insist that the difference between the saint and the sinner then is not that they never fail and we do, but the speed with which they seek forgiveness and begin again immediately no matter how many times they fall. This takes great humility and is how true humility is learned.

"When you stop falling then you are in heaven, but when you stop getting up then you are in hell. In the trying is the dying, and in the dying is the rising that draws us up into the mystical body of Christ and into his mystical contemplation of his Father" (Peter Calvay Hermit).

Chapter 68

Into the Redeeming Christ

When my first fervour was over the only priest I asked gave me good advice. He asked me whether or not I loved my mother as much when she was ill, as when she was well. I told him that in one sense I loved her more when she was ill. Only a year before when she had been ill for two months and spent four weeks confined to bed, I did all the shopping, the cooking, the cleaning and all the other household tasks for her. The priest told me that I had to do the same for God now, as I did for my mother before when she could not show her love for me in the way she did before. I was now being offered the same opportunity to do for God what I did for my mother. I had shown my love for her by what I did, not just for what she did for me in the past, but because she was my mother. Go back to your prayer he said and show just how much you love God, not for what you got out of him in the past or hope to get out of him in the future, but because he is God. To this end he said never give less time to him in prayer than you gave in the past and try to support the desire that you still have to love him with acts of love even though all the feelings that you had before have deserted you. He then gave me a copy of *The Cloud of Unknowing*, and encouraged me to persevere come what may, as I did until what came next after very many months of journeying on in darkness, as I have already explained.

Only gradually I came to realize that although I could no longer meditate I had in fact been led into contemplation. It is because the simple desire for God, the desire to simply gaze upon him is so subtle, so unclear and so muddled to begin with that the searcher doesn't think they are praying at all, and to call this action contemplation seems totally inappropriate. However, it is appropriate, because that is what it is, and that is what it has been called from the beginning. Those who persevere, come what may, using a short prayer originally called the "prayer of the heart" to express their love for God are persevering in the contemplation that St John of the Cross describes as "Obscure Contemplation".

How can such a simple way of praying be called mystical contemplation? Is this the end to which all that I have written been leading, the apotheosis of all my teaching and the teaching of the great mystics, from whom I have learnt so much? Is it merely trying to make simple acts of love in a spiritual wasteland where endless temptations and distractions try to draw me away from trying to do God's will and do it to the end? The answer is yes. This is precisely what Jesus Christ was doing on the Cross. Here in terrible physical pain and interior darkness, writhing in the agony of suffering the most terrible death that man could devise for him as he was being slowly tortured to death, he was making simple acts of love that mixed, merged and mingled into what became the greatest act of love that wrought the salvation of the world. When led into obscure contemplation at the beginning of the dark night of purification, the believer is being asked to begin participating in a new and deeper way in the very act of our Redemption, by experiencing in kind, albeit on a much lower level, something of what Christ had to endure on the Cross. As this strange new form of prayer deepens as it always will with perseverance, those who have committed themselves to following Christ will now be asked to participate in his act of redemption. Their hearts will begin to beat with his heart, their acts of love will syncretise with his acts of love, as the two gradually become one with years of selfless self-sacrificial loving. What seems at first to be endless, pointless spiritual drudgery, will in God's time and when he feels we have been sufficiently purified, be suddenly filled with the experience of God's love to shattering degrees of intensity. This gives the believer the help and strength to return to the darkness to participate even more deeply, even more fully, in the redemptive action that Christ performed on the Cross. And so, the journey continues.

It is essentially so simple, even though sometimes so painful, because it consists in acts of love, made sometimes in darkness sometimes in light. The simplicity of these acts of contemplative loving do not change, they just become less and less obscure, as the act of loving that is its very essence is perfected. As a series of acts of loving develop into a habit of loving, an inner disposition of loving is brought to perfection that can be practised both inside and outside of prayer. That is why the highest and most powerful form of prayer, contemplation, is so simple and therefore for everyone, because everyone can love, and everyone can make simple acts of love. If what St Paul said is true then the humblest and simplest at the bottom, have a head start on everyone else. He insisted that God's power works most perfectly in weakness.

As the mystical purification that takes place draws towards its completion then something surprising suddenly begins to happen. Through the inflow of divine love that purifies the inner faculties of the mind, meditation is made possible again, but in colour as it were, and in far higher definition than before, and in such a loving and tender way that the mystic is regularly moved to tears. So, for those who make it to the heights of mystical transformation in this life, meditation returns, but not usually for too long before the receiver is spiralled upwards into ecstatic bliss when for a time they are taken up and into the heights of contemplative loving, in Christ's mystical body, and together with him and through him into his mystical contemplation of his Father. These two types of all-absorbing loving, the one that draws us into the Son, and the one that draws us, in, with and through the Son to gaze on the Father, inspire one another. At one moment it is our human nature, now transformed through purification, that finds its fulfilment in the human nature of

Christ. At another moment it is in this new oneness that brings us together as never before, that enables us, in with and through him, to gaze upon the glory of God, in brief moments of ecstatic bliss. In the famous passage from 2 Corinthians 12:1–3, St Paul describes how he has had visions and revelations that came from Christ, while at another time he was lifted up out of himself into what he called the "third heaven", that was clearly into a mystical experience of God when he neither saw nor heard anything but experienced what cannot be put into human words. As we have seen, the same sort of thing happened to St Francis, when he received a revelation shortly before he saw the vision of Christ Crucified, and then went on to be lifted up and out of himself into ecstasies, both before and on his way back to Assisi after he had received the Stigmata.

These two profound ways of experiencing the love of God, the one through his son, and the other, through his son, of the Father, can be seen most clearly in the lives of all the great saints when their purification is brought ever closer to completion. As these experiences became almost commonplace for them, they came to realize that the love that swept them up from the son into the father, and then released them again to descend into the son, was none other than the Holy Spirit. In short, even here in this life they were being caught up into something of the vortex of loving that had united the Father to the Son from all eternity. They were in effect experiencing the life of the Holy Trinity in action – in his act of loving. Thanks to the incarnation and the hypostatic union, Christ was able to draw others into himself, to experience, through his divinized human nature, something of what he had experienced before his incarnation, namely the love of the Three in One. This is God's plan conceived from all eternity for us, so that we would find our ultimate destiny in eternal life and everlasting loving, in what, as we have seen, St Paul called God's secret plan, the *Mysterion*.

When his apostles saw Christ transfigured on Mount Tabor

they were being given a preview, not just of what would happen to him after the Resurrection, but what would happen to his followers too, not just in the next life, but even in this life, if they persevered in the spiritual life that would lead then ever more deeply into his sacred humanity. For be sure of this, the spiritual life that we pursue in prayer takes us up, after purification, into his sacred and transformed and transfigured humanity to experience his perfect human love for us and to receive our purified human love of him. Further to this we also encounter there those loved ones who have also been taken up and into his glorified human nature. Nor do we travel on beyond his glorified body for this is the place where we reside to eternity, gazing in, with, and through him on the glory of the Three in One where he was begotten from eternity and only left briefly to take us back with him to the place where we were first conceived, and where we will find our ultimate destiny.

In this life the mystic who has reached, what the Eastern Fathers called divinization, will at one moment be transported physically by the love of their risen Lord, and at another moment be transported with him into the ecstatic joy of contemplating our Loving Father. The thrilling enthralment and transforming experience of human loving at its most perfect, can be suddenly followed by the supra human loving with which Christ loves his Father that often envelops a person and draws them into ecstatic bliss. It is here where only in an otherworldly silence, does God communicate what his Son came to give us. Words unite those who are separated from each other, but in the perfect union with God that has been our deepest desire from the beginning, there is a perfect infinite and blissful silence.

But all has not yet been said about our journey into the profound mystical vortex of loving that revolves between the Father and the Son. It is into this final mystery that we will all be caught up and to all eternity. I say "we" because we are not alone. We are at one too, with all who have chosen to enter into this ecstatic joy, with mothers and fathers, brothers and sisters, friends and lovers, children and grandchildren, and not just our extended family but the whole extended Christian family, living and dead. They are not just living with us in Christ, but travelling with us too, into never-ending beatitude. Our own personal joy and satisfaction is enhanced beyond our wildest dreams by re-meeting our own families again in Christ's own glorified and mystical body, and in knowing and loving them as never before. Even in the best of families, the pernicious cancer of selfishness prevented us loving each other as we would have wished while we were on earth. But now that the cancer has been purified away and we have been transfused with pure love. There is nothing to prevent us from becoming the genuine loving families, that we always wanted to be, but never really were on earth. Nevertheless, this supernatural and transforming reunion with our families in the next life is not the end of our journey, but the prelude to a new journey as we set out together upon our final and unending journey into eternal life and loving, where God's plan for us from the beginning, his *Mysterion*, is brought to perfection.

Together, we will, not just experience the fullness of ecstatic joy, but the ever more fulfilling joy of experiencing *Epecstasy*. In order to express our ultimate destination, St Gregory of Nyssa, the great mystical poet devised a new word by adding a prefix to the word ecstasy to create this new word, *Epecstasy*. This word means that we not only go out of ourselves into God through an ever-deepening love, but that we continually go out of ourselves and into God through love – through his infinite love and to eternity. For the more God's infinite loving enters into us then the more the capacity to receive even more love grows within us and continues to grow to all eternity as we relentlessly go beyond and supersede what was once our capacity for love. As this journey unfolds, our capacity to receive and give love never stops expanding, as we travel without any further let or hindrance, into the destiny designed for us by God from all eternity. The reward of the traveller is to go on travelling the solace of the searcher is to go on searching.

As this, our final journey opens out and expands, we are, together with all whom we love and hold dear, bonded ever closer together within Christ, within his hypostatic union, within the union of the divine and the human that constitutes his glorified human personality. Nor are we led into some sort of pantheism as some pseudo-mystics suggest, because love differentiates. In other words it makes us more ourselves than we ever were before, as it does for those loved ones who travel with us. So we continually rejoice at what infinite love is doing to us and to those whom we love. This adds to the ecstatic bliss that envelops us as we journey on together into infinite loving. It is always within him, and while we are loving him and drawing ever closer to him, that we are drawing ever closer to all who are in him. As this is taking place ever more deeply ever more fully we are all simultaneously loving God our common Father. We are drawing nearer and nearer to the blissful union with the pure unadulterated loving and goodness, that resides in Our Father – our divine and ever devoted dad who is in heaven. He is our true home, the home in which he first conceived us, and the home for which our whole being has been yearning, within the infinite loving that constitutes the Three in One. For, as St Augustine put it, our hearts have been created for God alone and they will never rest until they rest in him.

Lead, kindly Light, amid the encircling gloom,
Lead Thou me on;
The night is dark, and I am far from home,
Lead Thou me on;
Keep Thou my feet; I do not ask to see
The distant scene; one step enough for me.

About this Book

When love is lost within a family, catastrophic consequences follow. That is not just for the parents, but for the children and society at large. When the God-given love that Jesus Christ introduced into the first Christian family was lost, similar consequences ensued. Loveless men and women not only do damage to themselves, but to others too inside and outside of the Church. This last spiritual and supreme masterpiece of a great spiritual master explains and details how the love that was lost can be put back and flourish where it once flourished before. This book is the long-awaited watershed that can slake the thirst of the dry weary land that has been yearning to receive it.

The book begins by giving a practical summary of the early God-given spirituality introduced into the early Church by Jesus Christ, and how and why, it succeeded in transforming a Pagan Empire into a Christian Empire in such a short time. Then how, after the victory of Constantine, it gradually went into decline and how it was renewed by Monastic spirituality. A brief history of Christian spirituality then follows that shows how and why, after Quietism was condemned (1687) and love was taken out of Christian spirituality, it gradually escalated into the catastrophic decline and abuses everywhere in Christian Churches today. After showing the reader how they can return to the lay spirituality that prevailed in the early Church, religious orders are criticised for failing to love and therefore for failing to guide others in the profound mystical spirituality that they have forgotten. The salient feature of this book is that it shows everyone, a step-by-step guide how to practise the simple practical Christ-given spirituality that can change lives for the better.

Bio

David Torkington

David Torkington is a Spiritual Theologian, Author, Lecturer and Broadcaster, who specializes in Prayer, Christian Spirituality and Mystical Theology. For the past fifty years he has been communicating to his audience his profound love of the traditional and authentic Mystical and Biblical Theology that has inspired all his writings on prayer. He has done this through his ability to give inspiring lectures and retreats to religious and lay, both in England and worldwide in Africa, and in the heart of Christendom, in Rome. More recently he has concentrated on writing, blogging, podcasting and broadcasting to his audience which includes both Catholic and Protestant Christians who are all inspired by his ability to express profound truths simply and truthfully.

In the past he was asked to lecture on Mystical Theology at the Angelicum in Rome as the only speaker who had practical knowledge and experience in Mystical Theology. In his twelve-year tenure as Director of a London Retreat and Conference Centre he gained direct experience of the decline in the moral and spiritual life of the Church. He is the only author who directly confronts this problem, gives reasons and solutions and offers hope to those wishing to return to the Christ-centred spiritualty bequeathed to Christians by Jesus Christ himself.

CIRCLE
BOOKS

CHRISTIAN FAITH

Circle Books explores a wide range of disciplines within the field of Christian faith and practice. It also draws on personal testimony and new ways of finding and expressing God's presence in the world today.

If you have enjoyed this book, why not tell other readers by posting a review on your preferred book site. Recent bestsellers from Circle Books are:

I Am With You (Paperback)
John Woolley

These words of divine encouragement were given to John Woolley in his work as a hospital chaplain, and have since inspired and uplifted tens of thousands, even changed their lives.
Paperback: 978-1-90381-699-8 ebook: 978-1-78099-485-7

God Calling
A. J. Russell

365 messages of encouragement channelled from Christ to two anonymous "Listeners".
Hardcover: 978-1-905047-42-0 ebook: 978-1-78099-486-4

The Long Road to Heaven,
A Lent Course Based on the Film
Tim Heaton
This second Lent resource from the author of *The Naturalist and the Christ* explores Christian understandings of "salvation" in a five-part study based on the film *The Way*.
Paperback: 978-1-78279-274-1 ebook: 978-1-78279-273-4

Abide In My Love
More Divine Help for Today's Needs
John Woolley
The companion to *I Am With You*, *Abide In My Love* offers words of divine encouragement.
Paperback: 978-1-84694-276-1

From the Bottom of the Pond
The Forgotten Art of Experiencing God in the Depths of the Present Moment
Simon Small
From the Bottom of the Pond takes us into the depths of the present moment, to the only place where God can be found.
Paperback: 978-1-84694-066-8 ebook: 978-1-78099-207-5

God Is A Symbol Of Something True
Why You Don't Have to Choose Either a Literal Creator God or a Blind, Indifferent Universe
Jack Call
In this examination of modern spiritual dilemmas, Call offers the explanation that some of the most important elements of life are beyond our control: everything is fundamentally alright.
Paperback: 978-1-84694-244-0